GEORGIANS REVEALED

LIFE, STYLE AND THE MAKING OF MODERN BRITAIN

Arrest

GEORGIANS REVEALED

LIFE, STYLE AND THE MAKING OF MODERN BRITAIN

Moira Goff, John Goldfinch, Karen Limper-Herz
and Helen Peden

With an introduction by Amanda Goodrich

The British Library

First published in 2013 by
The British Library
96 Euston Road
London NW1 2DB

On the occasion of the British Library exhibition
Georgians Revealed: Life, Style and the Making of Modern Britain
8 November 2013–11 March 2014

British Library Cataloguing-in-Publication Data
A catalogue record for this book is available from the
British Library

ISBN 978 0 7123 5714 2 (paperback)
ISBN 978 0 7123 5713 5 (hardback)

Note to the Reader
The original spelling, punctuation and capitalisation have been preserved in captions throughout this book. Square brackets in the captions indicate bibliographical information that can be inferred, but is not printed in the original texts. British Library shelfmarks are given at the end of each caption to an item in the Library's collection; catalogue details are provided where possible for items loaned from other institutions.

Opposite, from left to right:
King Georges I–III, National Portrait Gallery, London;
George IV, Fenton House, the Goff/Fitz-Clarence Collection.
National Trust Images/Jonathan Gibson.

Designed by Andrew Shoolbred
Printed in Italy by Printer Trento S.r.l.

Contents

Introduction

Amanda Goodrich

The term 'Georgian' describes the reign in Britain of the Hanoverian monarchs, originally German, namely George I to George IV, from 1714 to 1830. The Georgians, of all levels of society, are celebrated here in recognition of the tercentenary of the Hanoverian Succession in 2014. The monarchy certainly has a part to play in the story told by this book and the exhibition. But they also explore the period more broadly, encompassing cultural, social and economic perspectives. Through a unique mix of exhibits, both printed material and objects from the period, the exhibition aims to capture a slice of Georgian life, something of the essence of the time. Consequently, rather than provide a conventional linear history of the period, it explores a set of themes and connections through displays of items that create a network, an intricate spider's web, of texts and objects.

James Gillray, *A Connoisseur Examining a Cooper*, 1792. British Museum. George III examines a portrait of Oliver Cromwell by the famous seventeenth-century miniaturist Samuel Cooper. In 1792 the Revolution in France was turning towards republicanism, and Gillray suggests here that the king could suffer the same fate as Charles I.

In common with all conventionally delineated past eras, the Georgian period is not a piece of the past preserved in the aspic of a static history. It is, rather, a moment in time that is constantly reviewed and reshaped in relation to the present experienced by historians and their audience. It speaks to our lives today, and many interesting and relevant comparisons can be made. History does not exactly 'repeat itself', as is often suggested: rather, issues emerge today that in some way reflect those grappled with in the past, albeit in a very different environment.

The exhibition and this book draw on the British Library's exceptionally rich collections of texts by contemporary authors, both those well known to us and others less familiar, to reveal a unique set of thoughts and ideas. Many of these still resonate today. Such texts provide insight into the views of the time and contain interesting details of everyday Georgian life and the ways in which Britain was growing and developing. Numerous texts in the collections are now also available online in digitised form. While texts are prominent in the exhibition, other objects from the period also make an important contribution. The history of material culture, in other words the history of 'things', enhances our knowledge of contemporary life; the lived experience.[1] Things have histories, as people do, and historians today study the genealogies and biographies of objects to ascertain their origins, patterns of use and the interconnections between objects and people. Many objects survive far longer than their original owner, and carry with them a history of ownership, place and value that may not be easy to extract. Contemporary texts assist in revealing such details and Georgians certainly wrote much about the things they owned, as texts in the exhibition illustrate. Moreover, the things people own help to define who they are and how they see themselves; many acquisitions in the Georgian period were made with that in mind. The exhibition, then, brings together texts and objects that interact to provide a vivid picture of Georgian life.

An Age of Freedom

This chapter considers more broadly the threads and themes that emerge from the exhibition within relevant contexts. It looks at the ideas that influenced the texts and the style of the objects on display, and links material culture to other histories. As the exhibition illustrates, the Georgian period was a vibrant and exciting time of considerable change in many areas of life. In particular it heralded a new consumer society that was furiously getting and spending, shopping and socialising, and enjoying ever more

James Gillray, *A Voluptuary under the Horrors of Digestion*, 1792. British Museum. Here the Prince Regent is depicted as a large, dissipated glutton, lounging in his chair. Empty bottles lurk under the table and gaming dice lie on the floor, confirming the reputation of the Prince as a profligate and degenerate representative of the elite.

PORT
VELNOS
Vegetable
SYRUP
Butcher's
Bill
Debts
of
Honor
unpaid
FARO

lavish public entertainments. It is sometimes described as the coarse and brash century, one of profligacy, dissipation, gaming and gambling, in which bawdy houses and molly houses (illicit meeting places for homosexual men) were open for business, and the Duke of Devonshire lived openly with his wife, his mistress and all their children.

A new celebrity culture emerged, with a variety of men and women claiming celebrity status, from Grimaldi the famous clown to socialite Elizabeth Chudleigh, actor, playwright and theatre manager David Garrick and the notorious dandy Beau Brummel. Even criminals such as thief Jack Sheppard, renowned for his dramatic escapes from Newgate, the criminal gang leader Jonathan Wild and the 'gentleman' highwayman James Maclaine achieved considerable notoriety and were celebrated in the press. John Gay's *The Beggar's Opera* (1728) incorporated fictitious characters modelled on such criminals, and proved highly popular entertainment. The Georgian period may appear to have been an era when 'anything goes', a time of considerable new freedom. A characteristic of the changes in Georgian culture was indeed increased freedom, and this is the main theme explored in this chapter. Yet it needs to be examined within a broader context than that of personal gratification within a buoyant consumer society.

In fact, the Georgian focus was very much on improvement and progress in many areas of life. The period has been identified, among other things, as the 'age of reason' and 'the age of revolutions'. The first refers to influences on modes of thought, in particular by the Enlightenment, and in relation to philosophy and religion. Indeed, this is a time as important for ideas as it is for material change. The revolutions that have been identified during a broader period within which the Georgian era falls, from the end of the seventeenth century to the middle of the nineteenth century, include not only a consumer revolution but also others in agriculture, finance, science, industry, and politics in the American and French Revolutions. The period has also been termed 'the age of modernity' and this label largely incorporates the other two. Together they reflect a number of concepts of freedom.

Today we tend to think of 'modern' as reflecting our own twenty-first century society, in which democracy and a host of rights and freedoms are taken for granted. But 'modernity' is a tricky concept for historians, much debated in terms of when it can be applied and what it describes. In relation to the Georgian period, it is associated with the shift away from an *ancien regime* society in Britain, characterised by a primarily rural economy and domination by monarchy, aristocracy and the Anglican Church.[2] This old society was structured in terms of hierarchical ranks, with an elite of nobility and gentry and then everyone else: the people.

Georgian modernity implies moves towards a more industrial, commercial and urban society with greater political engagement by ordinary people, greater religious freedom and the development of the nation state. This society saw the emergence of a middle class who presented a challenge to the established elite. Consequently, a more modern society, a 'polite and commercial people', began to develop.[3] That is not to suggest that society became free of concepts of rank and deference. The nobility and gentry continued to dominate, and there was a notable divide between the propertied and property-less. Yet Britain, unlike other European countries, had no legal bulwark dividing the different ranks. Moreover, the growing middle class was at the forefront of industrial and commercial development, with a few becoming richer than many of the nobility.[4]

Politics and Religion

In terms of government Britain had, in theory at least, a more 'modern' constitution than any other European monarchy. The people of England certainly thought so, celebrating the English liberty they perceived as superior to the absolutism and popery of the neighbouring enemy, France. Such liberties were rooted in English history, stretching back to Magna Carta, and included the rule of law, trial by jury, representative government and a mixed constitution of king, lords and commons. The Glorious Revolution (1688–9) and the enhanced parliamentary government it introduced were also much celebrated. The Hanoverian succession to the British throne was further limited by the Act of Settlement (1701). This statute claimed in the full title that it was 'An Act for the further limitation of the Crown, and better securing the rights and liberties of the subject', making clear that those from abroad who were invited to take the throne did so under the control of Parliament and the people. This statement reflects contemporary fears about foreign monarchs who may not always act in the best interests of British people, as indeed William III had failed to do. (In particular, he had angered his subjects in Britain by fighting wars in Europe in which they had no interest.) The statute sought to ensure that the people's rights under the law were protected and the independence of the legislature and the judiciary were strengthened. Thus in comparison to other eighteenth-century European societies the English were blessed with unusual liberty: no other monarch was part of a mixed constitution or compromised by such statutes. Astonishingly, perhaps, it was only in October 2011 that the government proposed an amendment to the Act of Settlement to introduce gender equality in the succession so that the first-born child, whether male or female, succeeds to the throne. The amendment also enables the heir to the throne to marry a Roman Catholic (although the monarch may still not be a Catholic). Memories of the crypto-Catholicism of the later Stuarts linger on.

It is notable, though, that in reality during the Georgian period the mixed constitution did not reflect an equal balance between the three constituents of monarchy, aristocracy and democracy. The king still retained considerable political power should he choose to invoke it, although the Hanoverian monarchs tended to interfere less in political matters than their Stuart predecessors.[5] Indeed, George III was known for his domesticity and nicknamed 'Farmer George' for his interest in agriculture. Both houses of Parliament were dominated by the nobility, with seats in the House of Commons rarely freely available to those who were not connected in some way to the nobility. Party politics was established with the Whigs and the Tories, but this resulted in something of a Whig oligarchy dominating between 1715 and 1760. There was little democracy as we understand it today; very few of the population, only about two per cent, actually had the right to vote. Politics was very much an elite and male domain, with only property-owning men qualifying for the franchise in most of Britain, or to stand as representatives in Parliament. Liberty was then firmly linked to property.

The period did, however, witness growing calls for greater political liberty and reform of government, first manifested in accusations of corruption against the Whig governments. Agitation for reform increased in response to the American War of Independence (1776–83) and then the French Revolution (1789–*c.* 1799), with reformers demanding greater changes. The most radical, such as Thomas Paine, believed a revolution was necessary in Britain in the 1790s, but the majority claimed that reform of the existing constitution, incorporating an end to government corruption, a fairer representation in Parliament (particularly for the growing towns and cities) and an increased franchise would be sufficient to remedy Britain's ills. Such calls for reform fell on deaf ears in Parliament, and no significant political reform legislation was enacted during the Georgian period.

Religion was of great importance to Georgians, and here too a move towards increased freedom of worship can be detected during the period, while reform of the established Anglican Church was also continually sought. Officially the state in Britain was tied closely to the Church, with the people legally obliged to attend Anglican worship. The Test and Corporation Acts passed after the restoration of Charles II strengthened the Anglican Church and offices in government or the military were reserved for Anglican communicants. Roman Catholics were excluded from the franchise, Parliament and all state offices until 1829. Yet there was an increasing toleration of Protestant Nonconformists (known as Dissenters). Under the Toleration Act of 1689 Dissenters were allowed to worship freely and could set up their own educational establishments. Nevertheless, during the latter part of the period many Dissenters joined political reformers to agitate for greater religious toleration and political rights. Religious reform and new religious freedoms were also sought by Evangelical groups emerging within Anglicanism. The most famous of these was Methodism, formed in the 1720s by John Wesley. Itinerant preachers travelled the country preaching to ordinary people the importance of a spiritual conversion to the true Methodist Christianity. Membership grew rapidly, particularly among the poorer sectors of society, and Methodism eventually broke away from the Anglican Church in the 1790s.

William Wilberforce led another influential Evangelical group and wrote an instrumental text, *A Practical View of the Prevailing Religious System of Professed Christians, in the Higher and Middle Classes in this Country, Contrasted with Real Christianity*. First published in 1797, it was much reprinted and ran to eighteen English editions by 1830. Here Wilberforce relayed his ideas about what he saw as real religion as opposed to the superficial and ritualistic Christianity practised within the Anglican Church. As an MP, Wilberforce also fought for the abolition of slavery on Christian grounds. Another Evangelical Christian was the poet William Cowper, who experienced a dramatic conversion in 1764. He subsequently expressed his new devotion through poems, the most famous being *The Task* (1785). As a result of such *ad hoc* departures from mainstream Anglicanism, historians tend to see Britain as increasingly religiously pluralist during the Georgian period.

Industrialisation, Urbanisation and Finance

The Georgians witnessed innovations in many areas of the economy, including agriculture and industry. These were aided by the expansion of capitalism, internal and overseas markets and improved communications. Rather than identifying an 'industrial revolution' in terms of a sudden 'take-off', historians now tend to think more in terms of 'industrialisation' reflecting a longer and slower process. Before the nineteenth century few places in Britain experienced the development of industry on the scale of the cotton spinning mills of Lancashire; much manufacture was still carried out in small workshops and cottage industries. Nevertheless, there were considerable developments in technical innovation for manufacture, regional specialisation and distribution.[6] These innovations were assisted by expansion of infrastructure, particularly the introduction of the turnpike road system and canal building, which both became popular with elite private investors. Such transport systems allowed a greater freedom of movement for goods and people.

In his lengthy *Tour Through the Island of Great Britain* (1724–26) Daniel Defoe extolled the virtues of new turnpike roads, which, introduced through legislation, had spread rapidly throughout England by the 1770s. He noted that the pot-holed, heavily rutted and frequently waterlogged roads of old were now being replaced by well-maintained turnpike roads that enabled increased travel for a small fee. Markets could be reached more quickly and cheaply, with the goods and livestock arriving in better condition. Fresh meat was now available in London all year round, rather than in limited seasons, because livestock could be herded along turnpike roads in winter as well as summer without undue stress and damage to the meat. Defoe also noted that towns and villages on turnpike roads, particularly those near London, experienced improvements as easy access meant 'the citizens flock out in greater numbers than ever to take lodgings and country-houses'. Buying a country property was popular among the newly wealthy middle class, and those who had made money in the colonies overseas.

Towns and cities also grew dramatically during the period, providing improved street design, buildings and amenities. England was the most rapidly urbanising society in Europe between 1750 and 1800; people migrated to towns and cities to find work and to enjoy the new amenities on offer. Consequently traditional kinship and community ties were loosened and urban dwellers could experience considerably more individual freedom. The urbanisation process was not always benign, however, particularly for the poor, many of whom moved to urban areas out of necessity rather than desire. Agrarian reforms brought the enclosure of common lands, to the benefit of elite landowners. The loss of rights to use common land and a reduction in rural labour requirements meant that old systems of rural subsistence could no longer be sustained. Many new urban-dwellers had to take low-paid work in towns and cities, often in service or industry, where working conditions were frequently harsh and living conditions poor. The unemployed found little to assist them in the poor laws, and often turned to crime out of necessity. And this was a time notable for its 'bloody code' which rendered many minor crimes, of theft in particular, capital offences.

The developments in commerce and industry were assisted by increased modern financial systems that we take for granted today: banking, credit, insurance and the development of the stock market. The Bank of England was established in 1694, initially as a private company providing limited financial services, particularly paper credit for the government. Lloyd's of London started in a coffee shop in the capital in 1688, and then formed the Society of Lloyd's in 1744 at the Royal Exchange on Cornhill. Maritime insurance played an important part in the spread of overseas trade and the empire, and also assisted the slave trade that thrived during much of the period.

The economic historian Julian Hoppit has claimed that financial innovations of the period, and particularly the creation of national debt, were some of the most significant and enduring developments of the age. They were not, however, without problems. Many complained that the national debt merely lined the pockets of a few rich financiers or corrupt politicians.[7] Indeed, criticism of those in the City is not just a present-day phenomenon: it was also common during the Georgian period. A browse of William Cobbett's *Weekly Political Register* on the British Library database *British newspapers 1600–1900* provides good examples. The issue of 22 November 1823, for instance, condemned as 'most execrable' that 'class of money-making vagabonds, who, favoured by a system of trick and fraud, make their half millions of money by watching the turn of the market'.

State lotteries were run by private companies to help finance the national debt and raise revenue to fund wars and public works, including the British Museum. They contributed significantly to the costs of the American War of Independence and the wars against France (1792–1815).[8] Lotteries were also marred by scandals, corruption and criminal prosecutions, and were condemned as state-sponsored gambling. Private lotteries were sometimes set up by those in need of financial support for a venture, although a private act of parliament was needed to do so. For example, print-seller John Boydell and botanist John Thornton held such private lotteries.

Financial scandals were common during the Georgian period, the most famous of which was the South Sea Bubble. The South Sea Company was set up in 1711 to consolidate and reduce national debt. In 1720, in an attempt to increase its share capital against a background of poor profitability, the company resorted to all manner of dubious practices including bribery, deceit and obfuscation. The price rose dramatically but then crashed, and many investors lost heavily. A parliamentary enquiry was held and politicians were disgraced, stockjobbers condemned and profits confiscated. Such speculative ventures were common in the early eighteenth century, but the scale of the South Sea Bubble fraud turned public opinion against such activity. The Bubble Act of 1720 brought an end to that particular kind of speculative project, although other spectacular collapses continued to occur throughout the nineteenth century. Comparisons can be drawn here with the financial crash of 2007 that turned the public against the City and its 'fat cats'.

Consumer Society and Material Freedom

One important aspect of this new, more modern society was what has been termed a 'consumer revolution'.[9] Historians have recently tended to downgrade this concept in similar terms to an industrial revolution, arguing that consumption developed over a longer period, and more slowly, than had previously been thought. Nevertheless, there were now more opportunities to make or earn money, and to spend it on a wider choice of goods and activities – many at lower prices than previously available. This denoted greater material freedom for many in Georgian society, and particularly the middle class. Some goods were mass-produced for the first time, such as Wedgwood earthenware and china, and so became available to a greater proportion of the public. Wedgwood used the classical designs that had been the preserve of exclusive products for his mass-produced items, and this brought elite taste to a wider audience.

New goods and materials were also flooding in from overseas. Many came from Europe and America, but there were also more exotic products such as sugar, rum and tobacco from the West Indies and tea, spices and luxury fabrics, most notably silk, shipped from the East by the East India Company. Fashion became of great importance to both men and women, and trend-setting high society, known at the time as the *beau monde*, was keenly observed by the rest of the population.[10] Access to fashionable clothing was aided by new magazines that provided details of the latest fashions to be copied, and the availability of new fabrics and accessories. Consumption also increased among those who worked for wages, particularly in towns and cities, although much of what they bought were everyday commodities such as bread, milk, vegetables and basic clothing – items that, in a previous rural existence, they would have made or grown for themselves. Yet even wage earners could increasingly afford such items as soap, tea and sugar to sweeten it, and other things which they enjoyed. Small general stores could be found in towns and cities to supply such necessities.

The objects people owned in their home reveal a great deal about the material culture of the time. Of course the rich owned more than the poor and, while the great houses of the nobility were stuffed with things that tell us much about the owners, the poor left a far fainter imprint. The amount and quality of furniture, glassware, tableware, bed linen, kitchen utensils, books, ornaments, guns, horses, equipage and other items gleaned from family account books and inventories indicate the occupational status and social rank of the owner. Carriages were clear status symbols, like cars today. The standard two-horse carriage was a fairly practical vehicle, while the barouche was somewhat aristocratic and owned only by the rich and the curricle was a sports car of the day. Moreover, the possession of items such as clocks, mirrors and window curtains may reveal not only the social standing of the owner, but also the geographical location of his or her home. In the earlier Georgian period in particular, those below gentry status and living in rural areas were less likely to own such items than those living in towns and cities.[11] This was primarily because they worked more with the rhythms of nature than by mechanical time, and they had fewer meetings with others that required precise timing. Curtains were not essential where the night was pitch black and no one was likely to peer in, and mirrors were less of a necessity where visitors were rare.

Print after William Hogarth, Plate 2 from *A Harlot's Progress*, 1732. British Museum.
The well-dressed woman in the picture has just kicked over the tea table. The small black boy on the right holding the kettle is a page, probably hired to serve the tea dressed in exotic style to enhance the ceremony.

The elite, increasingly followed by the middle class, purchased and displayed items in the home to reinforce their status, confirm their taste and in some cases show off their wealth. Certainly what people owned no longer reflected merely their inheritance; increasingly it made a statement about their own identity. Although the middle class often purchased items with aspirational aims that reflected elite fashions, they did not always do so. Many preferred, or could only afford, simpler products, or carefully chose durable and practical items to furnish their home. Hence the middle class gradually developed a material culture of its own.

One aspect of the greater sociability that marked this period was an increase in social visiting, particularly in urban areas. Visits by friends and acquaintances became important for displaying the newly acquired identity and, by also visiting, such middle-class people could observe others' acquisitions and taste. Callers might be served hot drinks from the colonies: tea, coffee and chocolate became important signs of social distinction, enhanced by ownership of china designed for the purpose. It became fashionable among the wealthy to have a male black servant or a small black boy as a sort of novelty page, dressed in an exotic style to serve such beverages or adorn the more public spaces in the home.

Georgians also experienced a greatly increased freedom of the press and print industry due to the lapsing of the Licensing Act in 1695. The Act had imposed heavy control over what and how much could be printed. This new freedom resulted in a burgeoning print industry with a profusion of texts published in the form of books, pamphlets, broadsides, squibs, handbills, prints, journals, magazines, newspapers, plays, poetry and novels. Texts on politics, science, agriculture, architecture, political economy, philosophy, religion and a myriad of other topics were available and keenly read by educated Georgians. Many gentlemen put pen to paper on learned topics and published their views, often on several subjects in one pamphlet. Newspaper titles proliferated, the first dailies emerged and many developed strong political allegiances. Journals and magazines such as *The Gentleman's Magazine*, founded in 1731, became popular for their elegant cultural essays, parliamentary reporting, society news and gossip. Manuals and conduct books also flourished that instructed those in trade or service – or anyone merely wishing to climb the social ladder – how to behave appropriately. Perhaps surprisingly to us today, the most published genre in the eighteenth century remained the sermon.

Notably, the Georgians were the first to read a novel in the form that we would recognise. The first of these were mostly highly moral tales or conduct novels that, by means of a rather dull narrative, instructed women in how to behave. Over time, however, the rather more lively culture of the age produced works familiar to us, including those by Henry Fielding, Fanny Burney and Jane Austen. Novels today are a part of everyday life and are accepted as culturally beneficial, but in the Georgian period they were often an illicit pleasure. Many viewed novel reading as frivolous, and likely to lead to a dangerous corruption of moral standards. What was read, and how audiences for certain texts grew, also tells us much about the spread of ideas geographically and through the ranks and interest groups within society. Book collecting was an important part of masculine consumption by the Georgian gentleman, who was generally expected to have an elegant library in his country mansion. The King's Library, originally the library of George III, is now housed in striking architectural style in the British Library, its volumes still available to readers today. The reading of novels, on the other hand, was deemed to be primarily the activity of women, both from the elite and the middle class. Subscription libraries were opening in towns and cities around the country, enabling many more people to gain access to texts of all kinds.

Of course reading and writing require education, and literacy figures for the period are difficult to calculate. How literacy should be measured is an initial obstacle, and much debated by historians. Yet evidence suggests that literacy was more common in those below the middle class than had been thought, and particularly in urban areas. Those in trade, retail and financial businesses increasingly needed literacy skills and clerks and apprentices needed to be able to write.[12] Books were expensive but were to be found in poorer homes, if only the Bible. Reading aloud was a common practice; one literate family member would read to the others, and newspapers or pamphlets were read aloud in alehouses or on street corners. Visual images in the form of prints, caricatures and chapbooks, which contained simple, morally improving tales

The Circulating Library, 1804. British Museum. Women are enjoying the books available at one of the new libraries. Judging by their dress they are elite or middle-class women, perhaps borrowing the latest novel.

with accompanying woodcut prints, would also convey meaning to the less literate. Shops that sold satirical and other topical prints of the day would keep a display of the latest prints in their windows, and these were a common attraction for all sectors of society. The consumption of printed material was an increasingly important part of everyday Georgian life.

Open Spaces and Entertainments

Georgians also experienced new freedom in terms of the spaces and places they could visit and occupy. An urban renaissance that had begun in the seventeenth century accelerated in the Georgian period, creating in towns and cities public spaces for leisure and entertainments open to those of different ranks.[13] New pavements, squares, parks and walks enabled people to walk outside without stepping in horse manure or general detritus. It became popular to promenade in such places, to see and be seen, to show off one's wealth and fashionable attire or to ogle those who had it. New shopping opportunities sprang up in towns and cities and, for the middle class in particular, shopping became a pastime of similar importance to today. Shops, especially in London, were renovated and increased their stock; eye-catching window displays with attractive lighting developed, and service improved.

Moreover, much that had been largely exclusive to the king's court or the aristocratic mansion could now be found in new public spaces in towns and cities. High culture and the arts moved into coffee houses, debating societies, concert halls, theatres, museums, galleries and subscription libraries.[14] Bringing culture into the public domain became the mission of institutions such as the Royal Academy (formed in 1768 in Pall Mall and then opening at Somerset House in 1780), the British Museum (founded in 1753) and the Royal Institution (founded in 1799). The Royal Academy was one of the early venues to exhibit art to the public and exhibitions became very popular, with reviews beginning to appear in the press, while the British Museum was the first public and secular museum in Europe. It belonged to the nation and was open to all 'studious and curious persons' who wished to visit.

The Royal Institution sought to introduce science to the general public: to educate and inform by means of lectures and experiments. Its stated mission was to introduce 'useful mechanical inventions' and the applications of science 'to the common purposes of life', including agriculture and industry. Public demonstrations drew great crowds to the Royal Institution, with Humphry Davy's demonstrations of electricity and the effects of nitrous oxide (laughing gas) drawing large and mixed audiences.[15] More commercial demonstrations of new scientific discoveries such as electricity, mechanical inventions and ballooning were also held in large public venues such as the Pantheon in Oxford Street and the Lyceum on the Strand. In 1784 Mr Lunardi's famous hot air balloon was exhibited in the Pantheon.

Entertainments grew in type and availability to include dances, balls, masquerades, ridottos (entertainments with music and dancing), concerts, operas, ballet and other events. These were held in assembly rooms, new and enlarged theatres, at spas at Bath and other provincial towns and in pleasure gardens such as the famous Vauxhall, Kensington, Marylebone and Ranelagh in London. Such entertainments, particularly in the capital, competed for custom and became ever bigger, brasher and more spectacular. Novelty and technical innovation were at the forefront, dazzling their audiences with light shows, water cascades and fireworks. Spectaculars were hosted in the form of dioramas and panoramas that often boasted their astonishing size or technical novelty. Vast scenes could be viewed in the panoramas, often accompanied by music and including representations of famous battles and views of distant and exotic places, which most people would never visit.[16]

Sports such as hunting, bowling and cricket were also enjoyed around the country. Fox hunting became increasingly popular, with packs of hounds maintained by the elite or by local towns where hunt balls were also held in assembly rooms. Spectator sports also drew the crowds: cock-fighting remained a favourite, while horse racing developed more sophisticated facilities for a broader public to enjoy, race meetings offering food and drink, gambling opportunities and prizes to race winners. Many provincial towns such as Shrewsbury, Cheltenham, York and Worcester had race

James Gillray, *Scientific Researches*, 1802. British Museum. Here Gillray pokes fun at a demonstration at the Royal Institution and depicts Humphry Davy, at the bench, as a showman of science. The mixed audience appears spellbound.

courses, and Newmarket was also prominent. The Georgian period saw the introduction of the Triple Crown which was awarded to the horse that won in one season the St Leger (first run in 1776), the Derby (in 1780) and the Two Thousand Guineas (in 1809). The *Racing Calendar* was first published in 1727, listing 112 courses, and the Jockey Club was founded in 1750. Boxing, commonly known as prize-fighting, was a popular spectator sport with all sectors of society. This originally took the form of bare-knuckle fighting, with no rules and often held impromptu. The first English bare-knuckle champion was James Figs in 1719. In 1743 Jack Broughton introduced rules to protect the boxer, including the boxing ring, known as 'The Broughton Rules'. He also introduced the first boxing gloves, though these were not always worn by fighters. Many elite men were attracted to boxing as participants and Broughton was a popular coach. Spectator crowds grew during the Georgian period, particularly for prize fights; George IV and Lord Byron were both keen patrons of boxing. The fights between Daniel Mendoza and Richard 'the Gentleman' Humphries in the late 1780s drew huge crowds and much publicity.

This commercialisation of leisure brought more opportunities for ordinary people to seek entertainment in an enlarged public sphere, with freedom to roam, observe and take part as never before. Families were attracted to many such entertainments, some of which were considered educational. They were open to anyone who could afford to buy a ticket and many were inexpensive enough to attract great numbers and a broad social mix. The mixing of different ranks was at once exciting and shocking to contemporaries. The frisson of irregular contact at social gatherings was exploited by the masquerade, a popular form of entertainment that required the anonymity of those attending.[17]

Travel and tourism also became more common in the Georgian period, as the freedom of the open turnpike road beckoned. Visits to spas such as Bath, Tunbridge Wells and Buxton became popular for health and social reasons, as did the seaside. Such towns put on additional entertainments in their season. Brighton (named Brighthelmstone until the early nineteenth century) became a particular attraction for its sea bathing. The middle class who could not afford to travel on the Continent, or were prevented from doing so during the wars with France that blighted much of the period, chose instead to visit regions in Britain.

Areas of unchallenging beauty were conventionally the favourite with most tourists; anything wild was deemed inhospitable and too challenging. Such tourists would visit local sites of interest, including the country seats of the very wealthy and the nobility, which were sometimes open to the public upon application to the housekeeper. This enabled a filtering process to take place, ensuring that only the respectable gained access. By visiting such homes the middle class could view the style and taste of the elite at first hand, something they would not generally have the opportunity to do. In *Pride and Prejudice* Elizabeth Bennet's trip to Pemberley with Mr and Mrs Gardiner, while on a holiday in Derbyshire, represents such a visit.

Ideas and the Enlightenment

Such material changes did much to develop the environment within which Georgians lived and also influenced their view of themselves. Yet the political and cultural ideas that developed during the period were just as important in the making of a more modern Britain. An influential movement in ideas, and also for promoting greater freedom in Europe, was the Enlightenment. Historians are sceptical today about what this term means and when it may be applied – particularly in Britain, where it has been associated most closely with Scotland. Nevertheless, some general threads and themes that we may associate with an enlightenment, or enlightenments, may be drawn from the ferment of ideas that circulated around Britain's towns and cities, coffee houses and drawing rooms, even alehouses and street corners.[18]

The movement originated in France and during our period emerged in Britain, with some ideas taken from Europe and others more home-grown. It engaged with politics, philosophy, science, the arts, aesthetics and perceptions of civil society, and was generally a modernising influence. Enlightenment thinkers challenged the ignorance, dogma, superstition, injustice and oppression that they associated with contemporary European societies. They tended towards a secular and reformist view incorporating the concept of universal human rights. The Scottish philosopher David Hume was a critic of religious superstition and applied reason to religious concepts of the afterlife in his *On the Immortality of the Soul* (1775).

Science was also of great importance during the period, with new emphasis placed on empiricism, rational enquiry and the possibilities of human progress through the application of science. Humphry Davy's popular *A Discourse, Introductory to a Course of Lectures on Chemistry* (1802) reflects such ideas. His invention of the miners' safety lamp suggests an enlightened concern for the good of humanity. The classical world of ancient Rome and Greece was also revered, and a recurring source of inspiration in art, architecture, politics and society. A set of rules about composition, based on the classical forms, were followed to great effect by artists and architects such as Sir John Soane, who produced many neoclassical designs such as the exterior of the Bank of England. The neoclassical style was dominant in architecture during the period, and many people today associate the term 'Georgian' most closely with elegant London squares, Palladian country villas and the crescents and terraces of towns such as Bath, Cheltenham and Edinburgh. Neoclassical style is still linked to the Georgian nobility who built many of the London squares that bear their names, such as Bedford, Onslow and Devonshire.

Georgians also believed Nature was a force to be controlled and empirically observed, as illustrated by garden design of the time. Gardens of the elite were no longer set out in the formal geometric patterns favoured in the seventeenth century; instead they were landscaped by designers such as Capability Brown to reflect a planned prospect of tranquil sweeping lawns, water features and carefully placed ornaments and follies. Attempts were made to define what constituted the beautiful and the sublime in nature. Edmund Burke, in his *Philosophical Enquiry into the Origin of our Ideas of the Sublime and Beautiful* (1757), equated beauty with feelings of warmth, affection and even (non-sexual) love.

James Gillray, *Copenhagen House*, 1795. British Museum. Here the popular radical orator John Thelwall addresses a large audience at an outdoor meeting.

Yet the most intense and powerful aesthetic experience was the sublime. Burke associated it with such elements as obscurity, power, vastness and infinity that would provoke passions of astonishment, apprehension, horror or terror in the viewer. He did not, however, envisage an uncontrollable form of the sublime; it was, rather, to be experienced from a place of safety and explained in a philosophical manner.[19]

Although many of the ideas we associate with a European Enlightenment were originally shared among an intellectual elite, they did spread more widely in Britain and were of considerable influence in Georgian society and politics. Moreover, the general Enlightenment mission, to increase human happiness and progress for the good of all humanity, embraced the whole of society, in theory at least. For example Adam Smith, a leader of the Scottish Enlightenment, applied such ideas in *An Inquiry into the Nature and Causes of the Wealth of Nations* (1776), much proclaimed today as the first work of modern economics. Robert Owen famously introduced humanitarian ideals to his cotton mills at New Lanark, radically improving the material lives of his workers while keeping a close eye on the profits. He recorded his ideas in essays entitled *A New View of Society*, published together in 1816, and promoted more widely social improvement through community living. Radical scientists such as Joseph Priestley and Thomas Beddoes believed that the development of science would bring social progress and new political egalitarian freedom. The ideas of Enlightenment thinkers, particularly those of Jean-Jacques Rousseau, were later taken up by leaders of the French Revolution (although that was not Rousseau's aim) and fed into the political ideas that developed in Britain. The *Encyclopédie* compiled by the French philosophers Denis Diderot and Jean Le Rond d'Alembert (1751–65), the seminal text of the Enlightenment, condemned slavery on humanitarian grounds. Such ideas were influential upon the British movements to abolish the slave trade and slavery from the 1780s to the 1830s.

Moreover, increased communication, freedom of speech and the press enabled ideas to spread and develop more swiftly. The period saw a shift in views about the place of ordinary people in the world, and their rights and freedoms. The long-standing reverence for the English constitution and the liberties it enabled was challenged as reformers began to recognise the limitations of such liberties. Calls for political reform in Britain were underpinned by political ideas from America and France, focused upon a broader conception of liberty, equality and greater democracy. The cry of the rebellious Americans, 'no taxation without representation', and the French revolutionaries' call for 'liberty, equality and fraternity' struck a chord in Britain. A new 'people power' began to develop as ordinary people became engaged with political ideas that related directly to them.

While popular action can be traced back at least to the Peasants' Revolt of 1381, it was bolstered in the eighteenth century by this new sense of the people. The growth in urban living, and consequent loosening of local patrician control, contributed to the development of this popular voice, and the expansion of the press led to a new focus upon public opinion. The Georgian era was certainly a period when the people went out on to the streets, claiming space and a place to make their presence felt and their voices heard.

An increasingly organised, extra-parliamentary politics developed. Reformers formed societies, marched across cities, held outdoor meetings and signed petitions to

Parliament and the king in greater numbers than ever before. In 1787 the first mass petition, against the slave trade was signed by nearly one-fifth of the population of Manchester.[20] Radical societies around the country compiled petitions for reform of government; signed by thousands, these were presented to Parliament in 1793. Crowds of thousands attended mass meetings in cities such as Manchester, Sheffield and London to hear radical orators such as John Thelwall and Henry Hunt inform them of the political rights they had been denied and the equality they deserved. An estimated sixty thousand protestors gathered in St Peter's Fields, Manchester, in 1819 to demand the right to vote.[21] The reforms demanded all promoted freedom of one sort or another. Many pamphlets, broadsides, squibs, satirical prints, songs and verse were published, produced by those involved in the debates that raged between reformers and loyalists (those who defended the status quo). Indeed, a battle of ideas developed in print over political and religious reform and slavery. For example, in the debate in Britain in response to the French Revolution, Thomas Paine's *Rights of Man* (1791–2) was probably the most influential radical text, with Edmund Burke's *Reflections on the Revolution in France* (1790) representing, in passionate prose, the loyalist position. Such texts swelled the volume of printed material available to a wide audience.[22]

How effective such people-power proved to be in reality in bringing reform is difficult to determine, particularly as there were also many people, equally vociferous, who opposed such ideas. Yet, perhaps most importantly, this engagement of ordinary people with reform suggests an increased engagement with altruistic issues, and an understanding of contemporary ideas about their rights – in particular the concept of freedom as a universal human right. Moreover, in each of these areas reform of varying degrees was introduced in the early nineteenth century. Legislation for greater religious toleration was enacted in 1828 and 1829, while the Reform Act of 1832 achieved somewhat limited political reform. The slave trade was abolished by statute in 1807, and slavery in British colonies ended in 1833.

Romanticism

Perhaps inevitably, the Georgian period also experienced a reaction in Europe against the strictly rational and empirical approach of Enlightenment thought and the rules of classicism. This took the form of a move towards a greater sensibility, emphasising the importance of emotion and imagination. While Enlightenment ideas did not as a consequence disappear, they were mediated, paradoxically, by a need for greater freedom: freedom of expression emotionally, artistically, aesthetically and to assert greater individuality. This reaction and the ideas it promulgated can most closely be identified with Romanticism, a movement, particularly in the arts, that developed from about 1780. In contrast to the rationalism of the Enlightenment, this movement embraced the spiritual, the supernatural, melancholy, the Gothic, the exotic and the oriental, essentially promoting feeling over reason.

Such ideas associated with Romanticism can be identified in Britain in the later Georgian period. This brought an increased emphasis on the sublime, and consequently the wilder aspects of nature became more popular. The Scottish Highlands, the Lake District and the Alps became fashionable tourist destinations for their steep mountains and inhospitable weather. The desire for a more intense sublime experience was expressed through cliffs and waterfalls, thunderstorms, snowstorms, darkness and obscuring fog, all identified as evoking a powerful, sublime response. Close proximity to the source was advocated, with people encouraged to walk within the mountains rather than view them from a safe distance, so that they could experience the vastness and confusion of nature at first hand. These ideas were expressed in art and literature, for example J. M. W. Turner's painting *Snow Storm: Hannibal and his Army Crossing the Alps* (1812) well illustrates this more Romantic conception of the sublime. In 1816 Lord Byron, Shelley and Mary Shelley visited the Alps, where Mary Shelley wrote her disturbing Gothic tale *Frankenstein*. In his famous poem *Childe Harold's Pilgrimage*, Byron described the Alps as unequivocally sublime:

J. M. W. Turner, *Snow Storm: Hannibal and his Army Crossing the Alps*, 1812. Tate. Photo: The Art Archive/Eileen Tweedy. This painting depicts Hannibal and his men diminished by the towering power of nature. The great swirls of storm clouds dominate the painting and represent the obscuring, terrifying Romantic sublime.

> '...The palaces of Nature, whose vast walls
> Have pinnacled in clouds their snowy scalps,
> And throned Eternity in icy halls
> Of Cold sublimity, where forms and falls
> The avalanche – the thunderbolt of snow!
> All which expands the spirit, yet appals...'
> Canto III (1816), stanza 62.

Eastern societies (often termed 'oriental' at the time) also became an object of fascination for their exotic difference – in particular, as a source of fantasy about sexual desire and transgression. In the later part of the period it became fashionable for the elite avant-garde to dress in the oriental style. Byron, the ultimate English Romantic, frequently adopted such dress and also wrote the exotic poem *The Giaour: A Fragment of a Turkish Tale* (1813). Texts we might identify as Romantic include novels by Sir Walter Scott and Thomas de Quincey's *Confessions of an Opium Eater* (1822), a somewhat surreal diary of his opium-induced dreams. Romantic influences can also be identified in music and ballet.

The Prince Regent indulged his exotic fantasies in Brighton Pavilion, his bolthole from parental pressures and royal responsibilities in London. This extraordinary building reflected in part the Romantic sublime in an eclectic design. As well as some classical elements, the Pavilion incorporated a number of Eastern styles and motifs from, for example, Moghul India, Islam, China and Egypt. Inside the Pavilion the oriental theme continued with a mix of brilliant and exotic decoration, dazzling lighting and lavish furnishings and heating. Some visitors found it overwhelming, intoxicating and decadent. Romantics were perhaps the thrill-seekers of their day, seeking new ways to stimulate and excite the senses. But they were also pushing at the boundaries of what was acceptable and breaking established and classical rules – most notably in art, architecture and literature.

Taste, Politeness and 'Luxury'

Ideas were also important in shaping the constraints Georgian society imposed on the excesses of its flamboyant consumer culture and the new social freedoms it enabled. Indeed, the classical world was the source of codes and ideals about elite behaviour, civility and decorum that influenced Georgian ideas on taste and politeness, and the excesses of luxury. Consequently, taste and politeness developed exacting requirements and meant so much more than they do today.[23]

To have good taste was a mark of esteem in society, but developing it was not straightforward. It was necessary to reveal cultural superiority discreetly, through one's home decorations and personal style. Anything 'too vulgar' that tended towards 'luxury' was condemned as morally reprehensible. Good taste was formulated by the nobility, often upheld as arbiters of taste and connoisseurs of the arts. It was presumed that their 'good breeding' in terms of a classics-based education, natural talents and character, together with experience as young men of the aristocratic Grand Tour around Europe, prepared gentlemen for their natural roles. As well as compiling libraries, they often developed collections of art and artefacts, many gathering initial items from sites on the Grand Tour.

Moreover, members of the nobility had always asserted their power and position through the display of wealth in their homes, and by rich and fashionable dress when out and about. The fact that this privilege was now encroached upon by the middle class led to some anxiety, and a greater need to define more clearly what did, and what did not, amount to good taste. There was much snobbish derision of parvenus, 'nabobs' (those who had made their wealth in the colonies and come home to flaunt it) and 'mushroom men' (those who had been granted a title rather than inherited one). Thus taste was an exclusive concept; it was important socially not to display what we might today term 'bling'.

Yet in this environment of growing commerce and consumption, in which retailers and wholesalers competed for prime position, ideas about taste were also reinterpreted by shopkeepers, entrepreneurs, journalists and writers. Increasingly the middle class was also developing its own values and ideals, often reflecting Christian restraint and moral rectitude and centred on respectability and civility. What constituted 'good taste' consequently became more diverse and difficult to determine. It took up many pages of print in journals and magazines, and was a frequent point of discussion among those who felt themselves suitably superior to know.

Similarly, the concept of politeness was associated by contemporaries with ideas about 'good breeding', 'gentility', 'refinement' and 'sociability'.[24] Some historians have argued that politeness, like taste, was a way for the elite to differentiate themselves from the increasingly encroaching hordes of everybody else, to reinforce social barriers that were being eroded. Others believe that Georgian politeness was a means to enable communication between different ranks in more open social or commercial situations.[25] In fact, as contemporary sources indicate, politeness came to represent a number of varied ideas about correct behaviour.

In an article on 'Manners in Town and Country' that appeared in *The Spectator* (1711), the famous social commentator Joseph Addison claimed that a 'very great Revolution' had happened in manners in 'the Fashionable World'. The manners 'of the last age' that had enabled the elite to distinguish themselves from 'the Rustick part of the Species' had become too restrictive and cumbersome. He wittily declared that 'Forms of Conversation, like the *Romish* religion, was so encumbered with Show and Ceremony that it stood in need of a Reformation … to restore it to its natural good sense.' The Modish World had thrown aside much of this formality and adopted a new free and easy 'Openness of Behaviour'. Manners now 'sit more

James Gillray, *Exaltation of Faro's Daughters*, 1796. British Museum.
This print, showing two fashionably dressed ladies in the stocks, satirises the gambling obsession of the Georgian elite.

James Gillray, *Politeness*, 1789. British Museum. Here the stout John Bull, with his pint and the large cut of beef alongside, represents a contemporary 'Britishness'. In contrast the Frenchman, perched on a spindly chair, though fancily dressed, is feeble and effeminate and has only vermin to eat. The robust British bulldog intimidates the skinny, cowering French whippet.

loose upon us' and 'nothing is more modish as an agreeable negligence'. He lamented that such old-fashioned forms of politeness still lingered among the rural gentry, which rendered visiting them a tortuous experience. Going for a walk was marred by deference to hierarchy as to who should walk in front and who behind. The time-consuming formalities of seating arrangements and ceremonial meant that the dinner was cold by the time he could eat it.

Lord Chesterfield, however, took the matter of politeness far more seriously in his endless letters to his son. He linked 'good breeding' to good manners, and conventionally resorted to the classical world as the source of much that was admirable. He declared that only 'the strictest and most scrupulous honour and virtue', along with 'learning', could 'make you esteemed and valued by mankind'. Also required was a 'genteel and easy manner, and carriage', which must be free of 'awkwardness'. In a later letter Lord Chesterfield warned against 'Loud Laughter' as this is 'the mirth of the mob, who are only pleased with silly things; for true wit or good sense never excited a laugh … A man of parts and fashion is therefore only seen to smile, but never to laugh'.[26] Politeness here seems somewhat burdensome and while, as Amanda Vickery has noted, it required the appearance of an easy poise, it was clearly anything but easy to acquire.

Politeness rigorously reflected rank and status, and still required considerable control of behaviour and the suppression of emotions. Nor was the practice of politeness restricted to the public domain: it was also important in the domestic world of the home. Conduct manuals were written for the aspiring middle class, businessmen and women and shopkeepers, to enable them to learn the requirements of politeness necessary and appropriate to business or social interactions. Thus it seems that politeness developed both as a way to ease what had become rigid and formal manners among the elite, and as a means of communication between those of different social standing. It enabled a lady to speak to a shopkeeper without mishap, and for those of differing social position to converse at a dance at the local assembly rooms. Such politeness did not, however, break down hierarchical social boundaries. Rather, it controlled the increasing sociability of Georgian society, ensuring that those who wished to take part were not free to enjoy themselves in the way that we are today.

Despite the controlling requirements of taste and politeness, many Georgians still abhorred what they perceived as the new, rapacious consumer society with its offending 'luxury', casual manners and, particularly, the mixing of people of different ranks and occupations. Fears of the effects of such social interaction were fuelled by rumours of prostitutes dressed like ladies frequenting London parks and pleasure gardens, and rowdy and inappropriate behaviour at assemblies and public entertainments. Fanny Burney expressed such concerns in her novel *Evelina* (1778), in which the heroine becomes lost in the infamous dark walks at Vauxhall pleasure gardens and is accosted by unsuitable young men of indeterminate rank.

Indeed, a lengthy debate about the evils of luxury on the general morals of society was sustained throughout the Georgian period, and comparisons were made with the decline of the Roman Empire. Christian restraint and morality were also at the forefront of such debates about luxury. Evangelical Christians such as Hannah More and William Wilberforce promoted a movement for the reformation of manners from the late 1780s. In her pamphlet *Thoughts on the Importance of the Manners of the Great to General*

Society (1788), More called on the elite to set a better example and cease gambling, having their hair done and holding concerts and dinners on Sundays. It was believed that the luxury and profligacy of the elite corrupted the 'vulgar', who consequently became lazy, weak and effeminate. William Hogarth captured the excesses of the times with a strong moral message in his print series such as *Marriage A La Mode, A Rake's Progress* and *A Harlot's Progress.* His *Gin Lane* provided a strong visual image of the dire effects of the gin craze on the London poor, prompting the government to outlaw the production of cheap gin by means of the Gin Act (1751).

In *An Estimate of the Manners and Principles of the Times* (1757–8), John Brown, a clergyman, condemned the young men of fashion in London (often termed 'macaronis') who tended towards excess and 'Effeminacy' in their dress and lifestyle. Brown complained that they would not 'cross the Street to Dinner, without the effeminate Covering and Conveyance of an *easy Chair'* (by which he meant a sedan chair). Contemporary town houses provided further evidence of an 'Excess of Effeminacy: Warm Carpets ... warm Hangings', with doors and windows tightly fitted to 'prevent the least rude Encroachment of the external Air'. Dinner was sheer 'Luxury' with the most expensive wines of the continent, 'High Soups and Sauces ... every Mode of foreign Cookery that can ... spur the lagging Appetite'. Indeed, the conventional nourishing and temperate English diet had been replaced with 'inflaming foods' that can only 'irritate'. Nor was the conversation at dinner going to be of 'weight or importance', since good breeding now required that guests merely 'trifle agreeably'. This 'effeminate show', with its 'Splendor of Dress, Equipage, Furniture, Entertainments', was all so 'enormously expensive' that the man of fashion must resort to '*Gaming* as a *Trade*'; and Brown observed darkly that 'on these foundations seems to rest the midnight Riot and Dissipation of modern Assemblies'.

Throughout the period that enduring enemy, the French, were condemned as the most effeminate nation – weakened by the excesses of an absolute monarchy, Popery and food tainted with garlic and rich sauces. In contrast, the English John Bull represented the down-to-earth English country squire: robust and hearty, thriving on country life and, of course, plain roast beef. Tobias Smollett in *Humphrey Clinker* (1760–5) also condemned conspicuous consumption and luxury. The main character, Matthew Bramble, was depicted as a typical Bull-like country squire for whom society was going to the dogs. A visit to Bath brought him into contact only with 'ostentation of wealth', extravagance and vulgarity. Taste was nowhere to be seen; all was 'racket and dissipation', overtaken by 'the tide of luxury'. Indeed, even the waters of the baths were contaminated by the 'vulgar', and had become a cesspool of disease and infection. A healthy country life of fresh air, plain food and simple pleasures was to be recommended.[27] Of course, concepts of 'sin city' and a rural Arcadia have existed throughout history, but they were much heightened during the Georgian era in response to fears about the significant changes in society. Moreover, such vociferous contemporary condemnation of social life suggests that many Georgians managed to enjoy themselves, despite the rigours of taste and politeness.

Conclusion

New ideas and material changes thus came together in the Georgian period to create a more open and modern society. Greater physical freedom was made possible by changes in the way people lived and what they could consume, while ideas about greater political, social and economic freedom spread through society and were taken up by a new public, one comprising ordinary people. Of course this was not a period of unadulterated progress, as so-called 'Whig history' would have it. The contemporary belief in an inexorable journey towards the pinnacle of civilisation within the foreseeable future was, as time has shown, misplaced. Progress was uneven and, as in all societies, there was a mix of innovation and continued adherence to hidebound tradition. Certainly there were still obstacles in the way of the sort of freedoms and the sense of modernity we take for granted today. In particular, life for a large sector of society was 'poor, nasty, brutish and short', to misapply Thomas Hobbes's *Leviathan* (1651), and democracy and equality of any sort were a long way off.

One obvious example of the contradictory aspects of Georgian society is slavery. The slave trade and slavery contributed to economic growth for Britain and her empire, and ensured the availability of exotic consumer items. It made some men very rich, and cities such as Bristol and Manchester were built on the profits of this trade. Yet slavery was regressive in humanitarian terms. Here, capitalism, and the insatiable desires of a consumer society, came up against prevailing ideas about freedom and reform. The British Atlantic slave trade and slavery continued into the nineteenth century, and the growing public voice against it took some considerable time to have an effect.

The role of women in society represents another example of hidebound attitudes. While free to enjoy the benefits of the consumer society, women had few rights. The 'rights of man' meant just that: calls for universal suffrage meant universal *male* suffrage, and this discrimination was applied not just in politics but to life in general. That is not to say that women had no agency: many engaged with politics and commerce, owned businesses and wrote published texts. But such activities were circumscribed by law and convention, and most, including Jane Austen, did not write under their own name.

Nevertheless, the essence of the period could be said to be one of exploration and innovation in many areas of life, with the Georgians displaying optimism and enthusiasm in their bold grasp of the new. As the exhibition illustrates, those who could afford it demonstrated an insatiable appetite for the latest trends in products for the home, fashionable clothing, entertainments and travel. Advances in industry, commerce, technology and communications fuelled this new consumer society. These factors, together with the spread of ideas in politics, science, philosophy and the arts and the focus on progress and improvement certainly contributed to the making of something we might tentatively call a modern Britain.

Notes

1. See Amanda Vickery, *Behind Closed Doors: At Home in Georgian England* (New Haven and London, 2009); D. Hicks and M. Beaudry, (eds), *The Oxford Handbook of Material Culture Studies* (Oxford and New York, 2010).
2. J. C. D. Clark, *English Society, 1688–1832: Ideology, Social Structure and Political Practice during the Ancien Régime* (Cambridge, 1985).
3. Paul Langford, *A Polite and Commercial People: England, 1727–1783* (Oxford, 1989).
4. See Penelope J. Corfield, *Power and the Professions in Britain, 1700–1850* (London, 1995).
5. Linda Colley, *Britons: Forging the Nation, 1707–1837* (London, 1994).
6. Pat Hudson, *The Industrial Revolution* (Oxford, 1992).
7. Julian Hoppit, *A Land of Liberty? England 1689–1727* (Oxford, 2000).
8. James Raven, 'The Abolition of the English State Lotteries', *The Historical Journal*, 34, 2 (1991).
9. N. McKendrick, J. Brewer and J. H. Plumb, *The Birth of a Consumer Society: The Commercialisation of Eighteenth-Century England* (London, 1982).
10. Hannah Greig, *The Beau Monde: Fashionable Society in Georgian London* (Oxford, 2013).
11. Lorna Weatherill, *Consumer Behaviour and Material Culture in Britain, 1660–1760* (London, 1988).
12. Susan E. Whyman, *The Pen and the People: English Letter Writers, 1660–1800* (Oxford, 2009).
13. Peter Borsay, *The English Urban Renaissance: Culture and Society in the Provincial Town, 1660–1770* (Oxford, 1989).
14. John Brewer, *The Pleasures of the Imagination: English Culture in the Eighteenth Century* (London, 1997).
15. Jan Golinski, *Science as Public Culture: Chemistry and Enlightenment in Britain, 1760–1820* (Cambridge, 1992).
16. John Brewer, 'Sensibility and the Urban Panorama', *Huntington Library Quarterly*, Vol. 70, No. 2 (June 2007).
17. Penelope J. Corfield, *Vauxhall and the Invention of the Urban Pleasure Gardens* (London, 2008).
18. Roy Porter, *Enlightenment: Britain and the Creation of the Modern World* (London, 2000).
19. Material here on the Enlightenment and Romanticism is influenced by the Open University published materials *Enlightenment to Romanticism, c. 1780–1830*, 7 Vols (2004).
20. Boyd Hilton, *A Mad, Bad and Dangerous People? England, 1783–1846* (Oxford, 2006).
21. Unfortunately, although their protest was peaceful, the authorities sent in troops and it ended in a massacre in which a number of protestors died.
22. Amanda Goodrich, *Debating England's Aristocracy in the 1790s: Pamphlets, Polemics and Political Ideas* (Woodbridge, 2005).
23. See George Dickie, *The Century of Taste: The Philosophical Odyssey of Taste in the Eighteenth Century* (Oxford, 1996).
24. Amanda Vickery, *The Gentleman's Daughter: Women's Lives in Georgian England* (New York and London, 1998).
25. See Paul Langford, 'The Uses of Eighteenth-Century Politeness', *Transactions of the Royal Historical Society* 12 (2002); Lawrence Klein, 'Politeness for Plebs' in A. Bermingham and J. Brewer (eds), *The Consumption of Culture, 1600–1800: Image, Object, Text* (London, 1995).
26. David Roberts (ed.), *Lord Chesterfield's Letters* (Oxford, 1992).
27. Susan L. Jacobsen, '"The Tinsel of the Times": Smollett's Argument against Conspicuous Consumption in *Humphrey Clinker*', *Eighteenth-Century Fiction*, Vol. 9, No. 1 (October 1996).

1 Homes and Gardens

During the long period in which the four Georges ruled Britain, people's living environments and leisure activities changed, especially for the middle classes, who enjoyed more opportunities for travel, larger houses and increased access to public entertainments and pleasure gardens. Many of these changes are still with us today.

The architecture of private and public buildings became more ordered and classical in style, with less regional variation. Architects such as Robert Adam, Sir John Soane and John Nash designed some of their most famous buildings, including the Adelphi, the Bank of England and the Royal Pavilion at Brighton respectively. Changes were also evident in the interior designs of houses. Wallpaper, for example, came into use as a cheaper alternative to fabric wall hangings, and Thomas Chippendale designed his famous pieces of furniture, which are desirable collectors' objects today. Having one's own garden, and the time to enjoy it, became possible for more and more people. While the London gardener Thomas Fairchild concentrated on giving practical advice to city dwellers, Humphry Repton and Batty Langley, among others, advised people with larger gardens in the countryside on possible new designs.

Growing prosperity among members of the middle classes brought with it social changes that enabled more people to have servants to take care of some of their day-to-day tasks in and around the home. This in turn gave people more leisure time to enjoy and more opportunities to educate themselves or learn new skills. Reading novels and newspapers became more common because the spread of printing and the rise of circulating libraries made printed fact and fiction more accessible to those who did not possess their own libraries. Larger numbers of people, and especially women, spent time learning to play an instrument and to paint or draw. Such accomplishments, which had always been traditional among the upper classes, spread rapidly through the middle classes. While enjoying time with family or friends indoors or outdoors, people increasingly engaged in the ritual of drinking tea, a new commodity that became very popular in eighteenth-century Britain.

Today we still enjoy weekend visits to country houses and gardens, and this leisure activity is another legacy of the eighteenth century. Some members of the upper classes were keen to open up their properties to other people, to show what they had and to enable other people to enjoy it; and trips to places such as Stowe, Wilton and Kew Gardens became widespread among the middle classes.

Underpinning all of these changes to people's daily lives was a deep desire for improvement and the social mobility that this could provide.

The Adam Style

When talking about 'Georgian architecture' the buildings designed by Robert Adam are among the first that come to mind. The Adam brothers, Robert and James, were born in Kirkcaldy, Fife, the sons of Scotland's most famous architect. They were architects, builders, designers and developers, as well as suppliers of building materials. Their architectural style is characterised by neo-Antique ornaments and typically eighteenth-century refinement and elegance. The Adam brothers made use of varied room shapes and intricate decorative plasterwork in their interior designs, as well as rippling facades on the exteriors of their buildings. The style was heavily influenced by Robert Adam's experiences and studies during his Grand Tour between 1754 and 1758, and, to a lesser extent, by James's experiences on his Grand Tour. Both brothers amassed antiquities and drawings that influenced the work they produced in London. On his return to Britain Robert Adam (1728–1792) and his younger brother James (1732–1794) settled in London. They developed what we now know as the Adam style of architecture, based on their knowledge and study of Roman antiquity, which provided direct inspiration for their designs. Their sources were Roman architecture ancient and modern, English, Scottish and French architecture, old and new, and the use of new elements was a key part of their designs.

Robert Adam was one of the most successful architects of his day. He initiated a new phase of the classical revival in England and Scotland and introduced neoclassicism to Britain. The focus of the Adam brothers' practice was the unity of their designs, often achieved by conceiving houses in their entirety, their exterior and interior designs as well as their furniture. However, they also designed interiors for existing houses and provided plans for exteriors. Some of their buildings still used elements of the Palladian style in their exteriors, but the interiors they designed were deliberately and distinctly new and different. Robert Adam also criticised the Palladian style in his writings.

Famous buildings designed by the Adam brothers include the Royal Exchange and Charlotte Square in Edinburgh, Pulteney Bridge in Bath, Osterley Park, Syon House and Kenwood House around London, and what was probably their most famous creation: the Adelphi, a multi-purpose development (now largely demolished) on the north side of the Thames. It was built between 1768 and 1772 and was funded by the Adam brothers with the intention of having aristocratic housing above wharfs, warehouses, and dwellings for workers. However, the project financially ruined the brothers.

Robert and James Adam, *The works in architecture of Robert and James Adam, Esquires*, 3 vols, London, 1778, 1779, 1822 (3.Tab.1).

The works in architecture were first published in parts from 1773 and then in three volumes, two of which were published in 1778 and 1779 and one posthumously in 1822. The volumes were intended to raise money and re-establish the Adam brothers' reputation after the disastrous Adelphi project and to promote the Adam style at a time of increasing competition. They illustrate the exteriors of buildings designed by the Adam brothers, and provide examples of their interior designs, such as ceiling decorations and chimney pieces. The volumes were also intended as entertainment and instruction for potential clients and fellow professionals, as the authors hoped that their designs would become popular and spark an interest in their work, leading to new commissions. Shortly after this venture the brothers moved their practice to the newly financially resurgent Scottish market.

OPPOSITE TOP AND BOTTOM
Robert and James Adam, *The works in architecture of Robert and James Adam, Esquires*, 3 vols, London, 1778, 1779, 1822 (3.Tab.1).

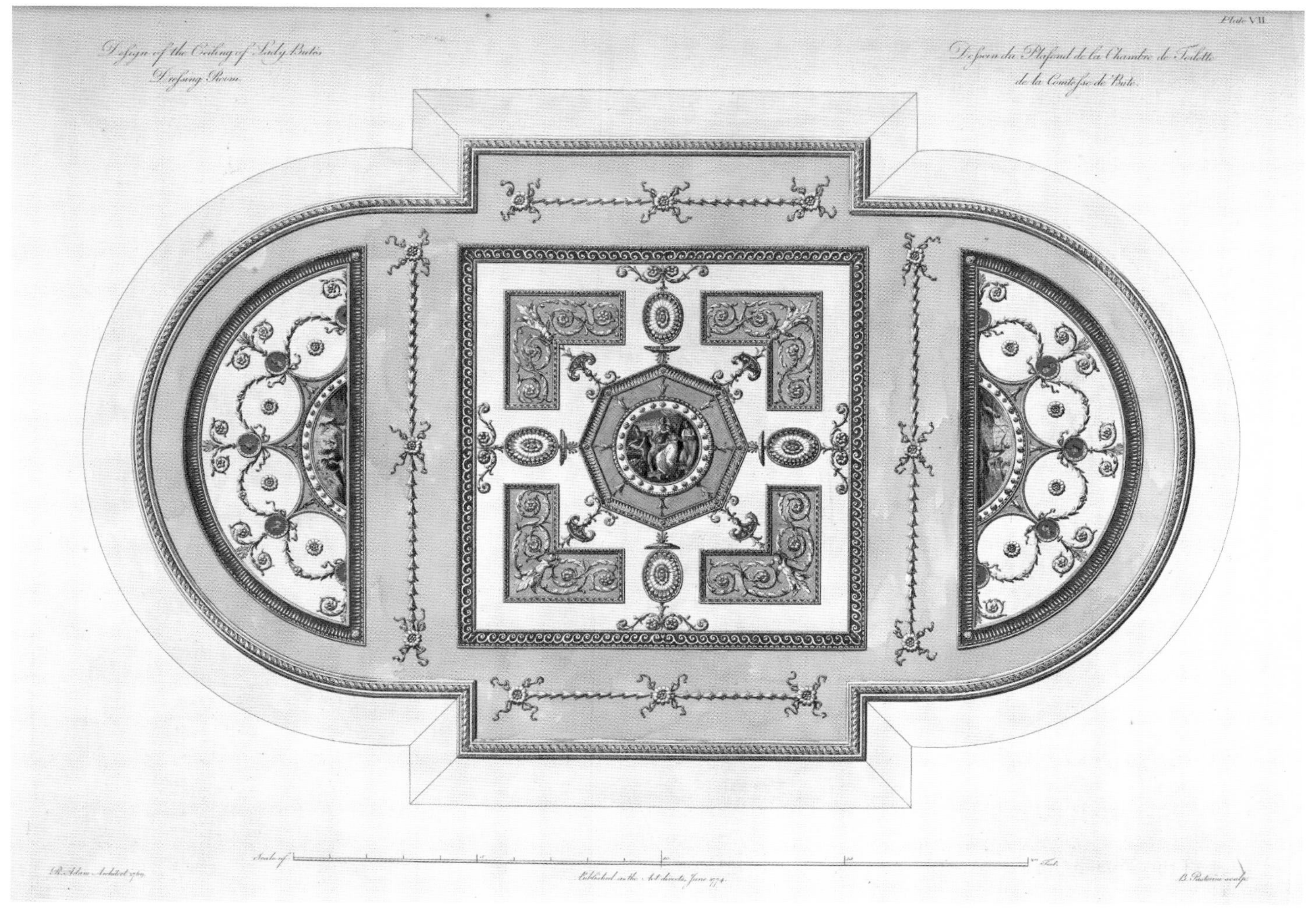

Plate VII.
Design of the Ceiling of Lady Bute's
Dressing Room.
Dessein du Plafond de la Chambre de Toilette
de la Comtesse de Bute.
Scale of
Feet.
R. Adam Architect 1769.
Published as the Act directs, June 1774.
B. Pastorini sculp.

Architectural Guides

William Pain (*c.* 1730–1794) was a prolific writer on architecture who published eleven books on the subject between 1758 and 1793. His works became bestsellers in America and were in higher demand than those of any other eighteenth-century English author. Most of them were small, pocket-sized pattern books, largely concentrating on designs for structural and decorative woodwork, and were very popular and published in several editions. All of his works were aimed at craftsmen, giving them guidance on how to work in the popular architectural styles such as Palladian, rococo or Gothic. All were also illustrated with easy-to-follow drawings and could also be consulted by customers looking for ideas for their existing or prospective properties. In *Pain's British Palladio* he included designs made by his son James, who had been apprenticed to John Nash and who, together with his brother George Richard, had built a number of private and public buildings in Ireland.

William Pain himself favoured the Palladian style of architecture, based on *I Quattro Libri dell'Architettura* by Andrea Palladio (1508–1580). The work was published in Venice for the first time in 1570 and then appeared in several editions, in Italian and in translation. Palladio himself had been influenced by classical architecture and the work of Vitruvius, and his *Quattro Libri* led to his ideas spreading throughout Europe well after his death. Books such as *Pain's British Palladio* contributed to the popularity of Palladio's ideas by making them accessible to, and achievable by, a wider audience.

William and James Pain, *Pain's British Palladio; or, the builders' general assistant. Demonstrating in the most easy and practical method, all the principal rules of architecture*, London, 1786 (1733.c.21).

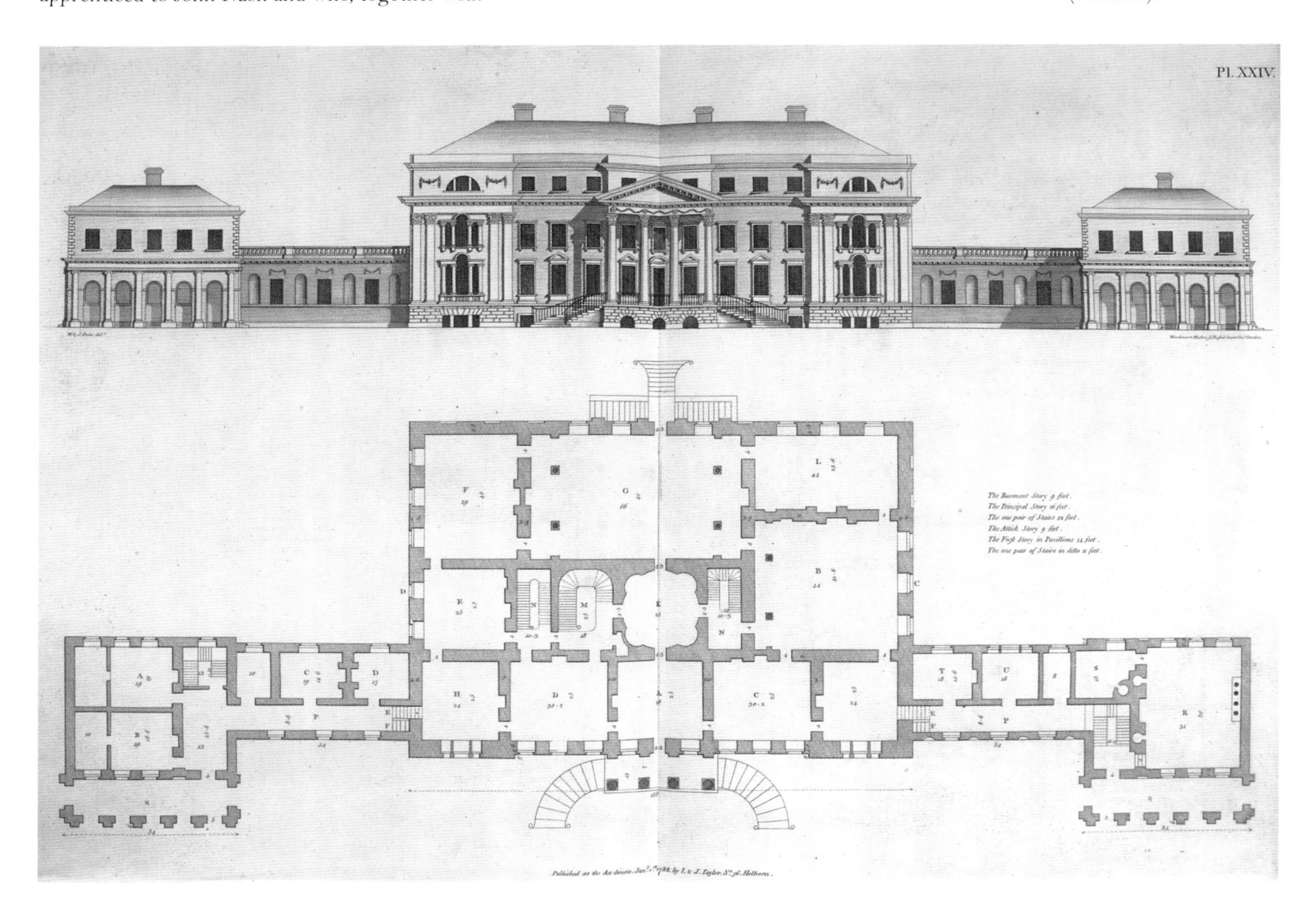

Architectural designs and practice were intended to be filtered down through society and the trade. Both *The gentleman's and builder's repository* and *The builder's magazine* were published with that aim in mind. The publications are both small formats and, like *Pain's British Palladio*, were intended for practical use by architects and builders up and down the country, and to provide inspiration for potential clients.

RIGHT
The builder's magazine: or monthly companion for architects, carpenters, masons, bricklayers, &c., London, 1774 (61.e.14).

BELOW
Edward Hoppus,
The gentleman's and builder's repository: or, architecture display'd, London, 1737 (C.175.dd.27).

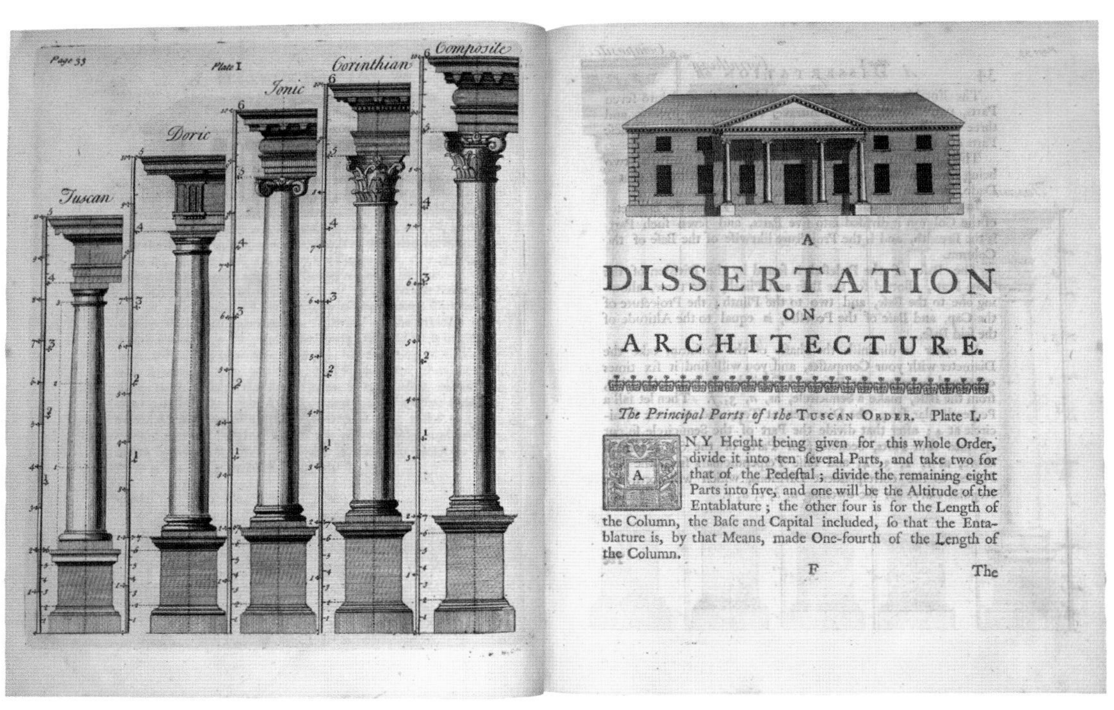

A

DISSERTATION

ON

ARCHITECTURE.

The Principal Parts of the TUSCAN ORDER. Plate I.

ANY Height being given for this whole Order, divide it into ten ſeveral Parts, and take two for that of the Pedeſtal; divide the remaining eight Parts into five, and one will be the Altitude of the Entablature; the other four is for the Length of the Column, the Baſe and Capital included, ſo that the Entablature is, by that Means, made One-fourth of the Length of the Column.

F The

A Unique Architectural Vision

Sir John Soane (1753–1837) is one of England's best-known architects, not least because he left his house in Lincoln's Inn Fields and its contents to the nation when he died. It is today one of London's most unusual and exciting museums.

Soane trained at the Royal Academy where he studied under the first professor of architecture, Thomas Sandby. He won the Gold Medal and was thereafter nominated for a Travelling Studentship for the most promising student of architecture. This paid him £60 a year for three years and enabled him to go on the Grand Tour, travelling to Italy to study Roman architecture at first hand. This experience shaped Soane's neoclassical architectural style. He bought his town houses in Lincoln's Inn Fields in 1792, 1808 and 1823, pulled them down, and rebuilt them to his designs. He acquired his country residence of Pitzhanger Manor in 1801 but sold it again in 1810. His town house famously holds his collection, including books, paintings, drawings, and antiquities.

Soane's biggest architectural project was the Bank of England, whose architect he became in 1788. His work also includes the Dulwich Picture Gallery, the first public art gallery in Britain, as well as the designs of the interiors of 10 and 11 Downing Street, which still survive, and the Board of Trade building. A number of his designs can be seen in his *Designs for private and public buildings*, published in London in 1828.

Soane became professor of architecture at the Royal Academy in 1806. His lectures were popular and accompanied by illustrations made by his pupils. Over 1000 of these illustrations survive. Soane's architectural style was often criticised during his lifetime and immediately after his death, and it was not until the beginning of the twentieth century that he was more universally regarded as the great architect he is known as today. His style was regarded as idiosyncratic, and Soane was at first mainly referred to in connection with the Bank of England, whose demolition in the early twentieth century helped to raise his public profile as an architect. Soane has since had a great influence on architects all over the world.

John Soane, *Description of the house and museum, on the north side of Lincoln's Inn-Fields, the residence of Sir John Soane*, London, 1832 (C.190.b.22).

John Soane, *Plans, elevations, and perspective views of Pitzhanger Manor House, and of the ruins of an edifice of Roman architecture situated on the border of Ealing-Green, London, 1802* [London, 1833] (C.190.b.22).

Redesigning Brighton Pavilion

In the early nineteenth century two men influenced the design of the Royal Pavilion at Brighton and its grounds as we know them today – Humphry Repton and John Nash.

The landscape gardener Humphry Repton (1752–1818) was the first man to plan a redesign of the Royal Pavilion at Brighton. His plans, some of which are shown here, were published in 1808. They were never executed in this form, however, although they influenced those of John Nash some years later.

Repton's designs contain a discourse of the prevailing styles of architecture – Greek, Gothic, and 'Modern' – as well as illustrations, in colour and black and white, showing his planned designs and a general layout of the Pavilion's grounds. In this publication Repton used the style of his famous 'red books' to illustrate his plans. They show the existing designs on so-called 'flaps' or 'fliers' which can be moved to reveal the planned new designs. Repton's plans as featured in this publication are not very detailed, but they show a recognisable

RIGHT AND BELOW
Humphry Repton, *Designs for the Pavilion at Brighton*, London, 1808 (55.i.4).

design for the Pavilion's exterior and its grounds. Repton's designs reflect his desire to move beyond established architectural styles to something more exotic and elaborate in response to his clients' needs.

The architect John Nash (1752–1835) was responsible for some of nineteenth-century Britain's most famous buildings and infrastructure developments. Between 1795 and 1800 Nash worked in partnership with the landscape gardener Humphry Repton, and their designs for fashionable villas and gardens in rural and suburban settings turned Nash into one of the most fashionable London architects of his age. Their partnership broke up in 1800 over a financial dispute. Both Repton and Nash aimed at achieving a picturesque effect, and both men worked with views and vistas to achieve maximum impact. The architecture of Nash's houses complemented the designs of Repton's gardens and vice versa, and their design approaches made small areas appear more spacious.

Nash's period of activity corresponded to a time when established architectural concepts and tastes were being questioned, and he could offer alternative designs to receptive clients, stressing his designs' exoticism and otherness. When he began to work for the Prince Regent in the 1820s, Nash stopped taking private commissions and concentrated on redesigning royal properties. His first commission was to redesign the Royal Lodge in Windsor Great Park and to design a number of rooms in Carlton House, at that time the Prince Regent's London residence.

His most important commission for the Prince Regent was that of rebuilding the Royal Pavilion at Brighton between 1815 and 1823. Nash turned the neoclassical structure designed by Henry Holland in 1787 into an 'Eastern' style to match that of the stable blocks redesigned by William Porden between 1803 and 1808. The inspiration for Nash's designs came from Mughal architecture

as well as the designs drawn up by his former partner Humphry Repton in 1808, which had never been executed.

Featured below is a cross-section of the building, illustrating both the layout of the rooms and the innovative structure, for which Nash employed technically advanced cast-iron domes. The music room shown on pages 24–5 was lavishly decorated by Frederick Crace and Robert Jones in an Eastern style, with a range of vibrant colours to match the exterior architecture.

While working for the Prince Regent, Nash was also responsible for the design of Regent's Park, including terraced houses for the middle classes on the periphery and Regent's Canal on the northern perimeter. He also planned Regent Street and designed some of its houses and the open space of Piccadilly Circus.

Nash's last big commission for George IV was less successful. In 1822 he was employed to redesign Buckingham House and turn it into what is now Buckingham Palace, the main London residence for the new king. However, the king kept changing his mind about the designs. Costs spiralled out of control, the designs were universally criticised, and when the king died in 1830 the building was left unfinished, fatally damaging Nash's career.

Nash wanted his architecture to give pleasure to people, and he has certainly had a lasting influence on buildings across Britain. Very much an architect of his time, he turned the decline of Georgian classicism to his advantage. He skilfully adapted his designs both to his clients' tastes and the buildings' locations to create dramatic and stylistically varied effects.

John Nash, *The Royal Pavilion at Brighton*, [London, 1827] (557*.h.19).

Garden Designs for Country and Town

The gardener, landscape designer, surveyor and architect Batty Langley (1696–1751) took exception to the very regularised garden designs in fashion at the end of the seventeenth and the beginning of the eighteenth centuries. He used his best-known publication, *New principles of gardening*, to advocate a free style of gardening with extensive views and vistas. Langley's book consists of seven parts and instructs its readers in designing and planting their own gardens and cultivating their plants. The work suggests geometrical layouts for a garden and provides information about the cultivation of fruit trees, forest trees, evergreens and flowering shrubs, as well as plants and herbs for kitchen gardens, with the latter section being by far the most extensive. Langley advocated a mixture of different plants and trees in a garden 'to make it look as if nature had planted them together', something that was unusual in English gardens at the time.

The book is illustrated with a number of plates, designed by Langley's brother Thomas and hand-coloured in this copy. They show garden layouts as well as designs for statues and decorative ruins. Langley saw both as vital components of a natural garden, where they provided entertainments for owners and visitors and marked the end points of walks and vistas.

Langley's book is dedicated to George II, and this copy, bound in red goatskin and tooled in gold to a panel design, featuring the royal coat of arms in the centre of both covers, may have been a presentation copy.

Owning and enjoying a garden was not only the privilege of people living in the countryside. The gardener Thomas Fairchild (1667?–1729) owned a nursery in Hoxton in London, specialised in exotic plants and used these to experiment and create new varieties. His gardens, known as the City Gardens, were popular for their size and the types of plants on display. They could be visited by people interested in finding out what kinds of plants could be grown in an urban environment.

Fairchild believed that people needed to have flowers around them to be happy, and was always concerned about the impact that pollution had on the plants in his city garden. He used *The city gardener* to pass on his knowledge to his fellow citizens and to provide information for the growing of plants in all kinds of urban environments. He described the plants suitable for squares and large open spaces in London and Westminster, discussed the difficulties of growing a garden near the Thames, described plants used for courtyards and enclosed spaces in London, and gave information about the kinds of plants people could grow on balconies and windowsills. The frontispiece to *The city gardener* (above) is thought to show Fairchild's own gardens, with one of the gentlemen in the foreground probably representing him. In addition to more native plants in the flowerbeds tended by the two gardeners in the plate, the four tubs in the foreground portray Fairchild's more exotic plants: an agave, a palm tree, a banana tree and a cactus. Fairchild was in contact with gardeners abroad, such as Mark Catesby in Virginia, who sent him seeds of plants that were not native to Britain for him to grow in London. Fairchild was one of the last men to have cultivated a vineyard in England, and was one of the first to have grown bananas in this country.

In his will Fairchild bequeathed money to the charity school and churchwardens of St Leonard's in Shoreditch to pay for an annual Whitsuntide sermon on the wonderful works of God and the creation. These sermons became known as the 'Vegetable Sermons'.

Thomas Fairchild, *The city gardener*, London, 1722 (234.e.28).

OPPOSITE
Batty Langley, *New principles of gardening*, London, 1728 (34.d.8).

Plate XXII. An Avenue in Perspective terminated with the ruins of an ancient Building after the Roman manner. T. Bowles Sculp

Shaping the Georgian Landscape

Humphry Repton (1752–1818) was a general merchant by training, but he moved to the countryside when his business failed. There he devoted most of his time to his garden as well as his talents for drawing and writing, and in 1788 he became a professional landscape gardener. He adopted the term 'landscape gardener' to describe his profession because, as he saw it, his work combined the 'powers of the landscape painter and the practical gardener'. He viewed gardens as works of art rather than works of nature.

Repton's first book, *Sketches and hints in landscape gardening*, is also his most famous work. When asked to design a garden or a garden's improvement for a client, Repton drew upon his so-called 'red books'. These contained plans and watercolour sketches showing a garden or landscape in its original and in its proposed new state. He achieved this by employing so-called 'flaps' or 'fliers', which showed the original landscape when in place and revealed the proposed improvement when opened. Repton's clients were mostly wealthy, and his improvements mainly concentrated on small changes with which he could achieve maximum effects. In contrast to other garden designers of his day, Repton did not usually organise the work – he acted as a consultant, with his 'red books' providing plans, records of his work and display copies for his clients. In *Sketches and hints in landscape gardening* Repton discusses general considerations to bear in mind when designing a garden, such as the location of the house, the use of water, park scenery and the approaches to a property.

Sketches and hints in landscape gardening also used this technique of the 'red books'. It featured facsimiles of designs that Repton had originally produced for his clients, although in this publication the plates were engraved in aquatint. The volume contains references to proposed plans for, among others, Holkham, Tatton Park and Welbeck.

Repton is today most famous for his writings and the use of 'red books'. His designs, however, often existed only on paper and were not always carried out.

ABOVE
Humphry Repton, *Sketches and hints in landscape gardening*, London, [1794] (61.e.18).

OPPOSITE
Humphry Repton, *Sketches and hints in landscape gardening*, London, [1794] (61.e.18).

Visiting Country Houses and Gardens

The gardens at Stowe are well known to visitors today, but they were already a popular tourist destination in the middle of the eighteenth century. Richard Temple, First Viscount Cobham, developed the gardens at Stowe, first to the designs of Charles Bridgeman in the 1710s and 1720s, and then to those of William Kent in the 1730s. The gardens also included ornamental buildings designed by Sir John Vanbrugh, and they began to attract visitors. Cobham was very keen for his gardens to be open to the public, and he sponsored the second and subsequent editions of the guide to Stowe, first published by Benton Seeley in 1744. After retiring from politics in the 1740s Cobham devoted his time to further improvements to house and gardens at Stowe under the auspices of Lancelot 'Capability' Brown.

This volume of engravings is from the collection of the Rt Hon. Thomas Grenville, whose brother George, Marquis of Buckingham, owned Stowe from 1770 until 1813. The book opens with a plan of the estate, followed by views of the house and the gardens from different vantage points, illustrating how people visited and enjoyed the gardens. The plate below shows musicians playing in the grounds.

All engravings in the volume are black and white, and give the viewer a true impression of what Stowe looked like in the eighteenth century – and still looks like today. The people and their clothes may have changed, but the gardens at Stowe remain very like the engravings in this volume.

A general plan of the woods, park and gardens of Stowe, [London?], 1739 (G.2886).

Stow: The gardens of the Right Honourable the Viscount Cobham contains plates showing Stowe, its gardens and descriptive texts of the buildings, as well as a dialogue between two visitors to the estate. The book would probably have been read at home rather than during a visit to Stowe. All buildings found in the gardens are accurately depicted and are thus recognisable to visitors today. The dialogue about a visit to Stowe is between two men: Polypthon, a visitor to the area, and Callophilus, a local of Buckinghamshire with a negative outlook on the world and on life in general. The reader follows the two gentlemen on their journey through the gardens and listens in on their conversation about what they see and what associations they have when viewing the buildings. The gardens offer something for everyone: contemplative walks for the thoughtful; beautiful nature for visitors just wanting to enjoy them; enchanting ideas for the romantic genius; noble entertainment for the man of true taste; and amusement for the trifling genius. The gardens are described as an epitome of the world in general, but while Polypthon sees them as an 'amicable Conjunction of Art and Nature', the more critical Callophilus says that 'the simplicity of Nature … was too much polished away'.

Stow: The gardens of the Right Honourable the Lord Viscount Cobham, London, [1751] (G.3413).

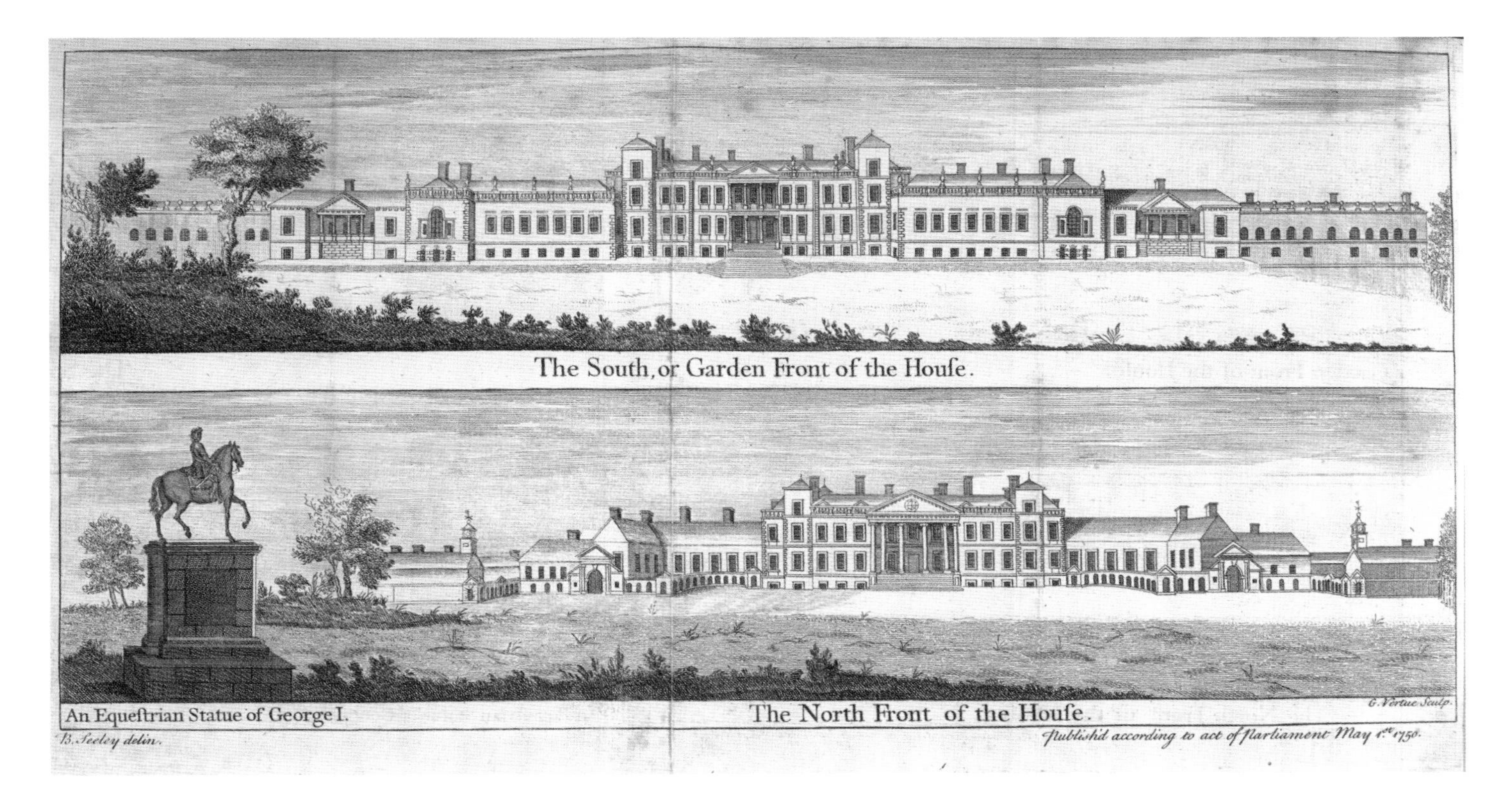

A description of the gardens of Lord Viscount Cobham, at Stow in Buckinghamshire, 6th edition, Northampton, 1749 (578.c.33).

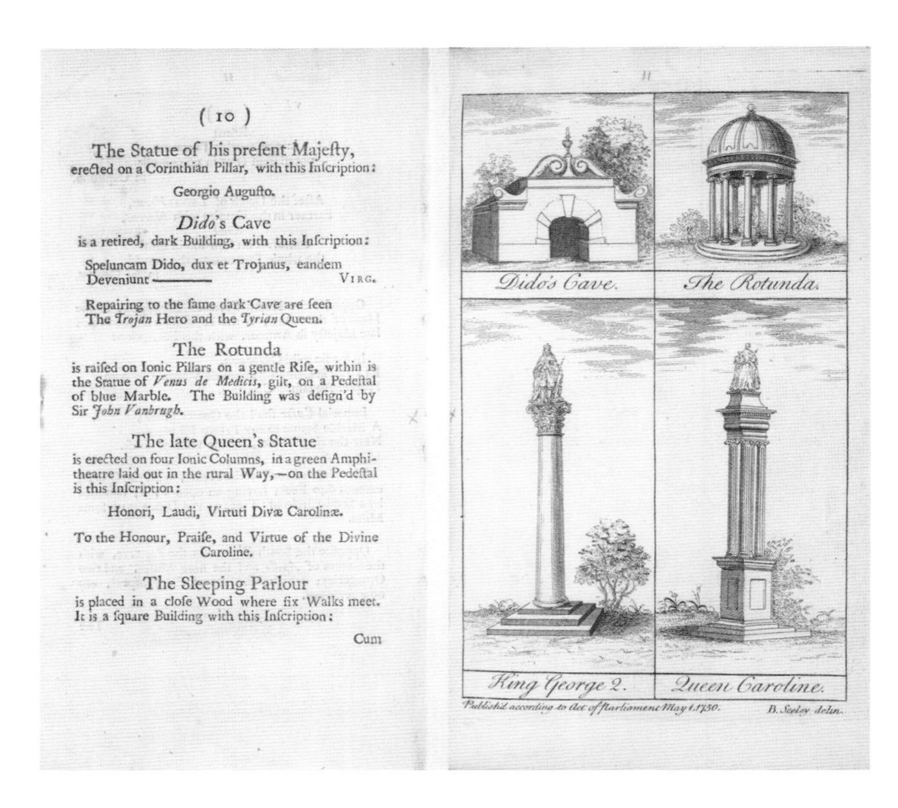

(10)

The Statue of his preſent Majeſty,
erected on a Corinthian Pillar, with this Inſcription:

Georgio Auguſto.

Dido's Cave
is a retired, dark Building, with this Inſcription:

Speluncam Dido, dux et Trojanus, eandem
Deveniunt ——— VIRG.

Repairing to the ſame dark Cave are ſeen
The *Trojan* Hero and the *Tyrian* Queen.

The Rotunda
is raiſed on Ionic Pillars on a gentle Riſe, within is the Statue of *Venus de Medicis*, gilt, on a Pedeſtal of blue Marble. The Building was deſign'd by Sir *John Vanbrugh*.

The late Queen's Statue
is erected on four Ionic Columns, in a green Amphi-theatre laid out in the rural Way,—on the Pedeſtal is this Inſcription:

Honori, Laudi, Virtuti Divæ Carolinæ.

To the Honour, Praiſe, and Virtue of the Divine Caroline.

The Sleeping Parlour
is placed in a cloſe Wood where ſix Walks meet. It is a ſquare Building with this Inſcription:

Cum

This pocket-sized volume is the sixth edition of the guide to Stowe which Viscount Cobham sponsored. It is recognisable to us as a guidebook to the estate, and could even be used when visiting Stowe today. It was designed to accompany the visitor during his tour of the estate, and consists of a number of accurate plates as well as descriptions of the different buildings. They allow readers to work their way around the grounds, either from home or with the book in hand during a visit. Cobham very much wanted his gardens to be appreciated by others, and his support for a widely available guidebook, which was published in numerous editions, is testimony to this aim.

While Stowe was famous for its gardens in the eighteenth century, Wilton was known for its large collection of antique busts and statues. This volume contains plates illustrating the objects, together with brief descriptions. It is testimony to the influence of the Grand Tour on the tastes of the upper classes. By publishing illustrations and descriptions of items acquired during the Grand Tour, the taste for classical antiquity was filtered down to the middle classes.

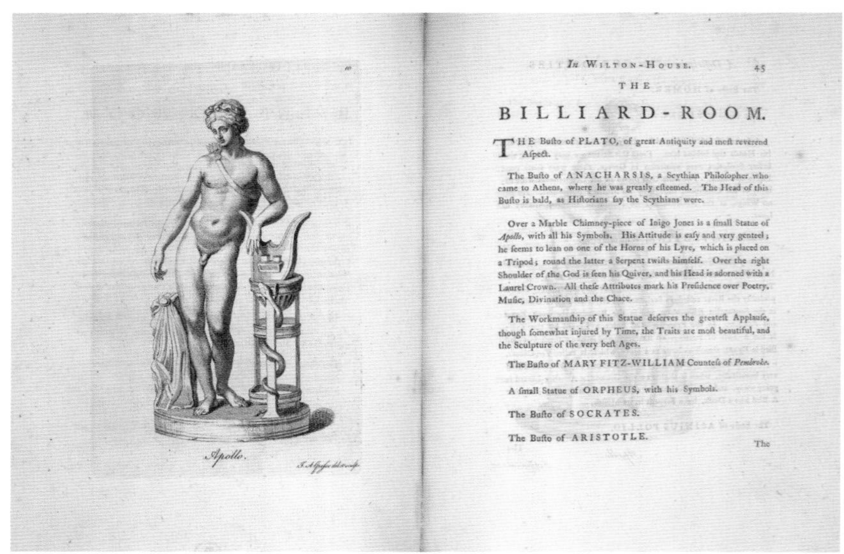

In WILTON-HOUSE. 45

THE

BILLIARD-ROOM.

THE Buſto of PLATO, of great Antiquity and moſt reverend Aſpect.

The Buſto of ANACHARSIS, a Scythian Philoſopher who came to Athens, where he was greatly eſteemed. The Head of this Buſto is bald, as Hiſtorians ſay the Scythians were.

Over a Marble Chimney-piece of Inigo Jones is a ſmall Statue of *Apollo*, with all his Symbols. His Attitude is eaſy and very genteel; he ſeems to lean on one of the Horns of his Lyre, which is placed on a Tripod; round the latter a Serpent twiſts himſelf. Over the right Shoulder of the God is ſeen his Quiver, and his Head is adorned with a Laurel Crown. All theſe Attributes mark his Preſidence over Poetry, Muſic, Divination and the Chace.

The Workmanſhip of this Statue deſerves the greateſt Applauſe, though ſomewhat injured by Time, the Traits are moſt beautiful, and the Sculpture of the very beſt Ages.

The Buſto of MARY FITZ-WILLIAM Counteſs of *Pembroke*.

A ſmall Statue of ORPHEUS, with his Symbols.

The Buſto of SOCRATES.

The Buſto of ARISTOTLE.

The

James Kennedy, *A description of the antiquities and curiosities in Wilton-House*, Salisbury, 1769 (G.4064).

H. Schutz, *A view in Kew Gardens of the Alhambra & Pagoda*, 1798 (K.Top. XL 46x).

Kew Gardens as we know it today dates from the initiatives of Princess Augusta and Prince Frederick in the 1750s and 1760s. Princess Augusta employed Sir William Chambers, who was responsible for building a number of follies in the gardens. The most significant of these was the Pagoda, the only one of his buildings that still survives; the others were built with cheap materials and have either not stood the test of time or been replaced by later developments. The changes initiated by Princess Augusta show the influences of the Chinese and of *chinoiserie*, as well of a revival of classicism made popular by the Grand Tour. The gardens were open to the public and included a pleasure ground, wilderness, formal gardens, exotics, animals and birds. Chambers's book publicised the gardens at Kew to the world, making them an example for gardens of this kind abroad, most notably probably the Garden Kingdom at Wörlitz in Germany. The latter was founded by Prince Leopold III Friedrich Franz of Anhalt-Dessau following a visit to Kew during his European tour in 1765–6.

Further changes to the gardens at Kew were made in the reign of George III, who united the gardens of Richmond and Kew. It was the botanist Sir Joseph Banks (1743–1820), who worked with George III and acted as superintendent to the gardens, who changed them from mere show gardens to a scientific arena with economic potential by planting samples collected from across the world. The gardens declined under George IV before they were reopened to the public by King William IV in 1831.

Designs for the Home

The text on this elaborate trade card reads: 'At James Wheeleys Paper-Hanging Warehouse Opposite the Church in little Britain & Aldersgate Street London Are manufactor'd & sold all sorts of emboss'd chints, & common papers for rooms, with great variety of papieé machee, & other ornaments for cielings, halls, staircases & c.– N.B. all kinds of furniture are exactly match'd and compleatly put up'. The card depicts the interior of Wheeley's shop, where the tradesman's assistant is showing an elegantly dressed couple and their child an elaborate floral piece of wallpaper. In the background we can see several rolls and books of wallpaper from which customers can select.

Wallpaper came into wider use in Britain in the later seventeenth century as a cheaper alternative to tapestry and other textile wall hangings. As wallpaper came in different styles and qualities, and was therefore sold at different prices, it was a form of interior decoration increasingly affordable to the middle classes. The investment made in wallpaper was not as great as that required for bespoke tapestries, so it was possible to change wallpaper when necessary or desirable – for example if fashions changed or a room needed to be redecorated. The production of wallpaper was flexible, and it could be manufactured to order. Wheeley's note, 'all kinds of furniture are exactly match'd', probably points to the bespoke nature of his products.

The cabinet-makers London book of prices, dedicated to the master cabinet-makers of London and Westminster, was written by the journeymen of London and Westminster in order to regulate

ABOVE
Trade card for James Wheeley's Paper-Hanging Warehouse, *c.* 1765–1809 (British Museum, Prints and Drawings, Heal 91.58).

BELOW AND RIGHT
The cabinet-makers London book of prices, [London], 1788 (C.125.de.16).

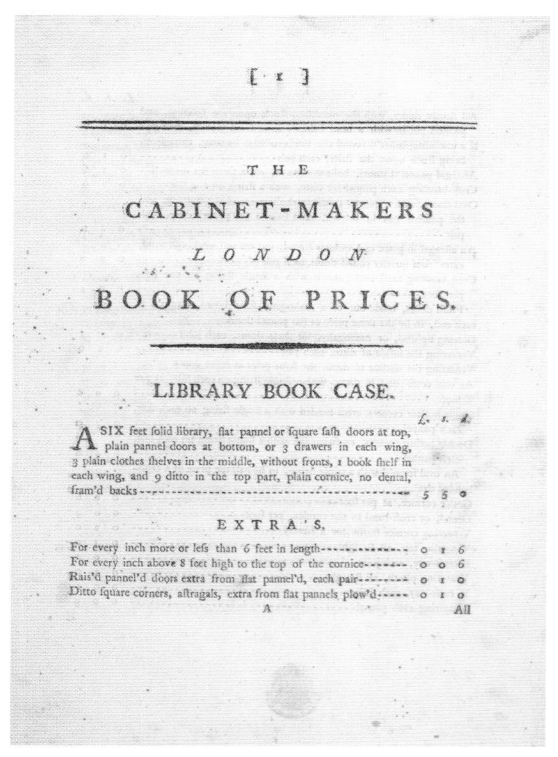

[1]

THE

CABINET-MAKERS

LONDON

BOOK OF PRICES.

LIBRARY BOOK CASE.

	£.	s.	d.
A SIX feet ſolid library, flat pannel or ſquare ſaſh doors at top, plain pannel doors at bottom, or 3 drawers in each wing, 3 plain clothes ſhelves in the middle, without fronts, 1 book ſhelf in each wing, and 9 ditto in the top part, plain cornice, no dental, fram'd backs	5	5	0

EXTRA'S.

For every inch more or leſs than 6 feet in length	0	1	6
For every inch above 8 feet high to the top of the cornice	0	0	6
Rais'd pannel'd doors extra from flat pannel'd, each pair	0	1	0
Ditto ſquare corners, aſtragals, extra from flat pannels plow'd	0	1	0

A All

the prices charged for the furniture produced by the members of the London Society of Cabinet-Makers. The book had been occasioned by the huge inequalities in payments received by members of the Society – some were paid much more than others for doing essentially the same work or, even worse, for less skilled or elaborate work. This publication, the authors hoped, would address these inequalities by giving guidelines as to what to charge for their labour. It contains exact measurements to be followed by craftsmen, especially by 'those who are unacquainted with Perspective'.

The book also contains prices for different types of furniture, such as bedsteads, bottle cases, card tables, commode dressing chests, dining tables, fire screens, gentlemen's travelling boxes, ladies' dressing tables and tea chests. There are prices for basic pieces of furniture and, if customers wanted to invest more, prices for additions; for example, 'a six feet solid library [bookcase], flat pannel or square sash doors at top, plain pannel doors at bottom, or 3 drawers in each wing, 3 plain clothes shelves in the middle, without fronts, 1 book shelf in each wing, and 9 ditto in the top part, plain cornice, no dental, fram'd backs' could be had for 5£.5s.0d. A customer could add 'Rais'd pannel'd doors extra from flat pannel'd, each pair' for 0£.1s.0d. Although the book was aimed at the trade as a guide, it could also be shown to clients to give them information about the different options available.

The cabinet-maker and furniture designer Thomas Chippendale (bap. 1718, d. 1779) was encouraged to write *The gentleman and cabinet-maker's director*, which publicised his own designs, because no furniture pattern books existed. As the title suggests, the book was aimed both at gentlemen clients to assist them in their choice of furniture and at fellow tradesmen who were encouraged to copy the designs and produce their own Chippendale furniture. The book opens with a discussion of the five orders of architecture and the rules of perspective – knowledge of which, according to Chippendale, was fundamental for furniture makers. He continues to describe and illustrate his designs on 160 plates. Furniture featured includes French, Gothic and Chinese chairs, Chinese sofas, canopy and Chinese beds, breakfast and writing tables, library bookcases, French commode tables, candle stands, tea chests and gerandoles (ornamental candleholders).

Chippendale employed a number of craftsmen in his workshop and it is thought that, despite being a cabinet-maker himself and familiar with all aspects of the production process, he worked as the proprietor and manager of the shop. His responsibilities were for overseeing the final products and taking care of his customers, rather than for undertaking the hands-on work.

Thomas Chippendale, *The gentleman and cabinet-maker's director*, London, 1754 (C.119.k.4).

We probably all have an idea of what Chippendale furniture looks like, but it was not until the beginning of the twentieth century that a genuine piece of Chippendale furniture could be identified. Even today most furniture described as Chippendale was based on the patterns in *The gentleman and cabinet-maker's director*, but was not actually made by Chippendale or his workshop.

Chippendale did not only supply furniture that he had designed; he also furnished complete houses, repaired existing furniture or hired out furniture, and he collaborated with architects such as Robert Adam to design pieces of furniture to fit the decoration of a room. Although his publication was aimed at gentlemen customers, not all furniture produced by Chippendale was expensive. He also made items to suit smaller budgets.

The gentleman and cabinet-maker's director was very popular and a second, slightly revised edition was published in 1755. A further enlarged edition was published in parts between 1759 and 1762, and a French edition also appeared around this time.

Chippendale set the trend for furniture pattern books, which was followed by A. Hepplewhite's *The cabinet-maker and upholsterer's guide*, first published in London in 1788, and by Thomas Sheraton's *The cabinet-maker and upholsterer's drawing-book*, first published in London in 1791. However, it is Chippendale's name that is now synonymous with a certain style of furniture, still very familiar today.

Gatherings at the Tea Table

This early example of the Georgian conversation piece was painted by Joseph Van Aken (*c.* 1699–1749) around 1720, shortly after he had come to London from Antwerp. It is probably a group portrait, although neither the family nor the individuals have been so far identified. The architectural backdrop may be fanciful rather than real, but is emblematic of the aspiring tastes of this middle-class family. The women are seated at the tea table, thereby acknowledged as their domain, while the men stand around it. The box for the precious tea is on the floor in front of the lady in black, who is carefully measuring some out from a caddy for the brew. A maidservant is poised ready to pour hot water into a small red teapot. The tea set on the table is fashionable blue-and-white porcelain, with the cups placed upside-down not yet ready to be filled. The moment depicted is formal, even ceremonial, but with the promise of refreshment and polite conviviality to come.

Joseph Van Aken, *An English Family at Tea*, *c.* 1720 (Tate Britain).

NUMB. IV.

THE

TEA-TABLE.

To be continued every *Monday* and *Friday*.

MONDAY, *March* 2. 1724.

AFTER Prayers were over, and we had ſeverally taken our Places at the TEA-TABLE, we proceeded to the diſpatch of ſundry weighty and important Affairs, which had a *long while lain before* us for that Purpoſe.

THE Humble Petition of our Chaplain the Reverend Dr. *Dolt*, was firſt preſented and read, ſetting forth the great Difficulties and Hardſhips he then labour'd under for want of a new Surplice and Common-prayer Book; and praying, That a Fund may be appropriated for that Uſe, and likewiſe for the better Payment of his Salary for the future, out of the Profits ariſing from the Sale of this Paper; or otherwiſe, in ſuch manner, and under ſuch limitations, as the TEA-TABLE, ſhall, in their great Wiſdom, think fit.

Order'd, That the ſaid Petition be rejected.

A Petition of *John James Heydegger*, by the courteſy of *England*, vulgarly ſtyl'd *Count Heydegger*, *John Rich* alias *Lun*, and —— *Fawkes*, in the behalf of themſelves and ſeveral hundred of others, *Eunuchs*, *Muſicians*, *Stage-Players*, *Tumblers* and *Dancers*, both on the high and the ſlack Rope, *&c.* was preſented and read, humbly praying and beſeeching, That the TEA-TABLE, will, according to their known Clemency and Goodneſs, take into conſideration the deplorable Caſe, and unhappy Circumſtances of the Petitioners, who will be reduc'd to the extreameſt Want and Neceſſity, and muſt either be oblig'd to beg their Bread, or become a Burthen to their reſpective Pariſhes, if ſuch kinds of Sports and Divertiſements, as are commonly known by the Name of Balls, and Opera's, and Hiccius-Doctius Tricks, and by which the ſaid Petitioners do at preſent make ſhift to get an honeſt and comfortable Subſiſtance for themſelves and Families, ſhou'd be prohibited by the TEA-TABLE.

Order'd, That the Age and Stature of each Petitioner be inquir'd into, and that our Secretary do acquaint the Secretary at * * *, that it is the Requeſt of the TEA-TABLE, that ſuch of the Petitioners as are able to bear Arms, may be entertain'd in his Majeſty's Service, in the quality of Private Centinels, and have the uſual allowance of Six-pence *per Diem* each, as is in ſuch caſe made and provided.

A Petition of *E*— *B*—— Eſq; and Sir *J*—— *W*———, and ſeveral other worthy Citizens, in their behalf, praying that if any Doubts or Differences ſhould ariſe between the Candidates at the enſuing Election for S——ſ, that the TEA-TABLE will be graciouſly pleas'd to be their Umpire, to whom both Parties have agreed wholly to leave the Deciſion of them.

Reſolved, That if any other Paper of Entertainment, as they are commonly call'd, News-Paper or Journal, ſhall either directly or indirectly meddle with, or have any thing inſerted therein, relating to the ſaid Election, or to any other Election hereafter of City-Officers, whether annual ones, as Lord-Mayor and Sheriffs, or for Life, as Aldermen and Alcconners; ſuch Papers are falſe, frivolous, vexatious, and ſcandalous, and the Authors thereof deſerving to be ſeverely reprimanded by the TEA-TABLE.

HOWEVER, theſe Orders and Reſolutions were not carry'd with that Unanimity as uſually attends the grave and cool Counſels of the TEA-TABLE. Debates aroſe! Words grew high! And the Members were loud and warm! The Chair ſtrove in vain to pacify them! That Authority which is at other times held ſo ſacred! Whoſe Orders it is impious and profane to diſobey! whoſe Nod is a Law to the whole TEA-

TA-

(Price Two Pence.)

The Tea-Table began publication on 21 February 1724 and was intended to appear twice a week. In the event it lasted for only 36 issues, ending in June the same year. It was the first periodical to be written and edited by the writer and actress Eliza Haywood (*c.* 1693–1756), who from the outset adopted the fiction that 'it is design'd to be carry'd on by one of the most agreeable and polite Assemblies in Town' from around the tea table. The second issue introduced readers to some of the ladies and the gentlemen who sat there to share their knowledge and wit. Haywood doubtless drew on members of her own circle for inspiration. She both capitalised on and subverted contemporary views of the tea table as a catalyst for female gossip and intrigue, as well as an emblem of polite sociability.

Eliza Haywood, *The Tea-Table*, [London, 1724] (Burney 237B).

The Pleasures of Reading

The eighteenth century was the first great age of the novel. Among the most successful was *Cecilia, or Memoirs of an Heiress* by Fanny Burney (1752–1840), which tells the story of a high-minded orphan heiress and her encounters with London society. Burney's novel is rich in eccentric characters and vividly describes social events, including a masquerade, a ball and a disastrous visit to Vauxhall Gardens. The author had become a celebrity following the publication of her first novel, *Evelina*, in 1778. *Cecilia* appeared in 1782 and was even more successful, running to three editions within a year. This copy of the third edition was bound in five volumes, probably around the time of publication. *Cecilia* was also Jane Austen's source for the title of her most famous novel, *Pride and Prejudice*.

Fanny Burney, *Cecilia, or Memoirs of an Heiress*, 3rd edition, London, 1783 (1608/1542).

An explosion of print culture in the eighteenth century produced new genres for reading, notably the periodical. *The Lady's Magazine*, which began publication in 1770, was among the new titles aimed at women. It contained serious pieces on a variety of historical and newsworthy topics, alongside such obviously feminine items as embroidery patterns. *The European Magazine* was aimed at men, and was credited to 'the Philological Society of London' when it began in 1782. It offered articles on fashion and gossip as well as essays on history and politics. Both appeared monthly and were illustrated by 'Copper-Plates', or engravings. These copies retain their original blue-paper wrappers, and are as they would have been when purchased from the bookseller.

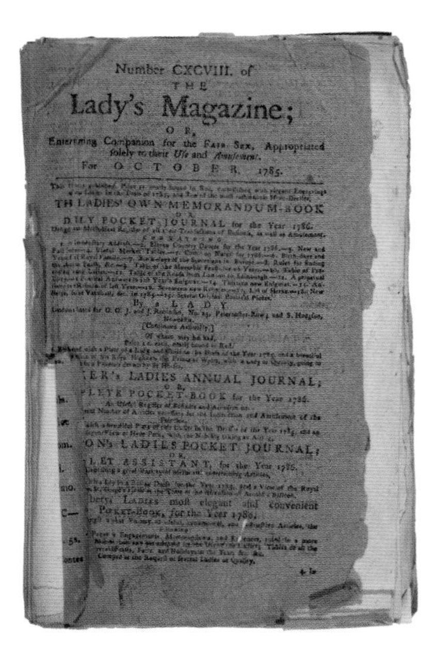

Number CXCVIII. of
THE
Lady's Magazine;
OR,
Entertaining Companion for the Fair Sex, Appropriated solely to their *Use* and *Amusement*.
For OCTOBER, 1785.

THE LADIES' OWN MEMORANDUM-BOOK
OR
DAILY POCKET JOURNAL for the Year 1786.

By a LADY.

LADIES ANNUAL JOURNAL;
OR,
POCKET-BOOK for the Year 1786.

LADIES POCKET JOURNAL;
OR,
ASSISTANT, for the Year 1786.

Ladies most elegant and convenient Pocket-Book, for the Year 1786.

The Lady's Magazine (October 1785 issue), London, 1770–1831 (1609/35).

Dedicated to the Prince of Wales.
No. 24.
THE
EUROPEAN MAGAZINE,
AND
LONDON REVIEW:
For DECEMBER, 1783.
BY THE
PHILOLOGICAL SOCIETY, of LONDON.

BOOKS printed for and sold by JOHN FIELDING, No. 23, Pater-noster-Row.

1. JOSEPH. In Five Books. By A. M. COX.

The European Magazine, and London Review (December 1783 issue), London, 1782–7 (1609/34).

Learning Through Play

The best methods for educating children were much debated in the eighteenth century. Was learning through play more effective than reading? The enterprising printer John Marshall combined the two in *The Infant's Library*, published around 1800. This set of 17 little books, held within a miniature wooden bookcase, is as much a toy as a collection of reading matter. Each volume, measuring approximately 55 mm by 45 mm and with a pretty cover of coloured paper, has tiny woodcut illustrations with facing texts. In some volumes the little pictures have been hand-coloured and are clearly meant to be the main focus of the child's attention.

The first two volumes of the library, dealing with the alphabet and reading and spelling, are obviously to aid learning. There are also volumes devoted to games for both boys and girls. Several of the books depict indoor scenes, with furniture and domestic objects, and outdoor scenes, showing gardens and landscapes; others introduce the child to birds, animals and flowers. Book 16, intended to be the final volume, contains 'A short history of England for the infant's library'; it features a series of portraits of English monarchs, culminating in George III and Queen Charlotte.

All these topics reflect the interests and values of polite society in Georgian Britain. Although John Marshall printed a number of editions of *The Infant's Library*, complete sets are rare; such tiny volumes and their fragile bookcase are vulnerable to loss and damage. The British Library holds a complete set, as well as additional copies of several volumes. Sadly, although the box with its pink paper lining survives, the sliding front, with its pretty image of a glass-fronted bookcase, has been lost.

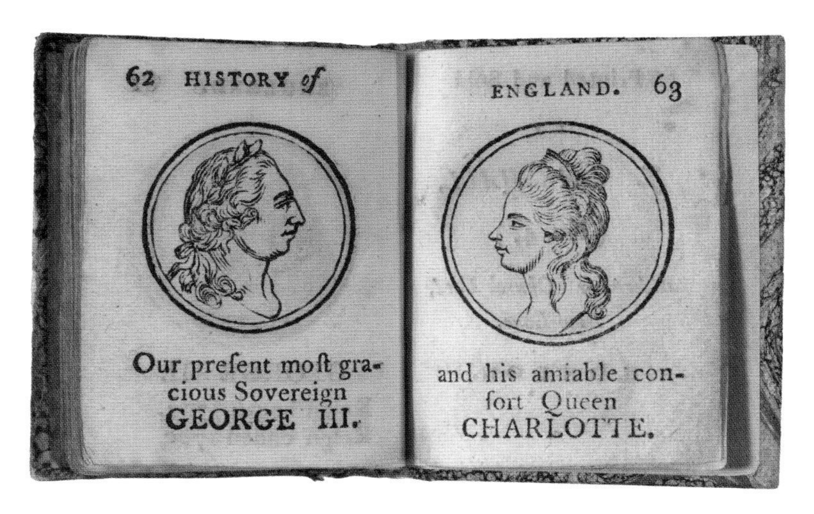

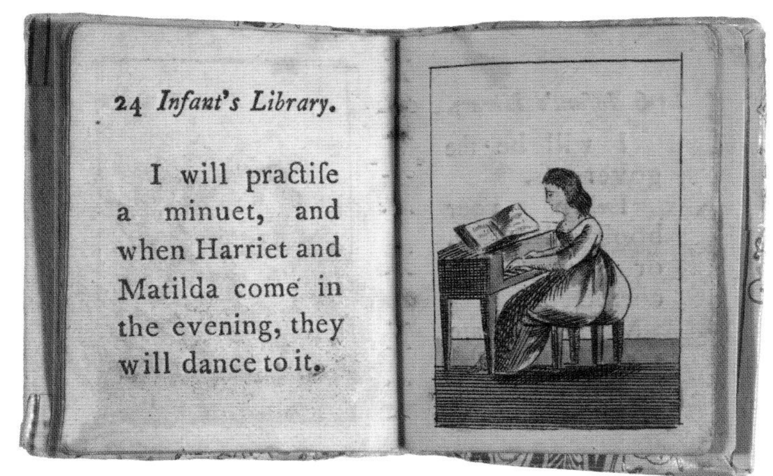

The Infant's Library, 17 parts, London, [1800] (C.194.a.945; Tab. 751.a.5).

The Arts of Writing and Conversation

This provincially printed handbook on the writing of letters begins with English grammar followed by some basic advice. In his preface the anonymous compiler declares that it is chiefly intended as a 'proper collection of letters, by eminent authors, upon subjects very various in their nature'. Although he names only a handful of his celebrity writers, the tone and content of a number of the letters suggest Lord Chesterfield's famous *Letters to his Son* as a source. The frontispiece, however, suggests that letter writing is a female activity, and some of the topics addressed (particularly those dealing with courtship and marriage) resemble excerpts from an epistolary novel.

The importance of the conversational arts to Georgian polite society is shown by the popularity of books devoted to them. Many of these works were formal in their language. Some had parallel texts, for example in English and French, designed to aid practice in other useful or fashionable languages. Jonathan Swift's (1667–1745) *Polite Conversation* was first published in 1738 but went through only a few editions. Like many of the other texts it is in dialogue form, although it is otherwise very different in tone. The pretty frontispiece in this later, small and cheaply printed edition shows polite gentlemen and ladies gathered round the breakfast table, but the sharply witty exchanges contain many less-than-polite sayings still in use today.

THE COMPLETE
LETTER-WRITER,
CONTAINING
FAMILIAR LETTERS
ON THE
MOST COMMON OCCASIONS IN LIFE.
ALSO A VARIETY OF
ELEGANT LETTERS
For the Direction and Embellishment of Style,
ON
Business, Duty, Amusement, Love, Courtship, Marriage, Friendship, and other Subjects.
TO WHICH ARE PREFIXED A PLAIN AND
COMPENDIOUS GRAMMAR
OF THE ENGLISH LANGUAGE,
DIRECTIONS FOR WRITING LETTERS, AND THE PROPER
FORMS OF ADDRESS.
AT THE END ARE GIVEN
FORMS OF MESSAGE CARDS.

DERBY:
PRINTED BY AND FOR HENRY MOZLEY, BROOK-STREET;
sold also by
GEORGE COWIE AND CO. 31, POULTRY, LONDON.
1824.

POLITE
CONVERSATION,
CONSISTING OF
SMART, WITTY, DROLL, AND WHIMSICAL
SAYINGS,
COLLECTED FOR HIS
AMUSEMENT,
AND MADE INTO A
REGULAR DIALOGUE.

By Dr. JONATHAN SWIFT,
Dean of St. PATRICK's, DUBLIN.

LONDON:
PRINTED FOR JOSEPH WENMAN,
No. 144, FLEET-STREET.
M,DCC,LXXXIII.

TOP
The complete letter-writer, containing familiar letters on the most common occasions of life, Derby, 1824 (1608/5456).

ABOVE
Jonathan Swift, *Polite Conversation, consisting of smart, witty, droll, and whimsical sayings*, London, 1783 (012331.de.77).

Royal Botanical Lottery

Botany, theoretical and practical, was among the most fashionable of late eighteenth-century hobbies. It encompassed flower painting as well as gardening and garden design, alongside more scientific studies. Robert John Thornton (1768–1837) was a physician who had a passion for botany. In 1797 he issued a prospectus for his *New Illustration of the Sexual System of Carolus von Linnaeus*, calling for subscriptions to an elaborate new edition to be published in parts. Each part would have '*at least* two superb plates printed in colours in imitation of paintings' and would cost the significant sum of one guinea.

The third volume of the work, entitled *The Temple of Flora*, proved to be Thornton's undoing. This was to be the most magnificent botanical work ever printed, with seventy spectacular colour plates. Thornton engaged the best artists and engravers that he could, including several who worked on paintings and prints for John Boydell's famous Shakespeare Gallery. Publication of *The Temple of Flora* came to a close in 1807, however, with only thirty-one plates complete.

Like Boydell, Thornton failed to attract subscribers owing to the economic downturn caused by Britain's wars with France. He largely financed the project himself, trying to raise money by exhibiting the paintings in a gallery in New Bond Street. This venture failed, and in 1811 he was forced to apply for an Act of Parliament to hold a private lottery. The Royal Botanical Lottery, held to dispose of Thornton's collection of paintings, drawings and engravings, together with copies of his books, offered tickets at two guineas each. The lottery was drawn in 1813.

Thornton's private lottery failed to raise the necessary funds, leaving him ruined. Today *The Temple of Flora*, with its exceptional plates showing flowers in evocations of their natural habitats, is one of the most celebrated botanical books ever published.

The Blue Egyptian Water Lily, plate from Robert John Thornton, *The Temple of Flora*, London, 1799–1807 (10.Tab.40).

Music for Gentlemen and Ladies

Listening to music was a tasteful and polite entertainment, whether at home or at public concerts. Music-making, however, was not so straightforward. It was, at best, a suitable accomplishment for women. For men, it might compromise their status by linking them with professional musicians. Lord Chesterfield, the politician and diplomat famous for the *Letters to His Son* published in 1774, advised the young man, 'If you love music, hear it … but I insist upon your neither piping nor fiddling yourself'. Despite such strictures, some men did play as well as enjoy music, among them the utilitarian philosopher Jeremy Bentham (1748–1832), who was proficient upon several instruments including the violin that still survives.

Many violin tutors were printed, intended for private study as well as to augment lessons with a music master. *The Compleat Tutor for the Violin* has a frontispiece showing a young man practising at home, his book set before him on the table. The text draws on a treatise by the famous violin virtuoso Francesco Geminiani (1687–1762), while the musical examples include 'God Save the King', songs and dances from the theatres and pleasure gardens, and music by Handel and Thomas Arne, among others.

The harpsichord was considered a particularly suitable instrument for women, and tutors for keyboard instruments were produced in large numbers throughout the eighteenth century. *The Compleat Tutor for the Harpsichord or Spinnet* has a frontispiece showing a girl seated at her keyboard with her pet dog in attendance (disconcertingly, the musical instrument she is playing is actually an organ). Most of the musical examples in this tutor are dance pieces, the sort of tunes that young women would be expected to play at home for the entertainment of family and friends.

Jeremy Bentham's violin, 1769 (Museum of London).

THE
Compleat Tutor
FOR THE
VIOLIN,
Containing the easiest and best Methods for Learners to obtain a Proficiency with some useful Directions, Lessons, Graces, &c. BY
GEMINIANI.
To which is added a favourite
Collection of Airs, Marches, Minuets, Song Tunes, and Duetts.
Price 1s. 6d.
LONDON
Printed & sold by S. A. & P. Thompson, No 75, St Pauls Church Yard.
Where may be had a new Edition of Instructions for every Instrument. Music and Instruments Wholesale Retail and for Exportation.

The Compleat Tutor for the Violin, London, [*c.* 1790] (b.105.b).

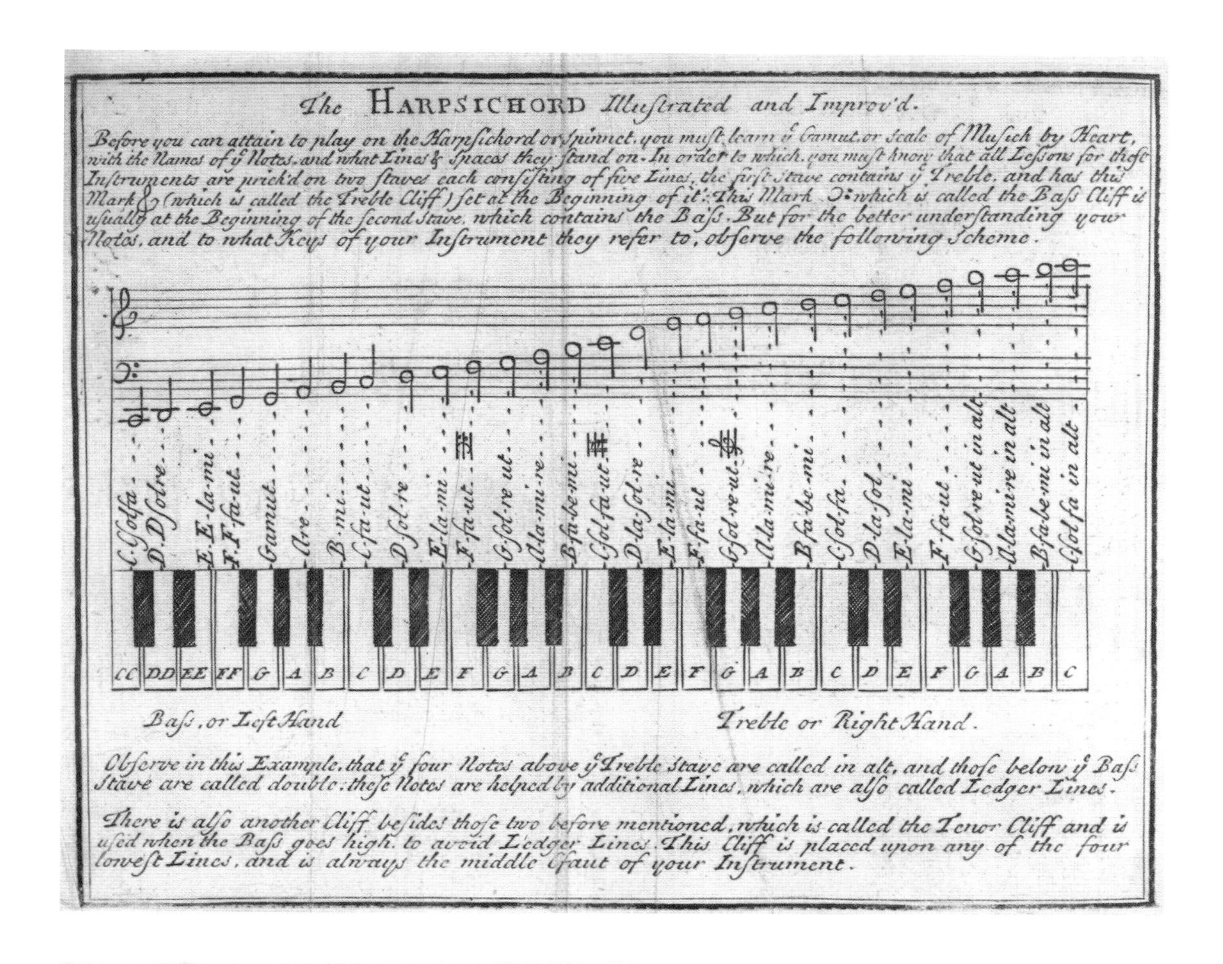

The HARPSICHORD Illustrated and Improv'd.

Before you can attain to play on the Harpsichord or Spinnet, you must learn ye Gamut, or Scale of Musick by Heart, with the Names of ye Notes, and what Lines & Spaces they stand on. In order to which, you must know that all Lessons for these Instruments are prick'd on two Staves each consisting of five Lines, the first Stave contains ye Treble, and has this Mark 𝄞 (which is called the Treble Cliff) set at the Beginning of it: This Mark 𝄢 which is called the Bass Cliff is usually at the Beginning of the second Stave, which contains the Bass. But for the better understanding your Notes, and to what Keys of your Instrument they refer to, observe the following Scheme.

CC DD EE FF G A B C D E F G A B C D E F G A B C D E F G A B C

Bass, or Left Hand

Treble or Right Hand.

Observe in this Example, that ye four Notes above ye Treble Stave are called in alt, and those below ye Bass Stave are called double: these Notes are helped by additional Lines, which are also called Ledger Lines.

There is also another Cliff besides those two before mentioned, which is called the Tenor Cliff and is used when the Bass goes high, to avoid Ledger Lines. This Cliff is placed upon any of the four lowest Lines, and is always the middle Cfaut of your Instrument.

The Compleat Tutor for the Harpsichord or Spinnet,
London, [*c.* 1745] (e.28.c.).

Drawing and Painting in Watercolours

Drawing was both a gentlemanly pursuit and a ladylike accomplishment. *The artists assistant in drawing* declares on the title page that it is 'adapted to the capacities of young beginners', but its text and its fold-out plates suggest that it is more suited to students intending to make art their profession. This little treatise deals with the basic skills of figure drawing and perspective, linking it to a tradition of English drawing manuals dating back at least to the early seventeenth century.

Flower painting was a skill deemed especially appropriate for ladies, both for its innocent subject matter and as an indoor pursuit. It was linked not only to needlework but also to botany, a subject much studied by women in the eighteenth century. *The delights of flower-painting*, with its many pretty, hand-coloured plates, was intended for 'the fair-sex' who could thereby represent 'an image of their lovely selves' using a nicely appointed watercolour box designed for women.

The progress of a water coloured drawing presented a new type of drawing manual that began to appear early in the nineteenth century. It did not deal with either figure drawing or perspective, but began directly with the depiction of a landscape. With the help of a series of plates, the author takes the student from an initial drawing through to a finished watercolour. Other similar manuals made good use of the new aquatint method of colour printing, but this treatise seems to have been hand-coloured.

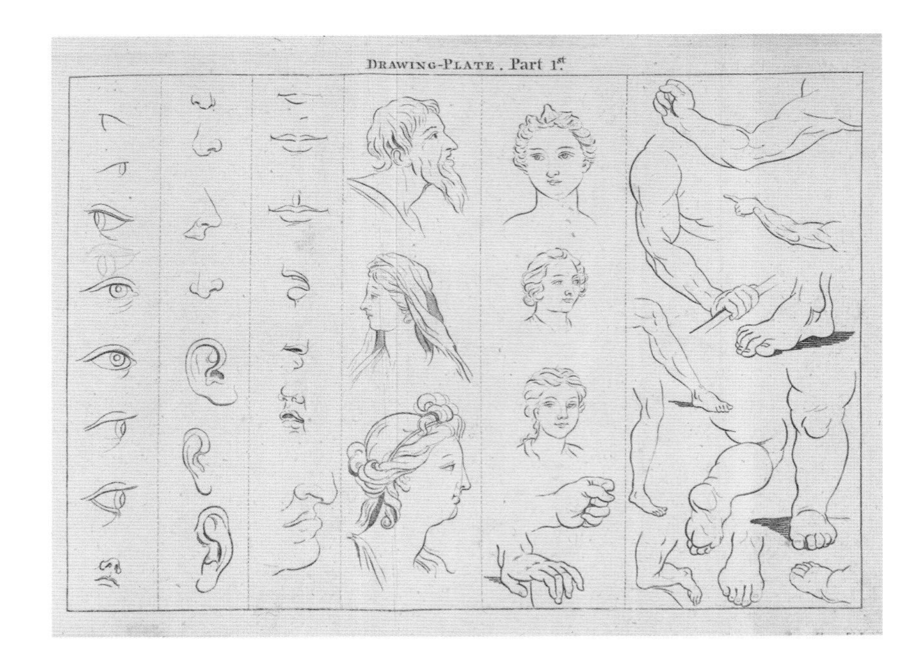

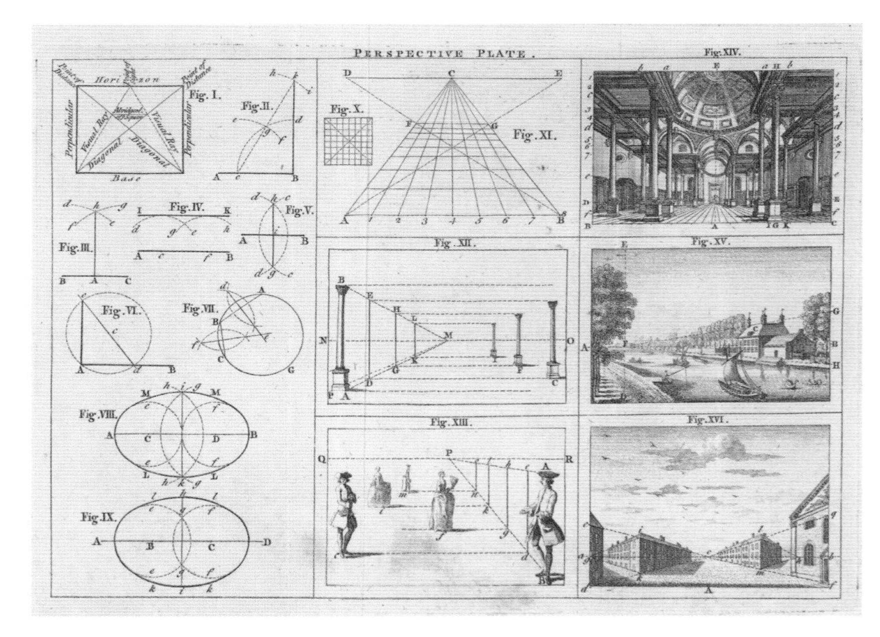

Carington Bowles, *The artists assistant in drawing*, London, [1770?] (1651/1692).

John Laporte, *The progress of a water coloured drawing*, London, [1812?] (564.a.16).

ABOVE
John June, *The delights of flower-painting*, 2nd edition, London, [1756] (C.119.c.9).

Drawing
of all Descriptions
Gold Size & Cement
ACKERMANN

2 Shopping and Fashion

> By Trade our Nation's Glory is maintain'd,
> By Trade ye Riches of the World are drain'd,
> O happy Britain! May thy Sons still rise,
> And fame and Wealth exalt them to ye skies.
>
> William Markham, *A General Introduction to Trade and Business*

In the eighteenth century Britain became a wealthy nation through trade. Exotic and luxurious goods were imported by the East India Company through its links with India and China, while at home a variety of manufacturers exploited new techniques to produce goods of equal quality, including silk, glass, porcelain, earthenware and furniture. Young apprentices were urged to serve their masters with particular regard to 'the Honour of God and the welfare of mankind', a code that justified commercial success. Tradespeople certainly comprised a particularly diverse and enterprising section of the middle classes, ranging from small backstreet workers to leading entrepreneurs – such as Josiah Wedgwood, Richard Twining, William Fortnum and Hugh Mason – whose businesses remain lucrative today.

Throughout the Georgian period people from all social classes continued to purchase everyday necessities at seasonal street fairs and markets. However, shops with fixed and permanent addresses in towns could offer a wider selection of goods and a more sophisticated environment. As towns were predominantly trading and meeting places, shops with elegant frontages and eye-catching window displays were well placed to attract custom from the busy streets.

Once inside, a customer would be engaged in a pleasant and sociable exchange by the shopkeeper and assistants, who would use all their professional skills to ensure a profitable purchase. A proliferation of printed advertisements announcing goods of finest quality, sold under the best terms, indicates a keen level of competition between shopkeepers seeking to capture a flourishing retail trade.

Improved production techniques enabled goods from the new British manufacturing industries to be sold for far lower prices than those of their imported counterparts. The main consumers of wares manufactured in Britain were the affluent middle classes, so it is perhaps not surprising that the designs and decorations chosen for their products reflected the themes that they found most attractive, whether these were based on classical motifs and references or characters from storybooks familiar from childhood. These British wares developed a refined style and beauty of their own, and it is appropriate that London, as the acknowledged centre of fashion and elegance in England, became their natural showcase.

English Trades

This popular guide to English trades, originally published in 1804, sought to present young people living in this commercial country with the most up-to-date accounts of each trade. The practical nature of each business is outlined in a series of factual accounts, accompanied by illustrations of the tradesmen as they conduct their work. The inclusion in the guide of so many trades relating to book production bears witness to a flourishing book trade.

The Book of English Trades, and Library of the Useful Arts, 7th edition, London, 1818 (RB.23.a.18153).

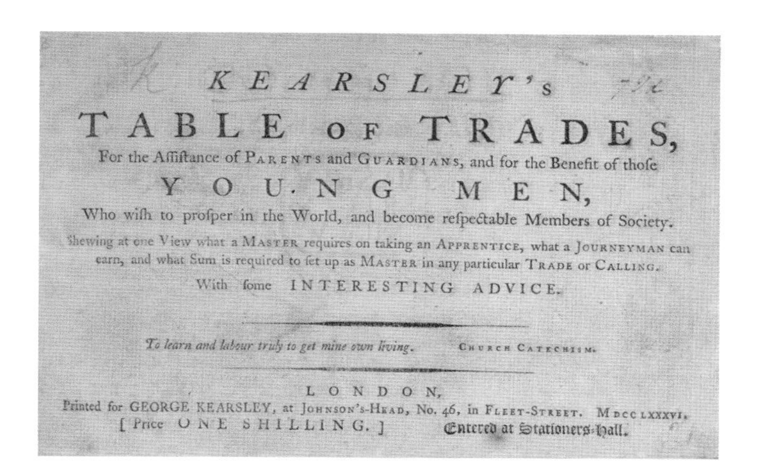

KEARSLEY's

TABLE OF TRADES,

For the Affiftance of PARENTS and GUARDIANS, and for the Benefit of thofe

YOUNG MEN,

Who wifh to profper in the World, and become refpectable Members of Society.

Shewing at one View what a MASTER requires on taking an APPRENTICE, what a JOURNEYMAN can earn, and what Sum is required to fet up as MASTER in any particular TRADE or CALLING.

With fome INTERESTING ADVICE.

To learn and labour truly to get mine own living. CHURCH CATECHISM.

LONDON,

Printed for GEORGE KEARSLEY, at JOHNSON'S-HEAD, No. 46, in FLEET-STREET. MDCCLXXXVI.

[Price ONE SHILLING.] Entered at Stationers-Hall.

(8)

TRADES, &c.	Apprentice Fee.		Sum required to fet up in Bufinefs.		What the Journeyman receives per Week, without Board.				Sum given per Year, with Board.		L. fignifies Laborious
	From	To	From	To	From		To		From	To	
	£.	£.	£.	£.	£.	s.	£.	s.	£.	£.	
Girdler	5	10	30	100	—	9	—	18	—	—	
Girth Weaver	5	10	50	100	—	10	—	14	14	18	
Glafs Houfe	3	10	1000	10000	—	18	1	10	25	40	L.
Glafs Grinder	5	10	50	100	—	15	—	18	18	25	L.
Glafs and Picture Frame Carver	5	10	20	100	—	18	1	1	—	—	
Glafs Seller	15	25	200	600	—	—	—	—	15	30	
Glazier	10	20	50	500	—	12	—	15	12	20	
Glover	10	50	50	1000	—	14	—	18	20	30	
Gold and Silver Wire Drawer	5	10	80	150	—	14	1	—	—	—	
Gold Beater	10	20	50	100	—	15	1	1	15	25	L.
Goldfmith	50	300	600	10000	—	—	—	—	20	50	
Grocer	20	200	100	5000	—	—	—	—	15	40	
Gun Engraver	10	20	40	100	—	16	1	10	—	—	
Gun Inlayer	10	20	40	150	—	14	1	4	—	—	
Gun Maker	5	20	100	1000	—	15	1	1	20	30	
Gun Stock Maker	5	15	10	30	—	12	—	18	—	—	
Haberdafher of Small Wares	40	300	300	1500	—	—	—	—	14	30	
Haberdafher of Hats	50	100	50	1000	—	—	—	—	20	40	

B 2

Kearsley's Table of Trades, London, 1786 (712.a.15).

The Polite Tradesman

These tables offer very specific and practical details of the costs involved in joining the apprenticeship system. A variety of trades are represented so that comparisons may be made between them. There is also an indication of whether the work is of a manual or 'laborious' nature.

George Kearsley, who edited the text, was a bookseller and stationer. He offers firm advice on the behaviour of an apprentice. He should be mindful that 'the laws of God are nothing less than the rules of happiness'. By adhering to this moral code, the apprentice will best ensure his good reputation, prosperity and future success in business.

Hannah More, *The Apprentice's Monitor; or, Indentures in verse, shewing what they are bound to do*, Bath, *c.* 1795 (1872.a.1(111)).

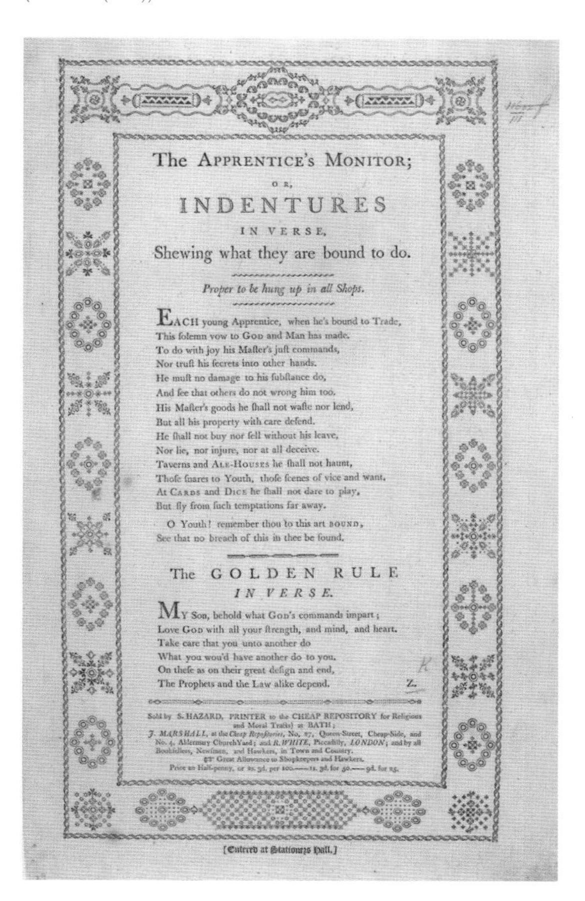

The APPRENTICE'S MONITOR;

OR,

INDENTURES

IN VERSE,

Shewing what they are bound to do.

Proper to be hung up in all Shops.

EACH young Apprentice, when he's bound to Trade,
This folemn vow to GOD and Man has made.
To do with joy his Mafter's juft commands,
Nor truft his fecrets into other hands.
He muft no damage to his fubftance do,
And fee that others do not wrong him too.
His Mafter's goods he fhall not wafte nor lend,
But all his property with care defend.
He fhall not buy nor fell without his leave,
Nor lie, nor injure, nor at all deceive.
Taverns and ALE-HOUSES he fhall not haunt,
Thofe fnares to Youth, thofe fcenes of vice and want.
At CARDS and DICE he fhall not dare to play,
But fly from fuch temptations far away.

O Youth! remember thou to this art BOUND,
See that no breach of this in thee be found.

The GOLDEN RULE

IN VERSE.

MY Son, behold what GOD's commands impart;
Love GOD with all your ftrength, and mind, and heart.
Take care that you unto another do
What you wou'd have another do to you.
On thefe as on their great defign and end,
The Prophets and the Law alike depend.

Z.

Sold by S. HAZARD, PRINTER to the CHEAP REPOSITORY for Religious and Moral Tracts) at BATH;
J. MARSHALL, at the *Cheap Repofitories*, No. 17, Queen-Street, Cheap-Side, and No. 4, Aldermary Church Yard; and *R. WHITE*, Piccadilly, *LONDON*; and by all Bookfellers, Newfmen, and Hawkers, in Town and Country.
☞ Great Allowance to Shopkeepers and Hawkers.
Price an Half-penny, or 2s. 3d. per 100.——1s. 3d. for 50.——9d. for 25.

[Entered at Stationers Hall.]

In this verse (right) Hannah More, educator, writer and social reformer, makes it clear that the contract binding an apprentice to trade also represents a solemn vow made by him to God, as well as to his master. The apprentice should therefore conduct his business with due regard to God's commands. If the attractively printed sheet had been displayed in shops as instructed, it would have provided an ever-present reminder of this golden rule for business.

The Melancholy History of the Apprentice George Barnwell

George Barnwell was an unfortunate apprentice who failed to follow the advised moral code of behaviour. His subsequent downfall was popularised throughout the eighteenth century to warn other young people against the evil effects of bad company and the temptations they might encounter on leaving home to set out in business.

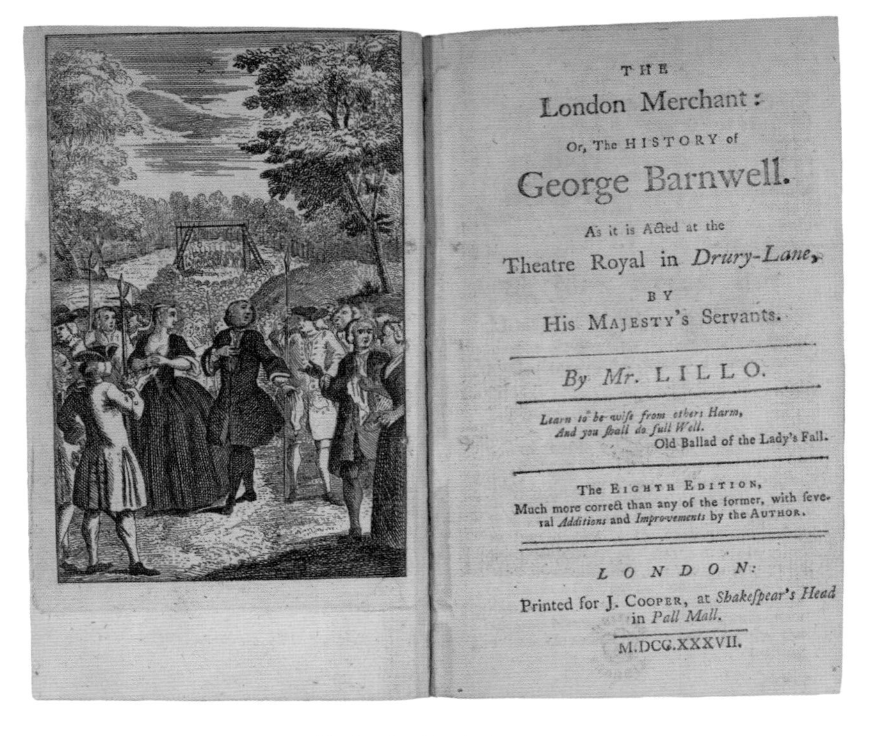

THE

London Merchant:

Or, The HISTORY of

George Barnwell.

As it is Acted at the

Theatre Royal in *Drury-Lane*,

BY

His MAJESTY's Servants.

By *Mr.* LILLO.

Learn to be wise from others Harm,
And you shall do full Well.
Old Ballad of the Lady's Fall.

The EIGHTH EDITION,
Much more correct than any of the former, with several *Additions* and *Improvements* by the AUTHOR.

LONDON:

Printed for J. COOPER, at *Shakespear's Head* in *Pall Mall.*

M.DCC.XXXVII.

The London Merchant: or, The History of George Barnwell, London, 1737. Frontispiece and title page (RB.23.a.28924).

The London Apprentice; or, The Melancholy History of George Barnwell, Derby, *c.* 1830. Hand-coloured frontispiece (RB.23.a.33744).

'Almost every man in Liverpool is a merchant'

In 1795 James Wallace commented that, 'Almost every man in Liverpool is a merchant'. This appears to have been the case in 1781, as *Gore's Liverpool Directory* records the variety of tradesmen required to maintain the shipbuilding and ancillary industries on which the great wealth of the city was founded. The trades listed here – the timber merchants, water bailiffs, mariners and sailcloth manufacturers – are all those either required for, or related to, the fitting out of the ships for their passage across the Atlantic.

Arthur and Benjamin Heywood are noted both as merchants and occupants of adjoining houses in Hanover Street. It was not uncommon for a merchant to maintain his warehouse and to conduct his business from the same building in which he and his family resided. Hanover Street was also near to the Old Dock, which would have allowed the Heywood brothers to keep a close watch over their shipping interests.

Ships sailing from Liverpool were packed with the products of the industries of the eighteenth century: textiles, metal goods, gunpowder, glass beads, spirits, tobacco and beer. The ships sailed firstly to the African coast, where their cargoes were unloaded and exchanged for slaves. During a second or middle passage, the slaves were taken to Barbados, the Leeward Islands, Jamaica or Surinam and there sold to work on plantations to produce sugar, spices, molasses, rum and tobacco; these products then made up the cargoes for the third and final passage to Britain, where they were sold for good profit.

Fortunes could be amassed through this self-supporting system of triangular trade by manufacturers, capitalists and plantation owners and also by financiers and agents, who enjoyed good returns on the money they lent to support each part of the operation.

The link between these trading activities and banking was a particularly close one, since a system of credit was required in order to finance the long-distance Atlantic trade. By 1781 Arthur and Benjamin are listed as both merchants and bankers. Richard Heywood, merchant, of 45 Castle Street, was Arthur's eldest son, and had taken up residence in Castle Street on the premises of the Heywood Bank after 1776, when it had been transferred there. The bank continued in the Heywood family for over a century. It was absorbed by Martin's Bank in 1883, then by the Bank of Liverpool in 1918. Finally, in 1968, it became part of Barclays Bank.

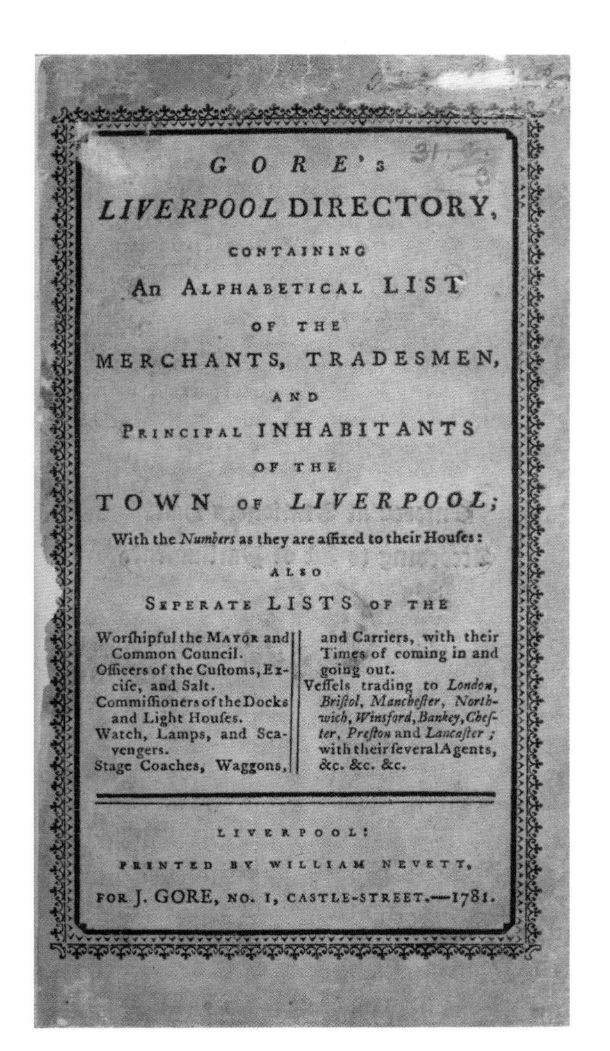

GORE'S

LIVERPOOL DIRECTORY,

CONTAINING

An ALPHABETICAL LIST

OF THE

MERCHANTS, TRADESMEN,

AND

PRINCIPAL INHABITANTS

OF THE

TOWN OF *LIVERPOOL*;

With the *Numbers* as they are affixed to their Houfes:

ALSO

SEPERATE LISTS OF THE

Worfhipful the MAYOR and Common Council.
Officers of the Cuftoms, Excife, and Salt.
Commiffioners of the Docks and Light Houfes.
Watch, Lamps, and Scavengers.
Stage Coaches, Waggons, and Carriers, with their Times of coming in and going out.
Veffels trading to *London*, *Briftol*, *Manchefter*, *Northwich*, *Winsford*, *Bankey*, *Chefter*, *Prefton* and *Lancafter*; with their feveral Agents, &c. &c. &c.

LIVERPOOL:

PRINTED BY WILLIAM NEVETT,

FOR J. GORE, NO. 1, CASTLE-STREET.—1781.

Gore's Liverpool Directory, containing an alphabetical list of the merchants, tradesmen, and principal inhabitants of the Town of Liverpool, 1781 (PP.2505.ycm (5)).

Hewit Robert, victualler, 7, *Old Shambles*
Hewit John, grocer, 1, *Cheapfide*
Heys Thomas, currier, 14, *Chapel-ftreet*
Heywood Arthur, merchant, 54, *Hanover-ftreet*
Heywood Benjamin, merchant, 53, *ditto*
Heywood Benjamin Arthur, merchant, 53, *ditto*
Heywood Nathaniel, merchant, 53, *ditto*
Heywood Richard, merchant, 45, *Caftle-ftreet*
Heywood Arthur, Son, and Co. bankers, 45, *ditto*
Heywood Arthur and Son, merchants, 4, *Gradwell-ftr*
Heywood Benjamin, counting-houfe, *ditto*
F

Markets and Fairs

While people from all social classes continued to purchase goods at street fairs and markets throughout the eighteenth century, shops with a fixed location and address could provide a range of goods for a growing number of affluent consumers. The depiction of Bartholomew Fair (right) suggests the festival spirit of the annual fair in Smithfield that ran for fourteen days from 24 August. The focus is clearly on entertainment and food. The image of Billingsgate (below) portrays a cross-section of English society buying fish at this famous London market.

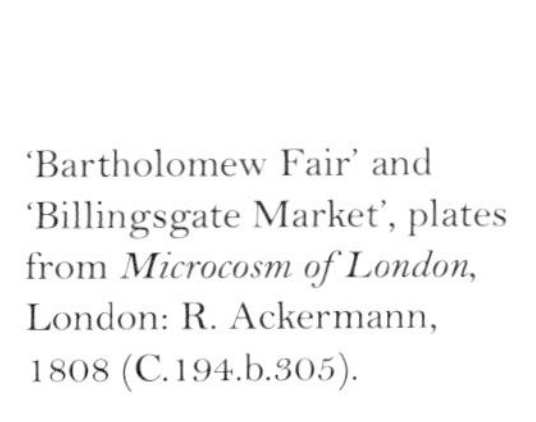

'Bartholomew Fair' and 'Billingsgate Market', plates from *Microcosm of London*, London: R. Ackermann, 1808 (C.194.b.305).

Buying and Selling

Although the spectators are the main subjects of this engraving (below), the prints in the shop window reflect the quantity and variety of the printer's work, and the way in which it has been displayed to catch public attention. The street view also shows some of the decorative features of the shop exterior, including an ornamental pillar and carved edging around the large glass window.

Spectators at a Print-Shop in St. Paul's Church Yard, London, 1774. Mezzotint with hand-colouring (British Museum, London, 1935,0522.1.16).

A Morning Ramble, or The Milliners Shop, London, 1782. Mezzotint with hand-colouring (British Museum, London, 1935,0522.1.31).

This satirical print reveals the flirtatious transactions between two fashionably dressed male customers and three equally elaborately dressed female milliners. This interior view shows the arrangement of the shop with its display of fabric draped across the window, a large mirror on the wall behind the milliner sewing a bonnet and an open box containing lace on the counter. Other storage boxes appear on shelves behind the milliners. Although it is not being used, the round stool has been placed for customers to sit comfortably at the counter.

John Pidler of Hotwells, Bristol, advertises a variety of goods to assist the comfort and pleasure of wealthy visitors to the Spa: lace for ruffles, stockings, gloves perfumes and syrups. He emphasises that his goods bear prices that are fixed 'plain marks' attached to each article, and that the customer can buy with confidence since these are already at their lowest and most reasonable. The need to state such terms, and to produce this printed advertisement, implies the existence of a number of other traders dealing in similar wares, and a keen level of competition and rivalry between shopkeepers.

It is interesting to note that John Pidler 'will remove to Bath next season'. While it would have been advantageous for him to remain in Hotwells during the summer months, he could only continue to turn a profitable trade once the season had finished by transferring to a spa resort such as Bath that could attract visitors all the year round. Many of the visitors to Hotwells would also have moved on to Bath at the end of the summer season. Pidler, who wishes to retain their loyalty, is keen to remind his fashionable customers that they will be able to continue to purchase his goods over the winter months.

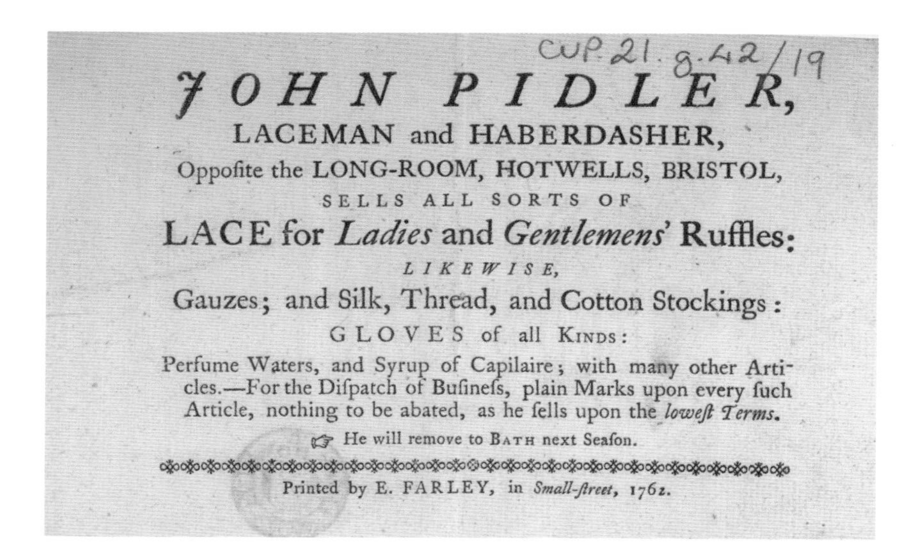

JOHN PIDLER,

LACEMAN and HABERDASHER,

Oppoſite the LONG-ROOM, HOTWELLS, BRISTOL,

SELLS ALL SORTS OF

LACE for *Ladies* and *Gentlemens'* Ruffles:

LIKEWISE,

Gauzes; and Silk, Thread, and Cotton Stockings:

GLOVES of all KINDS:

Perfume Waters, and Syrup of Capilaire; with many other Articles.—For the Diſpatch of Buſineſs, plain Marks upon every ſuch Article, nothing to be abated, as he ſells upon the *loweſt Terms.*

☞ He will remove to BATH next Seaſon.

Printed by E. FARLEY, in *Small-ſtreet*, 1762.

John Pidler, laceman and haberdasher, opposite the Long-Room, Hotwells, Bristol, 1762 (Cup.21.g.42/19).

This is the open plan of the haberdasher's shop from which Jane Austen's aunt, Jane Cholmeley Leigh Perrot, was accused of shoplifting in 1800. Mrs Leigh Perrot had purchased some black lace during her visit to Elizabeth Gregory's shop in Bath on 8 August 1799. A card of white lace that had also been on the counter was reported missing shortly after she left the shop and discovered in Mrs Leigh Perrot's pocket. The goods are portrayed invitingly draped over a brass rail, conveniently placed for interested customers to handle and examine them. While Jane Leigh Perrot was found not guilty, such an open arrangement would have made shoplifting a relatively straightforward crime to commit.

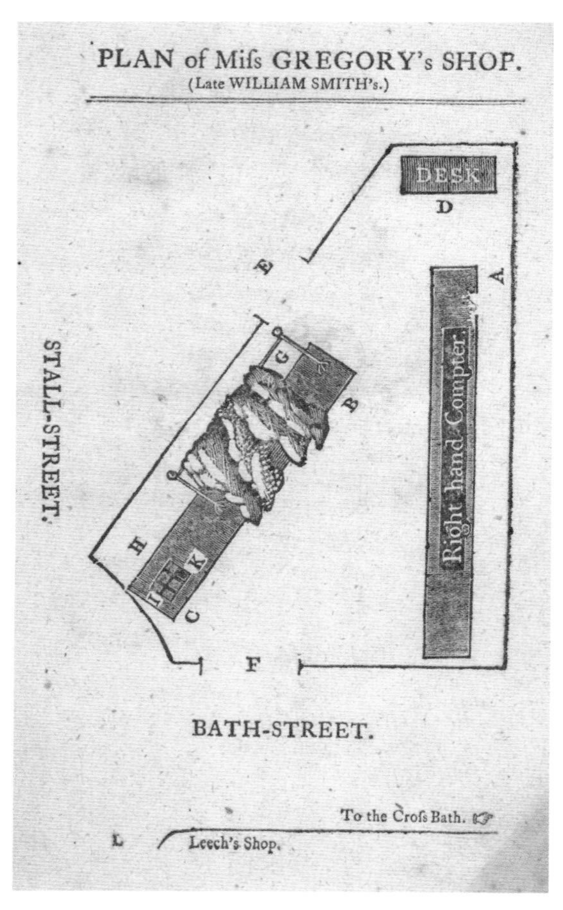

The Trial of Jane Leigh Perrot, wife of James Leigh Perrot … charged with stealing a card of lace, in the shop of Elizabeth Gregory, haberdasher and milliner, at Bath, Taunton, [1800]. Plan of Miss Gregory's Shop (6495.b.39).

In 1811 the Turnpike Trust of Kensington commissioned the artist Joseph Salway to produce a series of drawings to record the roads under its management. Salway's detailed plans included the little shops that supplied daily necessities along Kensington High Street, which retained its character as a village.

The view shown here, extending from Kensington Church Street to the gates of Kensington Palace, illustrates the neat and elegant appearance of the shop fronts. Their windows, made of small, flat panes of glass, blend with other architectural features such as columns, pilasters and fan lights. Other decoration may have included grained woodwork in imitation of dark, warm oak, as well as ornaments and lettering.

Kensington High Street, from *Plans and views of the several roads under the management of the Turnpike Trust of Kensington*, 1811. Coloured lithograph (Add MS. 31325. ff.27v–28).

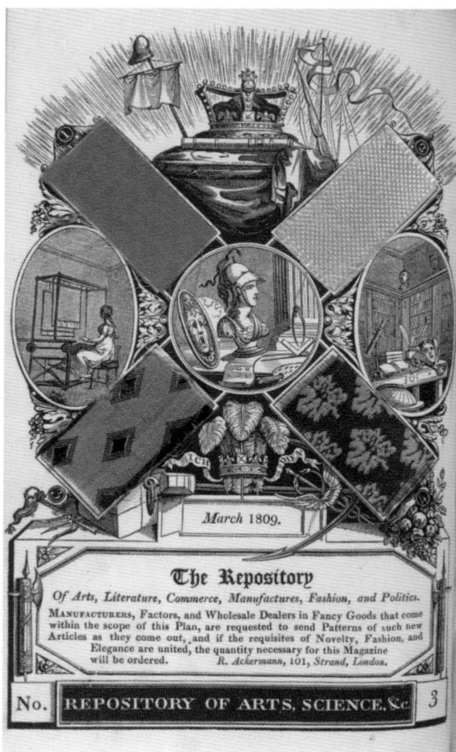

This is the seventh and enlarged edition of a most favourably received text, produced 'to acquaint the rising generation with our various trades, and their origin and history'. The descriptions of the trades include illustrations of customers as they browse, handle and closely scrutinise the goods to determine their quality (left). The customer and shopkeeper could then negotiate a satisfactory price and conclude the transaction.

In the first issue of *The Repository of Arts* Ackermann announced 'the commencement of a series of plates intended to exhibit the principal shops of this great metropolis'. The six plates do not only illustrate the variety of goods available for purchase, and the ways in which these were displayed in each featured shop; they also reveal how Georgian shopping could be a most pleasurable activity and leisure pursuit.

Each plate portrays the behaviour of customers as they respond to the impressive displays of high-quality, home-produced goods – arranged for them to handle and examine at close quarters. Seating areas on the shop floor enable the experience to be as leisurely as possible, encouraging customers to stay longer and purchase more. In such an environment shopping could certainly be 'a pleasure of the most refined nature'.

The goods on sale are themselves products of the new British manufacturing industries of the eighteenth century. Such wares could now be produced in large quantities and displayed en masse as elegant and desirable items.

Many of these products were inspired by the luxury goods imported from India and China. The fabric samples also included in *The Repository of Arts* champion the quality, style and ingenuity of British manufacture, and reflect an exotic influence in their names: 'India rib' and 'Oriental pink'.

ABOVE LEFT
The Book of English Trades, and Library of the Useful Arts, 7th edition, London, 1818 (RB.23.a.18153).

LEFT
Allegorical wood-cut, with samples of fabric furnished by Harding, Howell & Co., from *The Repository of Arts, Literature, Commerce, Manufactures, Fashions and Politics*, London: R. Ackermann, 1809–15 (C.119.f.1).

OPPOSITE TOP
Wedgwood's Rooms, York Street (now Duke of York Street), Pall Mall. From *The Repository of Arts* (C.119.f.1).

OPPOSITE BOTTOM
Harding, Howell & Co's Grand Fashionable Magazine, 89 Pall Mall. From *The Repository of Arts* (C.119.f.1).

John MacIntyre's Presents from China

These letters were sent from China by John MacIntyre to his wife 'Kattie' in England. MacIntyre was in the service of the East India Company, and at the time of writing was employed as a merchant at Canton, Macao and Penang.

His first letter, dated 9 December 1776, was sent from Canton. He had evidently been instructed by his wife to send home luxury goods, such as silk fabrics and porcelain, for her use. The letter indicates that a quantity of silk was sent to make gowns for several members of the MacIntyre family and their friends, and a 'cart load' of China ware was to follow. Such items were particularly desirable to the MacIntyre family – and to the British middle classes in general – as their quality and foreign origins evoked a sense of exotic luxury.

A further variety of fabrics, to be used for clothing and household furnishing, was sent in 1777. It was accompanied by boxes of tea, intended for consumption at home. When Kattie hosted her tea table for her female friends, she would probably have served her Souchong or Hyson tea from the thin, delicate cups of Chinese porcelain, complete with hand-painted decorations in blue and white, which had been sent the previous year.

some pleasant Spott either in England Scotland or Wales being
much in your way of thinking with respect to a Country Life.
If I stay here I will this year & every Year to come send some
Trifles to you and the Children to keep Poor Gaze a little in
your rembrance — I shall send by Mr Morgan or some other
hand a Speciment of my Teste in Silk for you to make a Gown,
a Piece of Longcloth to make any thing you Please, a Dark
Ground Large Pelempore, something to make my Dear little
Girls Thocks as my darling Charlotte used to call them —
[illegible] To Miss Selly, Jean & Mary Evans a Long Tea Silk
on their Joint Account, I shall send you no China ware
this Year as John is to send you a Cart load of it
John has never had the Oppatunity of doing so much
much for himself as he has now, having no body to Controul
him, & every body Somean the Supracargoes to assist & give
him every [illegible] in their power, so that I think
when he goes home this time, he may stay there —
Mr Neb has got a [illegible] but I Don't know whether
a Girl or Boy and he and his wife is doing vastly well
in the Mercantile way as the Mr Kerman used to say
Perhaps I will see them [illegible] year or two
I will w[illegible]

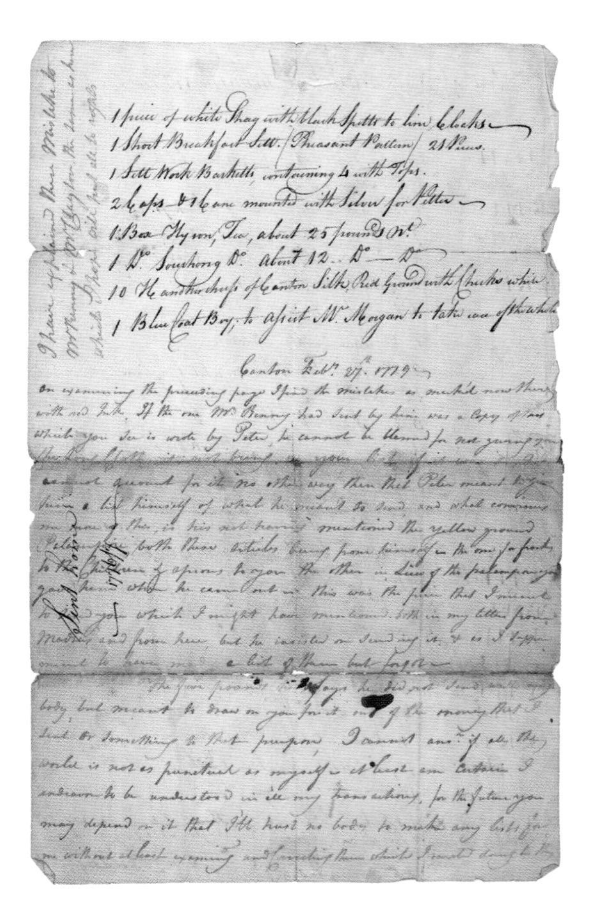

1 piece of white Shag with black Spotts to line Cloaks —
1 Short Breakfast Silk (Pheasant Pattern) 21 Pieces
1 Silk Work Baskett, containing [illegible] with Tops.
2 Caps & 1 Cane mounted with Silver for Peter —
1 Box Hyson Tea, about 25 pounds Wt.
1 Do. Souchong Do. about 12 .. Do — Do
10 Ps another piece of Canton Silk Red Ground with Checks white
1 Blue Coat Boy to assist Mr. Morgan to take care of the whole

Canton Febr 27. 1777

On examining the preceding page I find the mistake [illegible]

Papers of the MacIntyre and Anderson families, *c.* 1770–1882; letters 20, 23 relating to John MacIntyre, 1776, 1777 (IOPP/MSS Eur F 558).

Chinese Porcelain from the *Valentine*

On 16 November 1779 the *Valentine*, a ship of the East India Company, was wrecked on the Ile de Merchant, off the Channel Island of Sark. It had encountered a strong gale and fierce tide on its homeward voyage from India – a sad end to its fourth voyage to Madras, Bengal and Bombay.

While in India a large amount of Chinese porcelain had been transferred on to the *Valentine* from other East India Company vessels, to be taken back to England. Although the blue and white hand-painted designs are based on traditional Chinese scenes, and include figures, buildings, trees and rivers, they have been interpreted for the export market.

The broken edges of the fragments indicate that the cargo consisted of various qualities of porcelain, ranging from expensively thin, fine-edged pieces for an aristocratic table to those with thicker sides, intended for more general use. One piece is painted on both sides, indicating that it had once been a particularly fine cup or bowl.

Fragments of Chinese blue and white export porcelain (private collection).

English Ceramics

Josiah Wedgwood and Thomas Bentley had been in partnership since 1768. Together they specialised in producing a wide range of decorative items in durable, unglazed stoneware. This cup in the catalogue for 1787 was produced in the factory at Etruria, near Stoke-on-Trent, and, as described here, was made in the 'Jasper of two colours'. Jasperware was a type of fine-grained, unglazed stoneware that had been introduced by Wedgwood in 1774. Pieces made in this style were usually manufactured in two or three colours, from a range of blue, green, lilac, yellow, black and white. They were also made to such a fine finish as to be transparent. The illustration attempts to portray this delicate feature.

The cup is decorated 'chiefly after the antique', with Grecian and Etruscan ornaments. Archaeological discoveries at Pompeii and Herculaneum in the late 1730s and 1740s had inspired artists and designers to use motifs based on the ancient wall paintings and frescoes in their own work. Wedgwood's 'antique' decorations follow this taste for the neoclassical.

On the final page Wedgwood shrewdly draws attention to 'The Queen's Ware of Mr. Wedgwood's manufacture'. This type of cream-coloured earthenware had been named after Queen Charlotte, consort to George III, who had ordered a complete tea service from Wedgwood in 1765. Having been honoured by the Queen as 'Potter to Her Majesty' in 1762, Wedgwood realised the commercial advantage of promoting his royal connection. He continued to use his title, and endorsement, throughout his career.

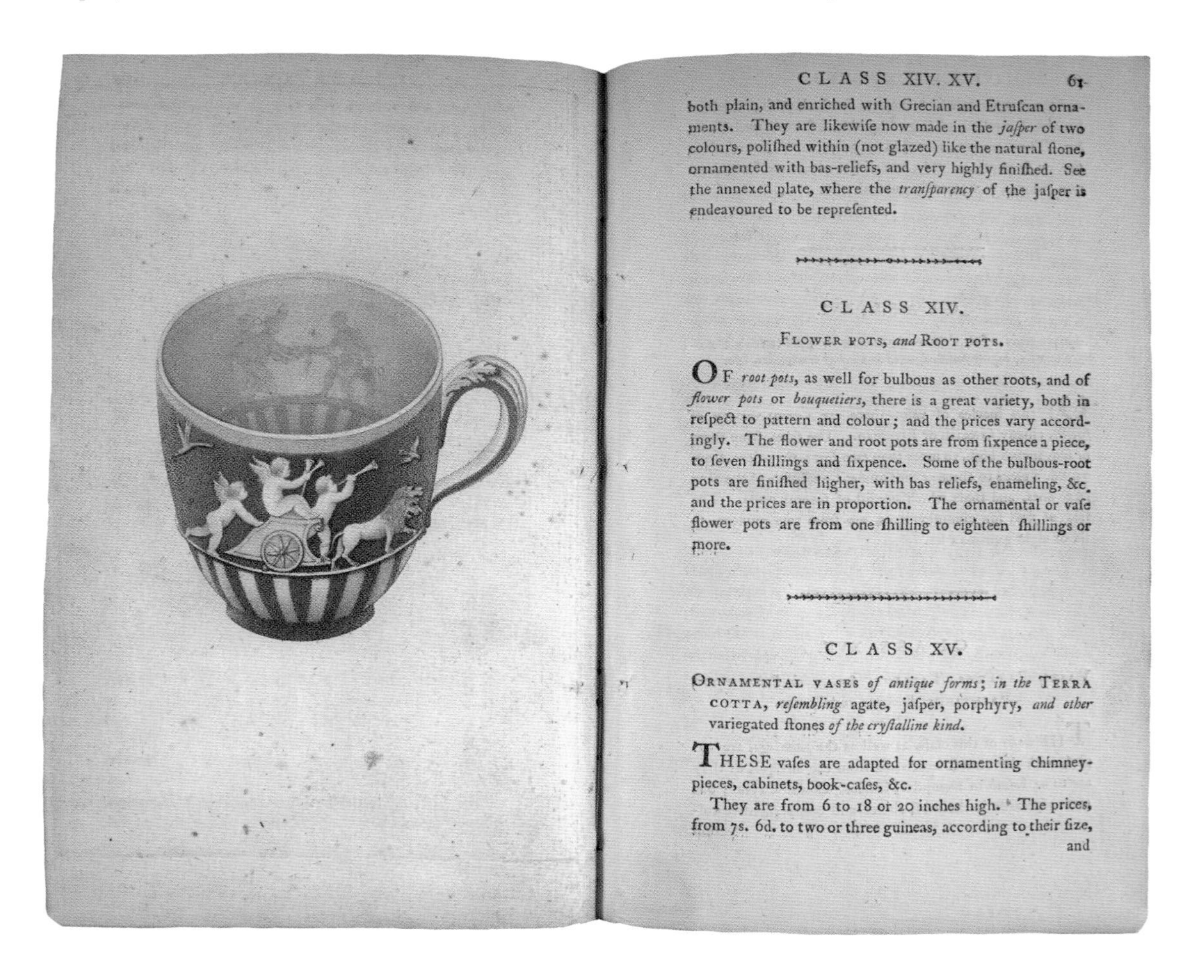

CLASS XIV. XV. 61

both plain, and enriched with Grecian and Etruſcan ornaments. They are likewiſe now made in the *jaſper* of two colours, poliſhed within (not glazed) like the natural ſtone, ornamented with bas-reliefs, and very highly finiſhed. See the annexed plate, where the *tranſparency* of the jaſper is endeavoured to be repreſented.

CLASS XIV.

FLOWER POTS, *and* ROOT POTS.

OF *root pots*, as well for bulbous as other roots, and of *flower pots* or *bouquetiers*, there is a great variety, both in reſpect to pattern and colour; and the prices vary accordingly. The flower and root pots are from ſixpence a piece, to ſeven ſhillings and ſixpence. Some of the bulbous-root pots are finiſhed higher, with bas reliefs, enameling, &c. and the prices are in proportion. The ornamental or vaſe flower pots are from one ſhilling to eighteen ſhillings or more.

CLASS XV.

ORNAMENTAL VASES *of antique forms*; *in the* TERRA COTTA, *reſembling* agate, jaſper, porphyry, *and other* variegated ſtones *of the cryſtalline kind*.

THESE vaſes are adapted for ornamenting chimney-pieces, cabinets, book-caſes, &c.

They are from 6 to 18 or 20 inches high. The prices, from 7s. 6d. to two or three guineas, according to their ſize, and

Catalogue of cameos, intaglios, medals, bas-reliefs, busts and small statues … By Josiah Wedgwood, 6th edition, with additions, Etruria, 1787 (679.d.22.(3)).

The Tea Party by Robert Hancock

A set of engravings by Robert Hancock, entitled *The Tea Party*, became some of the most popular motifs used in the decoration of eighteenth-century ceramics. Hancock perfected the process of transfer-printing, whereby an engraved design could be transferred to a ceramic surface. He continued to exploit this technique throughout his career at the factories of Battersea, Bow and Worcester, where he used it to mass-produce high-quality, decorated porcelain. Since transfer-printing was more cost-effective than painting by hand, a wider section of the public could now afford to buy porcelain.

This teapot is an early example of a transfer-printed engraving and depicts an aristocratic tea party. The scene includes a young African slave who pours hot water from a kettle into a teapot. He is expensively dressed to reflect the status, wealth and good taste of his rich master.

LEFT
Teapot and cover. Bow porcelain, 1755–6, showing *The Tea Party* engraving by Robert Hancock (Victoria and Albert Museum, C.426&A-1920).

BELOW
The Artist's Vade-mecum, 3rd edition, London, 1776 (1422.k.6).

BOTTOM
Cup and saucer, Worcester porcelain, *c.* 1765 (Victoria and Albert Museum, C.93&A-1948).

There were at least three different versions of Hancock's design. This cup and saucer has been transfer-printed from a variation later published in *The Artist's Vade-mecum*. This pattern book was intended to provide artists with examples and inspiration in 'the whole art of drawing'.

For most of the eighteenth century, tea was an expensive luxury item, enjoyed as a social drink by the upper class and wealthier members of the middle class. The drink was served at home by the lady of the house, who would prepare it at the table, in front of her guests. This cup and saucer with the image of an English upper-class tea party was intended for use by members of the middle class. The design may have been particularly attractive to them because it suggested a sense of aristocratic style and luxury – values that the middling classes wished to emulate at their tea tables.

Edward Eagleton's Tea

Some of the many varieties of tea are listed in these advertisements for Edward Eagleton's tea warehouses. Eagleton advertises his wares competitively, as being pure and of the best quality. He offers them 'for ready money only' to his middle-class customers in London and elsewhere ('country orders punctually executed'). The offer of a money prize encourages them to buy in larger quantities.

In 1777 tea was particularly expensive, largely due to a heavy import tax. The prices quoted here range from 4 to 15 shillings a pound in weight. At a time when a workman might earn around 10 shillings a week, this would have been a prohibitive price for him. He might have bought a less expensive adulterated tea instead, but there were risks involved as the added substances might include some that were poisonous.

Tea remained an expensive item until 1784 when the government, urged by tea merchants led by Richard Twining, finally reduced the tax. The lower price made tea a much more affordable drink for the middle and lower classes. As a result of the higher price of grain, tea also became cheaper than ale and malt liquors and gradually replaced them as a staple drink.

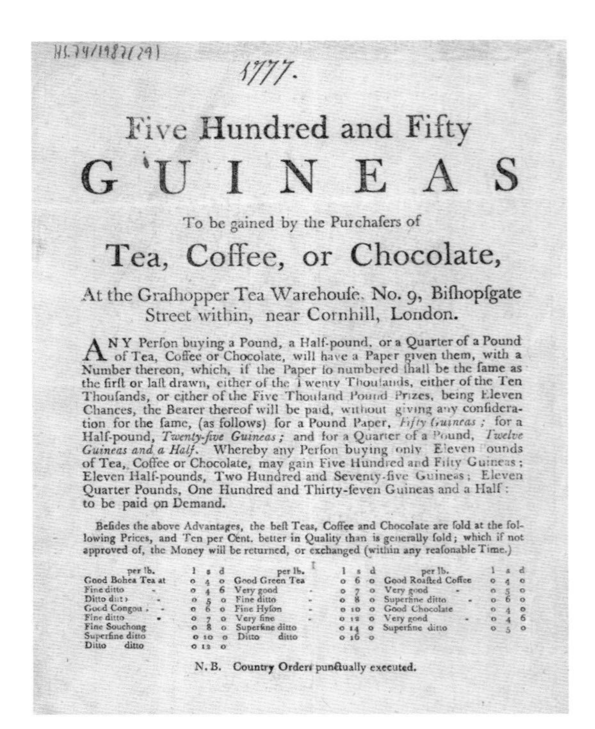

HS.74/1987(29)

1777.

Five Hundred and Fifty

GUINEAS

To be gained by the Purchaſers of

Tea, Coffee, or Chocolate,

At the Graſhopper Tea Warehouſe, No. 9, Biſhopſgate Street within, near Cornhill, London.

ANY Perſon buying a Pound, a Half-pound, or a Quarter of a Pound of Tea, Coffee or Chocolate, will have a Paper given them, with a Number thereon, which, if the Paper ſo numbered ſhall be the ſame as the firſt or laſt drawn, either of the Twenty Thouſands, either of the Ten Thouſands, or either of the Five Thouſand Pound Prizes, being Eleven Chances, the Bearer thereof will be paid, without giving any conſideration for the ſame, (as follows) for a Pound Paper, *Fifty Guineas*; for a Half-pound, *Twenty-five Guineas*; and for a Quarter of a Pound, *Twelve Guineas and a Half*. Whereby any Perſon buying only Eleven Pounds of Tea, Coffee or Chocolate, may gain Five Hundred and Fifty Guineas; Eleven Half-pounds, Two Hundred and Seventy-five Guineas; Eleven Quarter Pounds, One Hundred and Thirty-ſeven Guineas and a Half: to be paid on Demand.

Beſides the above Advantages, the beſt Teas, Coffee and Chocolate are ſold at the following Prices, and Ten per Cent. better in Quality than is generally ſold; which if not approved of, the Money will be returned, or exchanged (within any reaſonable Time.)

per lb.	l	s	d	per lb.	l	s	d	per lb.	l	s	d
Good Bohea Tea at	0	4	0	Good Green Tea	0	6	0	Good Roaſted Coffee	0	4	0
Fine ditto	0	4	6	Very good	0	7	0	Very good	0	5	0
Ditto ditto	0	5	0	Fine ditto	0	8	0	Superfine ditto	0	6	0
Good Congou	0	6	0	Fine Hyſon	0	10	0	Good Chocolate	0	4	0
Fine ditto	0	7	0	Very fine	0	12	0	Very good	0	4	6
Fine Souchong	0	8	0	Superfine ditto	0	14	0	Superfine ditto	0	5	0
Superfine ditto	0	10	0	Ditto ditto	0	16	0				
Ditto ditto	0	12	0								

N.B. Country Orders punctually executed.

Five hundred and fifty guineas to be gained by the purchasers of tea, coffee, or chocolate, at the Grasshopper Tea Warehouse, No. 9 Bishopsgate Street within, near Cornhill, London, 1777 (HS.74/1987(29)).

FOR READY MONEY ONLY,
RETAIL AND WHOLESALE,
SUGARS.
MOIST (ONLY) 8d. Per lb.
LUMP (ONLY) 12d. per lb.
BETTER SORTS CHEAPER IN PROPORTION.
TEAS,
ONE OUNCE TO THE POUND OVER WEIGHT.
GOOD CONGOU (ONLY) 4s. 8d. Per lb.
CAPITAL SOUCHONG (ONLY) 5s. Per lb.
BETTER SORTS CHEAPER IN PROPORTION,
BEST Raiſins, Currants, Starch, Blues, Durham Muſtards, RICE, SPICES, &c. Lower Than at Any Other HOUSES In LONDON.
AT EAGLETON and Co's.
ESTABLISHED *TEA-WAREHOUSES*,
The *Original Graſs-Hopper*, 42, CHEAPSIDE,
And 9, BISHOPSGATE-STREET,
Near *Cornhill*, LONDON.
WHERE Samples of SUGARS, TEAS, SPICES, &c. May be Seen.
*** Orders per Penny or General Poſt Coach, Carrier, &c—For TOWN or COUNTRY Duly Attended, to WHOLESALE and RETAIL. And ſent (As per Order) to Any Part, Place, Coach, Carrier, Inn, Wharf, &c. In LONDON.

For ready money only, retail and wholesale … at Eagleton and Co's. established tea-warehouses, London, *c.* 1780 (HS.74/1987(23)).

The Children in the Wood

This cup and saucer was mass-produced in the early nineteenth century to meet the growing demand of the middle classes for less expensive china. The unusual pointed handle is of the 'London shape' favoured by many British manufacturers between 1813 and 1825. They also liked to use the word 'London' to suggest the latest, most fashionable styles.

The transfer-printed design shows two scenes from *The Children in the Wood*, a story that had been available as a cheap publication throughout the eighteenth century. Printed on poor-quality paper, using old type and wood blocks, these chapbooks were produced in high print runs for a wide circulation.

The design on this cup and saucer can be seen to be very similar in style to the book illustrations. Members of the middle classes familiar with these illustrations would certainly have made the connection between these designs and their print culture.

Staffordshire 'London shape' cup and saucer, *c.* 1820. The pink, transfer-printed design is accented by pink lustre banding (private collection).

THE
CHILDREN
IN THE
WOOD:
A TALE FOR THE NURSERY.

WITH COPPER-PLATES.

REVISED AND CORRECTED, WITH ADDITIONS,
BY MARY ELLIOTT.

LONDON:
WILLIAM DARTON, 58, HOLBORN HILL.
1822.

Price Sixpence.

LEFT
Tragical History of the Children in the Wood, York, [1790?]. Frontispiece (RB.23.a.10048).

ABOVE
The Children in the Wood…, London: William Darton, 1822. Frontispiece (1578/3180).

New Shoes for Changing Styles

For the upper and middle classes, shoes were an expression of style as well as a necessary protection for the feet. Women's changing fashions in dress were mirrored by the shoes that went with them. As elaborate gowns in silk brocades gave way to plain frocks in simple muslin, so shoes slowly lost their heels and buckles and became flat pumps with ribbon ties. During the eighteenth century men's shoes gradually assumed a flat-heeled, lace-up style similar to that still worn, reflecting the simplification of men's suits towards today's sobriety.

Around the time that George I arrived in England, after his accession to the throne, ladies shoes were highly ornate. They had substantial curved heels, needlepoint toes and latchets (straps across the instep), which would be fastened by buckles. They were often of fine brocade, with matching clogs to be worn in the street as a protection against puddles and dirt. Their buckles, with sparkling stones of paste, were stored in a custom-made curved box to keep them safe and clean when not being worn, underlining their value to the wearer. Women's shoes kept their heels until late in the eighteenth century, although over time they became thinner and lower.

Shoes of the 1810s could hardly be more different from those of a century earlier. Often made of satin in black as well as white, with narrow ribbons to hold them on, they were plain, light and flexible. Such shoes are the ancestors of fashionable modern ballet pumps, as well as the ballet shoes still worn by dancers. The late eighteenth-century men's shoes, with very low heels and laces, are remarkable only because they are red leather rather than black (it has been suggested that they were leisurewear, intended for the seaside). Like other shoes of the Georgian period they are 'straights', with no left or right foot. This print of the 'fashionable shoe-maker' is perhaps less than subtle in its depiction of the delights of trying new shoes, particularly with a shoe-maker as attractive as this ultra-fashionable young man.

The fashionable shoe-maker trying on an Italian slipper, London, 1784 (British Museum, Prints and Drawings, 1935.0522.1.185).

Pair of men's shoes, *c.* 1790. Red leather with cream silk trimming and laces (Northampton Museum, 1968.44.8 P).

Staying A-la-Mode

Before the advent of the fashion magazine (or at least the reporting of fashions in the columns of newspapers) late in the eighteenth century, the only way to keep up with London fashions was to be there – or to hear from someone who was. Manuals of deportment and dancing, such as Nivelon's *The Rudiments of Genteel Behaviour*, depict the styles of their day, but they were soon out of date. The pretty plates in this book show the relative plainness and clean lines of early Georgian dress. The lady is tightly corseted, with a pointed stomacher and a hooped skirt to make her waist seem even smaller. Her dress appears to be a plain silk with little decoration. The gentleman's attire is more elaborate, with a three-piece suit and decoration on the waistcoat beneath his coat, and the full skirts of his coat correspond with the lady's silhouette.

The fashion plate began to emerge in mid-century, in the form of frontispieces in pocket-books for ladies. These tiny images show fashions for the past year in some detail. That in *The ladies' own memorandum-book* for 1769 displays the extreme elaboration attained by full dress: lace at neck and elbows, a ladder of bows on the stomacher and pleated ruching in serpentine lines on the petticoat and skirts of the gown.

Thirty years later, female as well as male fashions were greatly simplified. By the early years of the nineteenth century, women were wearing high-waisted gowns of classical simplicity. Men had begun to adopt modern trousers for day wear, even though knee breeches were still expected as part of formal evening attire. *Le Beau Monde* is only one of several magazines providing colour plates with the latest fashions for both sexes. With regular issues throughout the year, it was relatively easy to stay in style.

Francis Nivelon, *The Rudiments of Genteel Behaviour*, London, 1737 (1812.a.28).

The ladies' own memorandum-book; or, daily pocket journal, London, 1769. Frontispiece plate with fashions for the past year (RB.23.a.6835).

Le Beau Monde, or, Literary and Fashionable Magazine, London, 1806–8. Plate with gentleman in trousers (P.P.5141.d).

Gallery of Fashion

One of the earliest publications that can claim to be a fashion magazine in the modern sense is the *Gallery of Fashion*, published in London by Nicolaus Heideloff (1761–1837) between 1794 and 1803. Heideloff was a German who worked in Paris until the French Revolution, when he fled to London.

He set out his intentions in the introduction to the first volume, which appeared in 1794. The *Gallery of Fashion* was to be 'a collection of all the most fashionable and elegant dresses in vogue' which would appear monthly and contain as many as five full-length figures of ladies 'of rank and fashion' in each issue. Heideloff drew his fashions from the clothes worn by his patronesses and did not scruple to flatter them for 'that style of elegance, and that original taste, which is so peculiar to the British ladies'.

The *Gallery of Fashion* is sumptuous in its production. Each volume opens with an elaborately decorated cartouche containing the title, volume number and year, and the beautifully coloured images show the latest styles in accessories as well as gowns. It depicts morning, afternoon and evening dresses, as well as ball dresses and even court dresses, and some of the illustrations have been touched with silver or gold highlights. A full description accompanies each plate, providing details of fabrics, colours, hairstyles, jewellery and accessories, including parts of the ensemble which cannot be seen at all, for example shoes. Thus it should have been possible for gowns, with all their trimmings and additions, to be made up for those ladies who purchased the magazine and liked a particular style. The dresses and accessories become noticeably plainer and simpler over the few years that the *Gallery of Fashion* was published, as fashions developed away from the decorative complexity of eighteenth-century rococo towards a more severe, early nineteenth-century classicism. One exception to the changing styles was court dress. It maintained an incongruous pairing of a full hoop with much surface decoration on the petticoat (as worn in the mid-eighteenth century) with a fashionably high waistline throughout the 1790s and early 1800s.

Ladies were shown enjoying a variety of leisure activities in the magazine's pages. 'Two ladies, en negligé, taking an airing in a phaeton' are precariously perched in their small open carriage drawn by two horses. A lady is shown seated on her horse, stylishly dressed for riding. Another two ladies take breakfast in their dressing-room, while two more are shown at a fortepiano, considering the music to be played. Yet others appear in a box at the opera, or seated and standing in a pretty group dressed for the ball. Fashionable dress was even required for visits to the seaside, as demonstrated by the ladies standing on the cliff side above the seafront (bathing machines can be seen on the beach below). One of them has her hair 'undressed' (it cannot be seen in the picture) as a concession to the informality of the occasion, while the other wears a 'Quaker Dunstable hat'. Heideloff's *Gallery of Fashion* is not merely a costume parade; it also provides insight into every detail of changing styles, as well as the daily round of society ladies – a lifestyle that many young women wished to emulate.

ABOVE, OPPOSITE AND OVERLEAF
Gallery of Fashion, London, 1794–1803 (C.106.k.16).

Fig. 253.
Fig. 254.
Fig. 255.
Fig. 256.

Fig. 151.
Fig. 152.

3 Culture and Ideas

During the Georgian period public entertainments grew significantly in variety and popularity. The newly affluent middle classes, with time and money to spare, were eager to go to theatres, visit museums and art galleries and attend concerts and other events at the new charitable institutions.

London's theatre world dated back to the Restoration, but during the eighteenth century theatres grew larger and more opulent to cater to growing audiences. New genres of entertainment such as pantomime, circus and the ballet, alongside traditional dramatic fare, pleased Georgian tastes. Many of Britain's provincial towns acquired their own theatres at this time, with regular programmes of drama and other events. Leading players from London toured the provinces during the summer, so many who never visited the capital were able to see celebrity actors and actresses at first hand.

Britain's celebrities did not come only from the theatres, although talented performers with particularly appealing skills were among Britain's most famous people. Criminals all too often became the focus of popular attention, if they were daring or glamorous enough. Women in the public eye who were beautiful and stylish, respectable or not, became the subject of celebrity gossip and were often regarded as fashion icons.

Alongside the pleasures of theatre and other public entertainments was an impetus to both learning and charity. Enlightenment ideals fostered the foundation of art galleries and museums in London that are still with us today. Britain as a nation may have been becoming richer, but there were many who lost as well as those who gained, and very real poverty was still rife. Art exhibitions and music concerts were regularly used by newly founded philanthropic institutions to attract charitable giving.

Behind all these ventures lay advertising: in newspapers, through periodicals, in pamphlets and in handbills sold or distributed in the streets. Print culture, here as in so many other facets of Georgian life, had a crucial role to play.

Building and Rebuilding Britain's Theatres

The eighteenth century ushered in a great age of theatre building and rebuilding. At George I's accession in 1714, the Drury Lane Theatre (dating back to 1674) was the only playhouse in London for drama, since the King's Theatre in the Haymarket was devoted to Italian opera. The new king quickly gave permission for a second playhouse to open in Lincoln's Inn Fields. This was succeeded in 1732 by a new theatre in Covent Garden, the first on the site now occupied by the Royal Opera House.

The passing of the Licensing Act in 1737 limited London theatre-going to these two playhouses, for the King's Theatre continued to offer exclusively opera. As the century rolled on, both Drury Lane and Covent Garden were extensively altered and rebuilt, for ever-growing audiences. In 1775 Drury Lane saw major alterations by the Adam brothers, undertaken for the theatre's manager David Garrick; these gave Drury Lane a capacity of around 2,000. Just a few years later the building was entirely demolished, to make way for a new and much larger theatre designed by the architect Henry Holland (1745–1806).

This theatre was entirely destroyed by fire in 1809, and had to be rebuilt from scratch. The architect Benjamin Dean Wyatt (1775–1852) created an imposing neoclassical design for the exterior, with a series of richly decorated classical interiors. This building, which still forms part of the present Drury Lane Theatre, seated an audience of 3,060. Wyatt's *Observations* on his designs for Drury Lane, published not long after the theatre reopened on 10 October 1812, reveals the grandeur of its public spaces and auditorium, underlining the importance attached to theatre-going in the early 1800s.

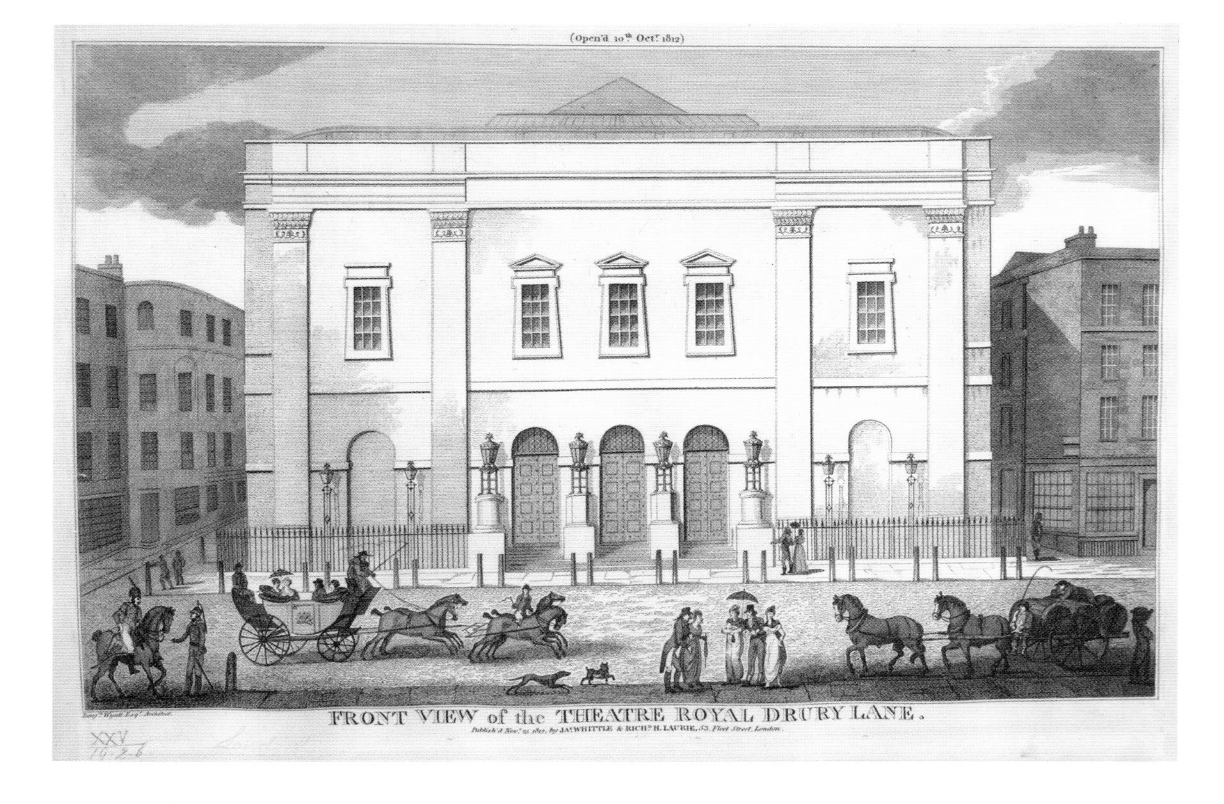

Front view of the new Theatre Royal, Drury Lane. Laurie and Whittle, 1812 (K.Top.25.19.2.b).

OPPOSITE
Plates from Benjamin Dean Wyatt, *Observations on the Design for the Theatre Royal Drury Lane, as executed in the year 1812*, London, 1813 (59.c.13).

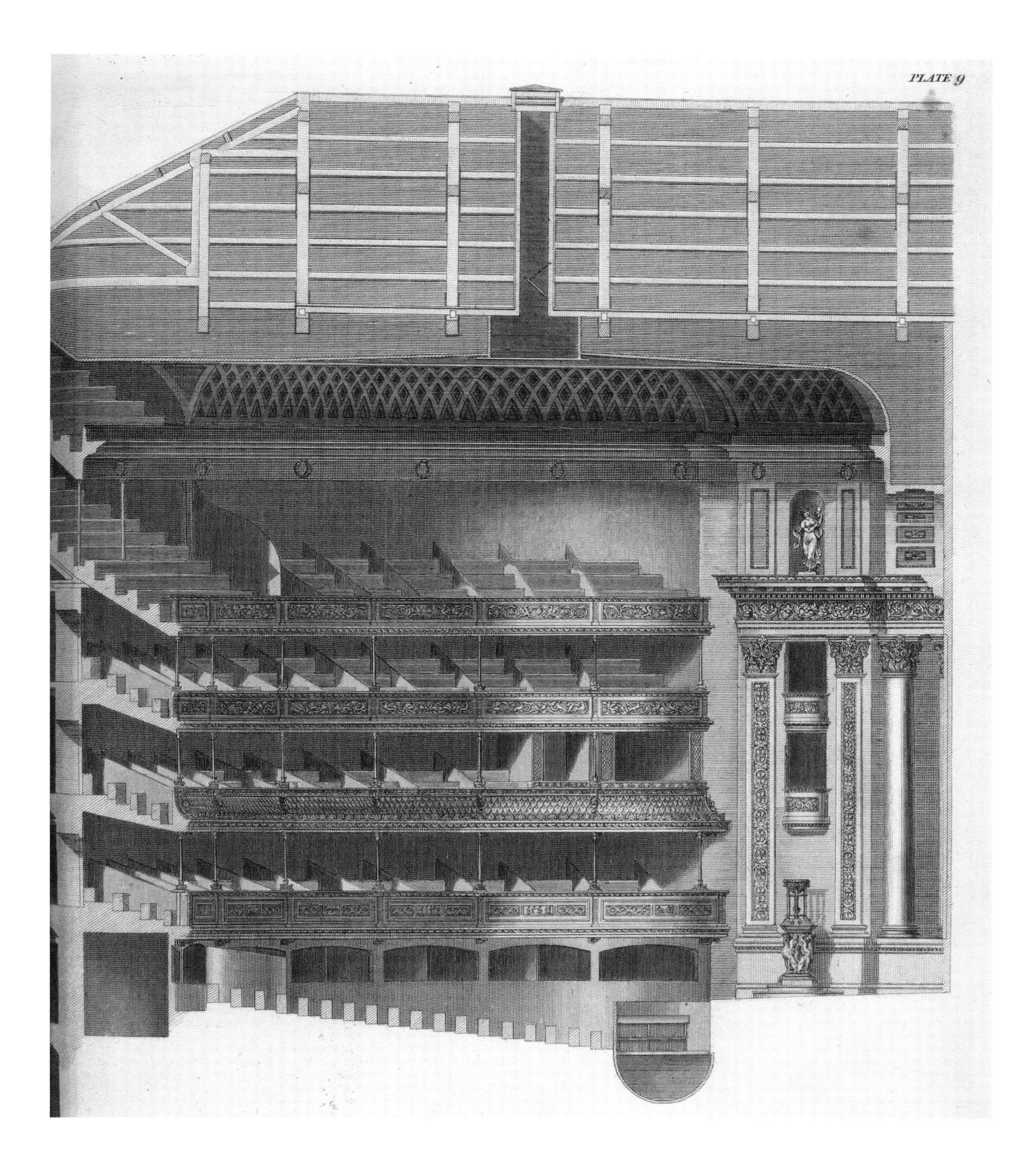
PLATE 9

Staging the Show

Theatres may survive, but their many performances leave few traces. Valuable evidence about scenery, costumes and staging during the Georgian period is provided by the rare surviving inventories of properties belonging to the playhouses. There are two such listings for the Covent Garden Theatre.

The first was made in 1744, when the manager John Rich (1692–1761) used his theatre and its properties as security for a large loan. This manuscript inventory is long and seemingly chaotic, as it is organised according to storage locations within the theatre. Mrs Horton (1698/9–1756) was a leading actress. Her dressing room contained her costumes as Imoinda in *Oroonoko* by Thomas Southerne (1660–1746) and Mary Queen of Scots in *The Albion Queens* by John Banks (1652/3–1706). Among the flats in the scene room were Medusa's Cave, probably from the pantomime *Perseus and Andromeda*, and two scenes for Hell, at least one of which may have been used in the pantomime *The Rape of Proserpine*.

Covent Garden was in financial trouble again in the 1820s, and the theatre was advertised for sale. The auction of its properties, including 'favourite panoramic views' from recent pantomimes and the wardrobe, with its colourful and exotic costumes such as a 'Harlequin's dress', a 'Magician's green dress', 'Chinese dresses' and a 'Persian dress', was set for 10 September 1829. In the event the sale did not take place, for the theatre was saved by public subscriptions and voluntary contributions.

ABOVE
Schedule of Properties Belonging to Covent Garden Theatre, 1744 (Add.MS. 12201, f. 61r).

LEFT AND OPPOSITE
Mr Thomas, *Theatre Royal Covent Garden. Catalogue of the valuable properties of this splendid establishment … which will be sold by auction*, London, [1829]. Title page, pp.58–59 (RB.23.b.4299).

THEATRE ROYAL COVENT GARDEN.

CATALOGUE
OF THE
VALUABLE PROPERTIES
Of this Splendid Establishment,

Unquestionably the BEST, as well as the MOST EXTENSIVE COLLECTION, in every department, that has EVER BEEN CREATED for the purpose of SCENIC REPRESENTATIONS.

THE BEST EFFORTS OF

ROBERTS, THE GRIEVE'S, WHITMORE, PUGH, PHILLIPS,

AND OTHER CELEBRATED ARTISTS,

Here abound in every Variety of Subject.

FAVORITE PANORAMIC VIEWS,

EXHIBITED IN THE RECENT PANTOMIMES,

AND MANY GRAND DROP SCENES.

THE

EXTRAORDINARILY FINE TONED ORGAN, BUILT by BISHOP,

At an expence little short of £1000.

The magnificent Centre Chandelier,

THOSE FOR THE PRINCIPAL ENTRANCE, LOBBIES, DRESS AND FIRST CIRCLES.

THE WARDROBE,

Embracing a MOST EXPENSIVE, ELEGANT, and GENERAL ASSEMBLAGE of DRESSES, and which cost, within a few Years, UPWARDS of £20,000.

EIGHTEEN BRILLIANT GLASSES,

In Gilt Frames, of the following dimensions, 79 in. by 68, 70 by 52, 50 by 45, 45 by 36, 42 by 36, 36 by 33, &c.

Furniture and Fittings of the Principal Dressing Rooms;

PORTRAIT OF MR. HARRIS,

AND OTHER VALUABLE EFFECTS;

WHICH WILL BE SOLD BY AUCTION, BY

MR. THOMAS,

In the Saloon of the Theatre,

ON THURSDAY, THE 10TH DAY OF SEPTEMBER, 1829,

And several following Days, at Twelve for One very punctually.

To be Publicly Viewed Three Days prior to the Sale, and [illegible]logues had, at 2s. 6d. each, (without one not a Person will be admitted,) at Mr. TH[illegible]'s Offices, 38, King Street, Covent Garden.

Printed by W. SMITH, *King Street,* [illegible]*even Dials.*

Theatrical Advertising

By 1714 London's theatres were advertising their performances not only through the long-established method of handbills and great bills distributed and displayed in the streets, but also in the growing number of newspapers. One of the very few surviving great bills, handsomely printed in red and black, is for a performance at the Theatre Royal, Covent Garden on 20 January 1776. Both the musical pasticcio *The Duenna* by Richard Brinsley Sheridan (1751–1816), and the anonymous pantomime *Prometheus* were new that season.

Covent Garden's auditorium was extensively altered in 1782 and again in 1792, increasing capacity to around 3,000. Playbills for the first performances after these significant changes draw attention to the 'New Theatre Royal' with a celebratory 'Occasional Prelude' – presumably created for the reopening. In 1782 the double bill consisted of revivals (*The Busy Body* from 1709 and *The Upholsterer* from 1758), and the playbill drew attention to changes to the theatre's entrances. In 1792 both *The Road to Ruin* by Thomas Holcroft (1745–1809) and *The Irishman in London* by William Macready (d. 1829) had received their first performances earlier in the year. The playbill was at pains to justify a 'small advancement of the prices of admission', as well as explaining further changes to the theatre's entrances. Apart from the usual advertisements, which give much the same information as the playbills, some newspapers carried quite lengthy accounts of the opening performance and the rebuilt and redecorated theatre.

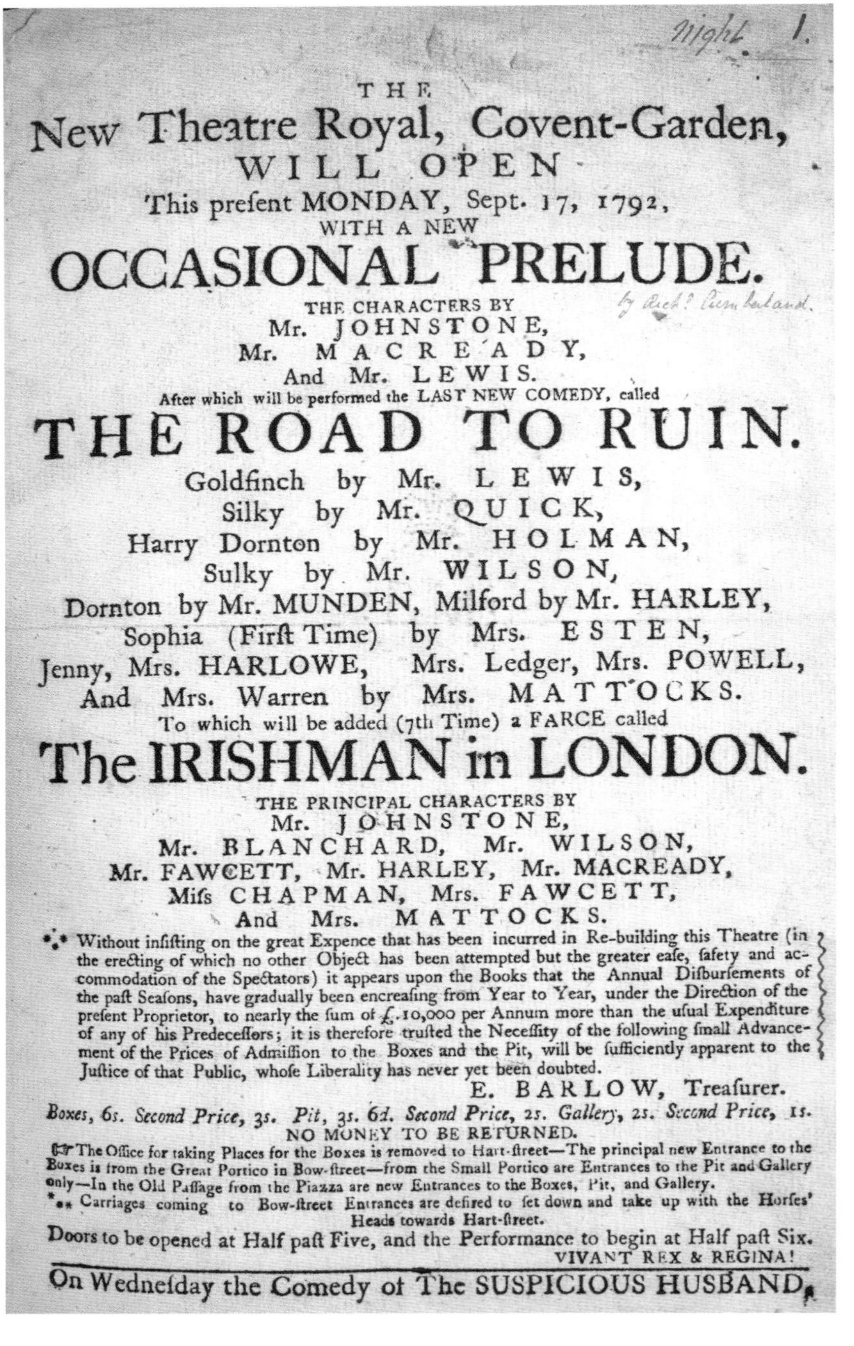

Night 1.

THE
New Theatre Royal, Covent-Garden,
WILL OPEN
This preſent MONDAY, Sept. 17, 1792,
WITH A NEW
OCCASIONAL PRELUDE.
THE CHARACTERS BY
Mr. JOHNSTONE,
Mr. MACREADY,
And Mr. LEWIS.
After which will be performed the LAST NEW COMEDY, called
THE ROAD TO RUIN.
Goldfinch by Mr. LEWIS,
Silky by Mr. QUICK,
Harry Dornton by Mr. HOLMAN,
Sulky by Mr. WILSON,
Dornton by Mr. MUNDEN, Milford by Mr. HARLEY,
Sophia (Firſt Time) by Mrs. ESTEN,
Jenny, Mrs. HARLOWE, Mrs. Ledger, Mrs. POWELL,
And Mrs. Warren by Mrs. MATTOCKS.
To which will be added (7th Time) a FARCE called
The IRISHMAN in LONDON.
THE PRINCIPAL CHARACTERS BY
Mr. JOHNSTONE,
Mr. BLANCHARD, Mr. WILSON,
Mr. FAWCETT, Mr. HARLEY, Mr. MACREADY,
Miſs CHAPMAN, Mrs. FAWCETT,
And Mrs. MATTOCKS.

*** Without inſiſting on the great Expence that has been incurred in Re-building this Theatre (in the erecting of which no other Object has been attempted but the greater eaſe, ſafety and accommodation of the Spectators) it appears upon the Books that the Annual Diſburſements of the paſt Seaſons, have gradually been encreaſing from Year to Year, under the Direction of the preſent Proprietor, to nearly the ſum of £.10,000 per Annum more than the uſual Expenditure of any of his Predeceſſors; it is therefore truſted the Neceſſity of the following ſmall Advancement of the Prices of Admiſſion to the Boxes and the Pit, will be ſufficiently apparent to the Juſtice of that Public, whoſe Liberality has never yet been doubted.

E. BARLOW, Treaſurer.

Boxes, 6s. *Second Price*, 3s. *Pit*, 3s. 6d. *Second Price*, 2s. *Gallery*, 2s. *Second Price*, 1s.
NO MONEY TO BE RETURNED.

☞ The Office for taking Places for the Boxes is removed to Hart-ſtreet—The principal new Entrance to the Boxes is from the Great Portico in Bow-ſtreet—from the Small Portico are Entrances to the Pit and Gallery only—In the Old Paſſage from the Piazza are new Entrances to the Boxes, Pit, and Gallery.

*** Carriages coming to Bow-ſtreet Entrances are deſired to ſet down and take up with the Horſes' Heads towards Hart-ſtreet.

Doors to be opened at Half paſt Five, and the Performance to begin at Half paſt Six.
VIVANT REX & REGINA!

On Wedneſday the Comedy of The SUSPICIOUS HUSBAND.

Playbill for performance at Covent Garden Theatre, 17 September 1792 (Playbills 84).

OPPOSITE
Great bill for performance at Covent Garden Theatre, 20 January 1776 (937.b.3).

The THIRTY FIFTH NIGHT.

At the Theatre-Royal in Covent-Garden,

This present SATURDAY, January 20, 1776,

Will be presented a New COMIC OPERA, call'd THE

DUENNA

OR, THE

DOUBLE ELOPEMENT.

The PRINCIPAL CHARACTERS, by

Mr. MATTOCKS,

Mr. QUICK,

Mr. WILSON,

Mr. DU-BELLAMY,

Mr. MAHON,

Mr. LEONI,

Miss DAYES,

Mrs. GREEN,

Mrs. MATTOCKS,

The MUSIC partly NEW and partly selected from the most EMINENT COMPOSERS

With a NEW OVERTURE, SCENES, DRESSES and other DECORATIONS.

To which will be added a New Pantomime (for the TWELFTH TIME) call'd

PROMETHEUS.

With NEW MUSIC, SCENES, DRESSES and MACHINERY.

The PRINCIPAL CHARACTERS by

Signor ZUCHELLI,

Mr. MAHON, Mr. BAKER,

And Mr. DAGUEVILLE.

Miss VALOIS,

And Signora VIDINI.

The VOCAL PARTS by

Mr. REINHOLD, Mr. DU-BELLAMY, &c.

The Overture and Music Composed by Mr. FISHER.

The Scenes painted by Messrs. DALL and RICHARDS

NOTHING under FULL PRICE will be taken

On Monday, DOUGLAS.

Douglas by a YOUNG GENTLEMAN. being his Fourth Appearance.

Theatrical Hazards

As a wholly commercial venture the theatre business was always financially precarious. One of the hazards to which theatre buildings were most vulnerable was fire. The Covent Garden Theatre was reduced to ruins by fire in 1808, followed by Drury Lane in 1809. These disasters were captured in print, and both theatres were quickly rebuilt. Fire insurance helped to ease the blow. The Drury Lane Theatre was presumably insured in 1809, for a receipt for a Westminster Fire Office premium survives signed by the manager, Richard Brinsley Sheridan, in 1789.

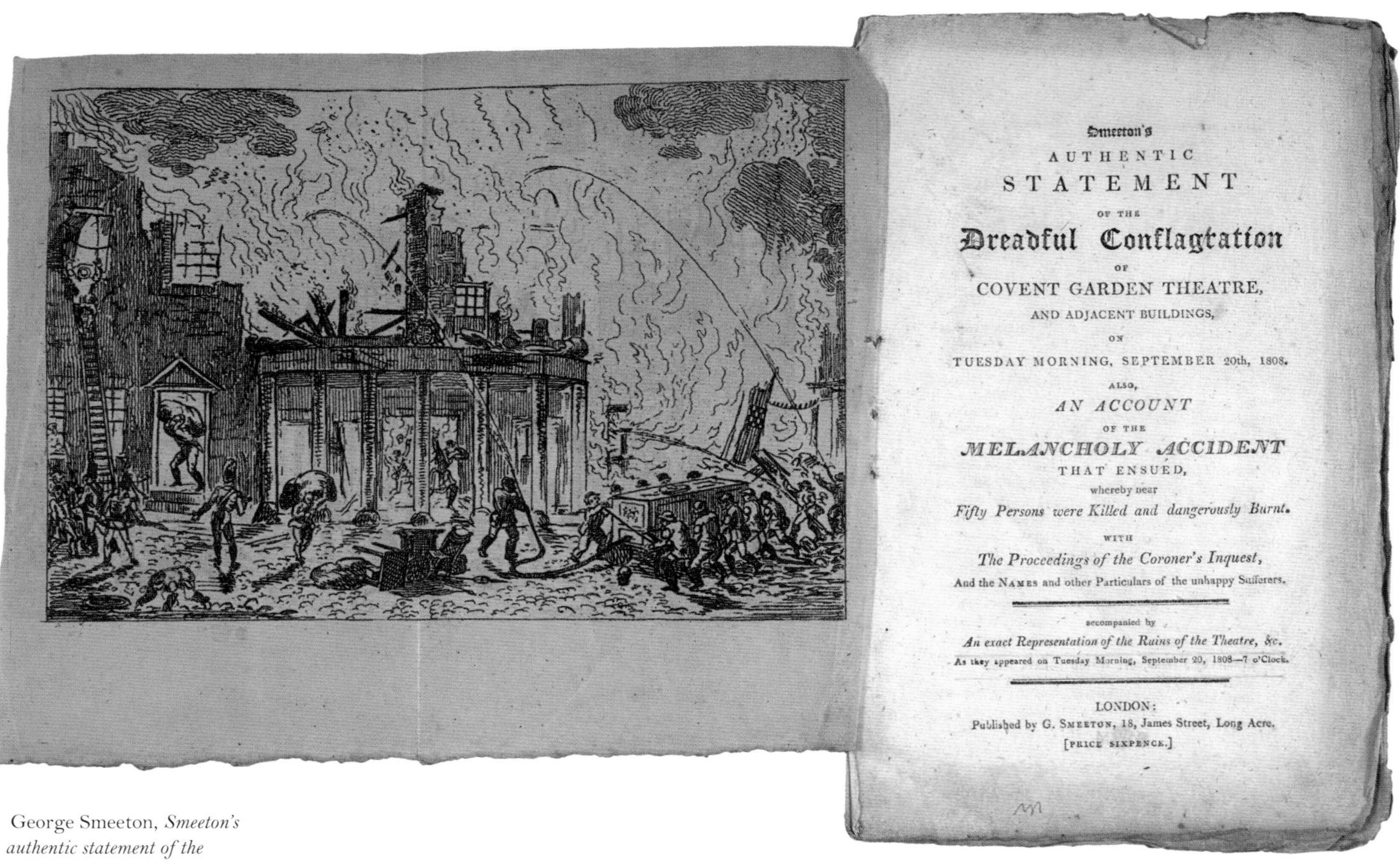

Smeeton's
AUTHENTIC
STATEMENT
OF THE
Dreadful Conflagration
OF
COVENT GARDEN THEATRE,
AND ADJACENT BUILDINGS,
ON
TUESDAY MORNING, SEPTEMBER 20th, 1808.
ALSO,
AN ACCOUNT
OF THE
MELANCHOLY ACCIDENT
THAT ENSUED,
whereby near
Fifty Persons were Killed and dangerously Burnt.
WITH
The Proceedings of the Coroner's Inquest,
And the NAMES and other Particulars of the unhappy Sufferers.

accompanied by
An exact Representation of the Ruins of the Theatre, &c.
As they appeared on Tuesday Morning, September 20, 1808—7 o'Clock.

LONDON:
Published by G. SMEETON, 18, James Street, Long Acre.
[PRICE SIXPENCE.]

George Smeeton, *Smeeton's authentic statement of the … conflagration of Covent Garden theatre*, London, 1808. Frontispiece (Dex.314.(1)).

Authentic account of the fire which reduced that extensive building of the Theatre-Royal, Drury-Lane, to a pile of ruins, London, [1809]. Frontispiece (1430.a.22).

A front view of the theatre in Birmingham on fire, 16 August 1792 (Maps K. Top 42.82.i.2).

Theatre Audiences

Theatre-going became an ever more popular pastime during the eighteenth century, but it was not always a polite entertainment, particularly as theatres grew ever larger. The Drury Lane Theatre built by Henry Holland, which opened in 1794, held more than 3,600, on five levels. When a favourite play or pantomime was given, or a celebrity performer appeared, managers tried to pack in as many people as possible. Performances by stars such as the actress Sarah Siddons (1755–1831) could provoke a very uncomfortable crush as people struggled to get in to see her.

In such conditions, it is not surprising that audiences could be fractious. Riots, while not frequent, did happen. One flashpoint for violence was ticket pricing: audiences hated any increase, for any reason. In 1809 the Covent Garden manager, John Philip Kemble (1757–1823), came under vicious attack for daring to raise prices following the rebuilding of the theatre after its destruction by fire. After enduring more than two months of rioting, Kemble was forced to give in to 'John Bull' and restore prices to their former levels.

Auditorium of the Drury Lane Theatre (1794 building) from Rudolph Ackermann, *The Microcosm of London*, London, [1808–10] (190.e.1).

Carington Bowles, after Robert Dighton, *The Pit Door* (*Drury Lane Theatre*), London, 1784 (British Museum, BM Satire 6769).

John Bull (pseud.), *Remarks on the cause of the dispute between the public and the managers of the Theatre Royal Covent Garden*, London, 1809. Frontispiece (840.d.10.(1)).

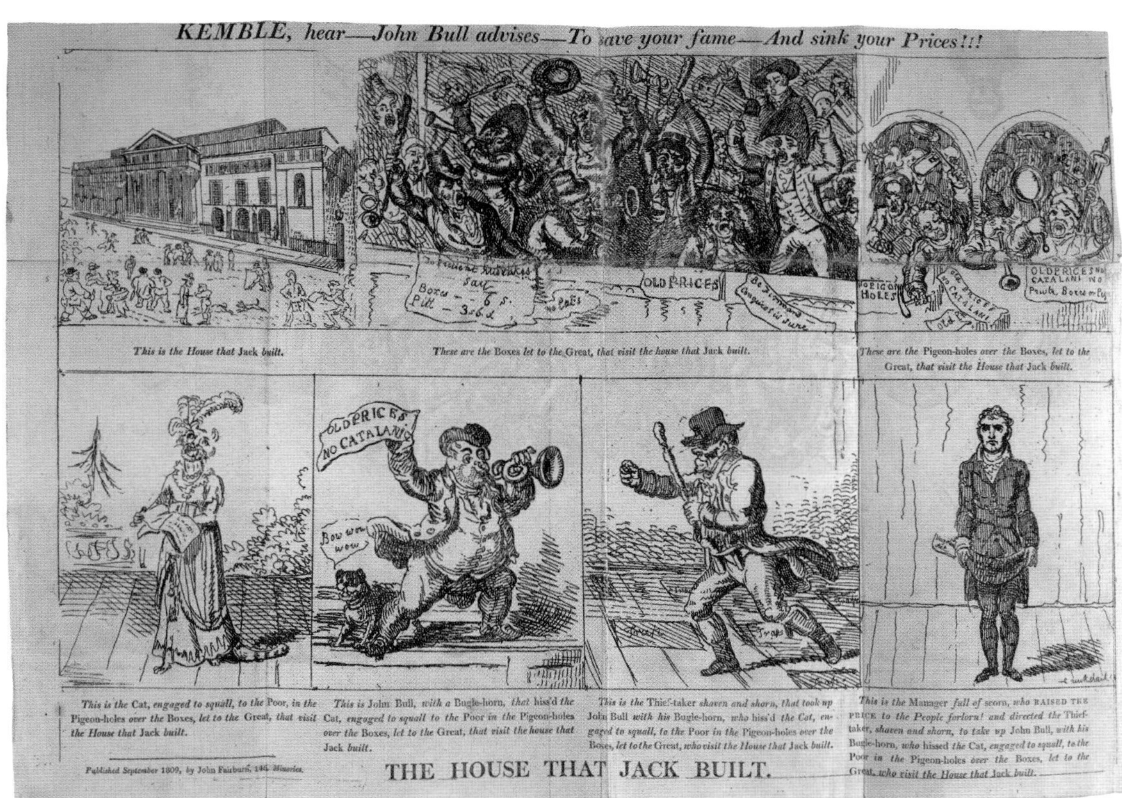

Margate's Theatre Royal

The Theatre Royal, Margate opened in 1787. James Winston, writing in 1805, was dismissive about the backstage facilities for the players, but he had to admit that the 'scenery is excellent'. According to him, seasons ran from July to October and the theatre was also occasionally used for masquerades put on by the management to make extra money. The original building still forms part of Margate's current theatre.

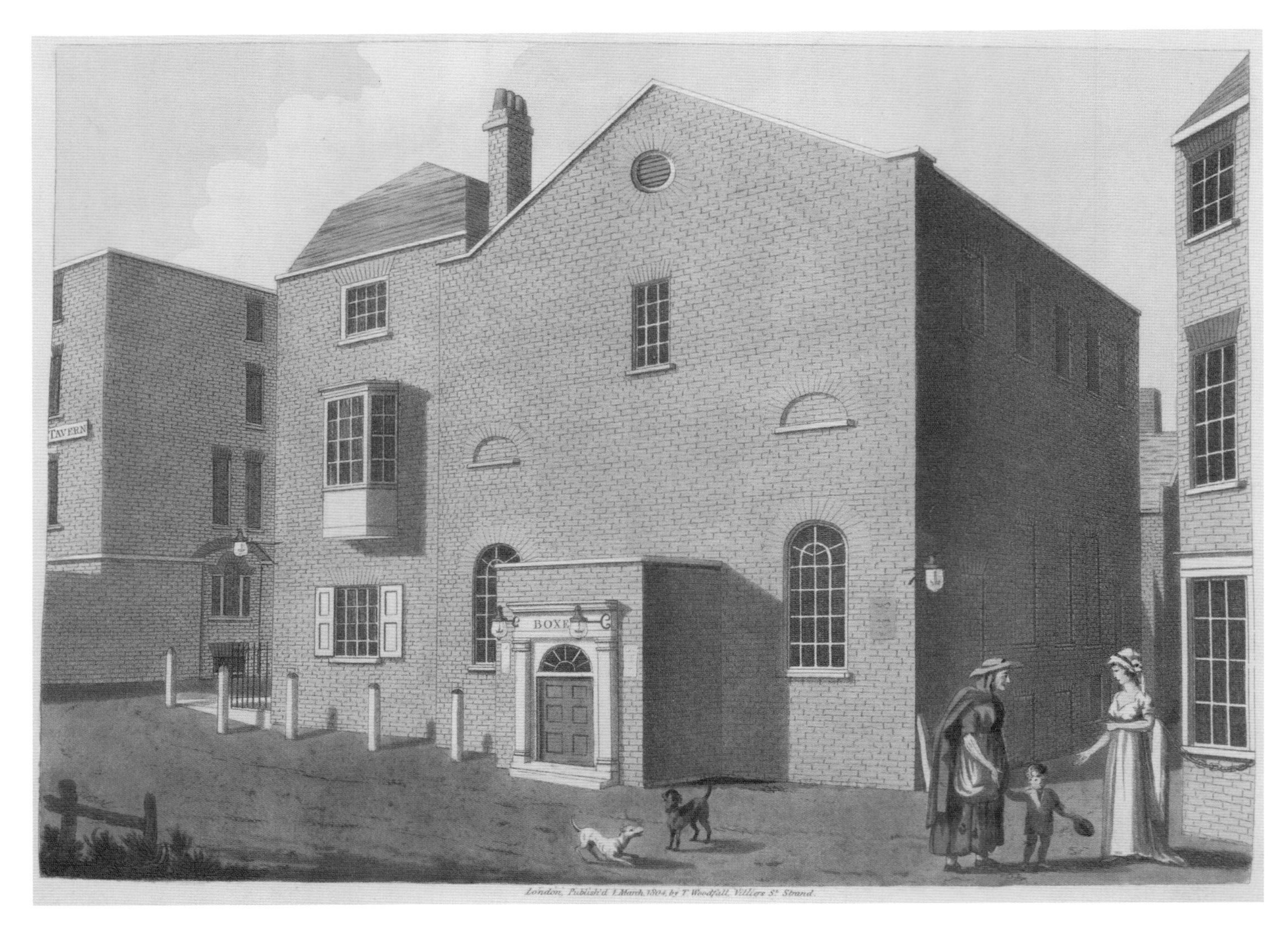

Margate Theatre, aquatint from James Winston, *The theatric tourist*, London, 1805 (78.l.15).

A volume of playbills for the Theatre Royal, Margate, is more than simply a collection of bills for performances long past. It provides a snapshot of the range of entertainments available to residents and visitors to the seaside town from summer 1800 to autumn 1801. The volume was probably bound soon after the collection was made. The various handbills it contains may all have been available at the theatre, making it a sort of tourist information centre as well as a venue for drama.

The playbills show the repertoire of plays and other entertainments enjoyed by local audiences. On 14 July 1800 there was a comedy, *The Suspicious Husband* by Benjamin Hoadly (1706–1757), followed by the farce *Miss in Her Teens* by David Garrick (1717–1779). Both plays dated back to the 1740s and remained staples of the London theatre. The playbill announced four playing days a week and advertised a special attraction for the next performance in the form of two players from Covent Garden. Mr Hill and Mrs Atkins duly appeared on 16 July 1800 in the comic opera by Isaac Bickerstaff (1735–1812), *Love in a Village*. This popular piece had been performed regularly in London since its first performances in 1762, but neither Hill nor Atkins had sung in it at the Covent Garden Theatre. Both had joined that company in the late 1790s, as singers as well as actors, and were middling-rank players there. Like many players of the period, they toured the provinces outside the main London season (which ran from September to the following June).

The bill on 12 October 1801 announced an extremely varied performance: a tragedy, *Douglas* by John Home (1722–1808); a farce, *The Village Lawyer* by George Colman (1732–1794); and a pantomime to end the evening with a flourish. *Harlequin's Descent from the Clouds* had not been played in London; it may well have been the invention of Mr Weston, who played Harlequin, for it included a couple of daring tricks by him. Theatre audiences in Margate could thus enjoy a range of theatrical entertainments comparable to London's for several months each year.

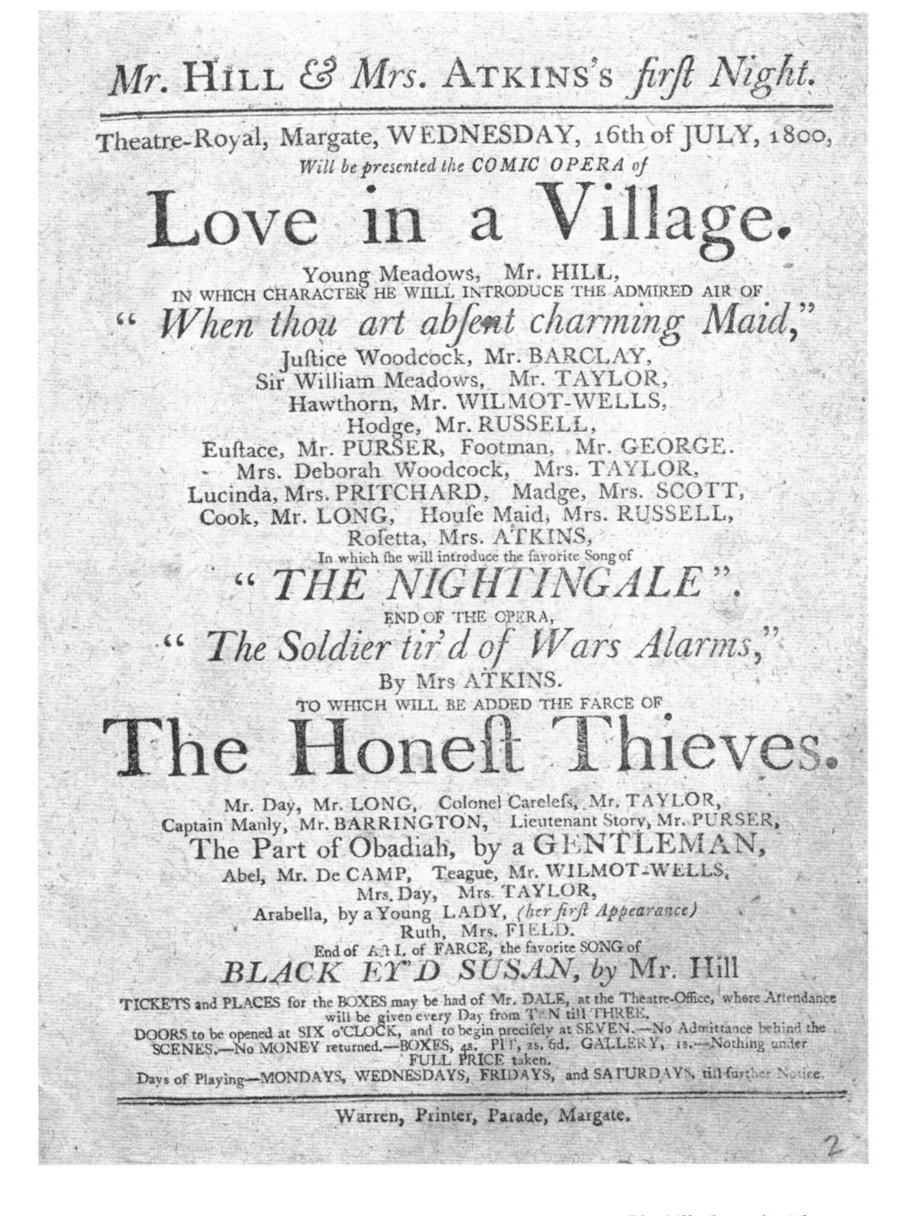

Mr. HILL & *Mrs.* ATKINS'S *firſt Night.*

Theatre-Royal, Margate, WEDNESDAY, 16th of JULY, 1800,
Will be presented the COMIC OPERA of

Love in a Village.

Young Meadows, Mr. HILL,
IN WHICH CHARACTER HE WILL INTRODUCE THE ADMIRED AIR OF
" When thou art abſent charming Maid,"
Juſtice Woodcock, Mr. BARCLAY,
Sir William Meadows, Mr. TAYLOR,
Hawthorn, Mr. WILMOT-WELLS,
Hodge, Mr. RUSSELL,
Euſtace, Mr. PURSER, Footman, Mr. GEORGE.
Mrs. Deborah Woodcock, Mrs. TAYLOR,
Lucinda, Mrs. PRITCHARD, Madge, Mrs. SCOTT,
Cook, Mr. LONG, Houſe Maid, Mrs. RUSSELL,
Roſetta, Mrs. ATKINS,
In which ſhe will introduce the favorite Song of
" THE NIGHTINGALE".
END OF THE OPERA,
" The Soldier tir'd of Wars Alarms,"
By Mrs ATKINS.
TO WHICH WILL BE ADDED THE FARCE OF

The Honeſt Thieves.

Mr. Day, Mr. LONG, Colonel Careleſs, Mr. TAYLOR,
Captain Manly, Mr. BARRINGTON, Lieutenant Story, Mr. PURSER,
The Part of Obadiah, by a GENTLEMAN,
Abel, Mr. De CAMP, Teague, Mr. WILMOT-WELLS,
Mrs. Day, Mrs. TAYLOR,
Arabella, by a Young LADY, *(her firſt Appearance)*
Ruth, Mrs. FIELD.
End of Act I. of FARCE, the favorite SONG of
BLACK EY'D SUSAN, by Mr. Hill

TICKETS and PLACES for the BOXES may be had of Mr. DALE, at the Theatre-Office, where Attendance will be given every Day from TEN till THREE.
DOORS to be opened at SIX o'CLOCK, and to begin preciſely at SEVEN.—No Admittance behind the SCENES.—No MONEY returned.—BOXES, 4s. PIT, 2s. 6d. GALLERY, 1s.—Nothing under FULL PRICE taken.
Days of Playing—MONDAYS, WEDNESDAYS, FRIDAYS, and SATURDAYS, till further Notice.

Warren, Printer, Parade, Margate.

2

Playbills from the Theatre Royal, Margate, 1800–1 (Playbills 422, 2).

Occasionally, Margate audiences did have the chance to see London's star actors at close quarters. Even Sarah Siddons and Dorothy Jordan (1761–1816) toured the provinces, to augment their salaries (all too often paid late by London's theatre managers) as well as to please admirers outside the capital. Mrs Siddons was renowned for her performances in tragedy, which were acknowledged to reach the sublime. She appeared in Margate from 25 July to 2 August 1800 in several of her most successful roles, including the title role in Nicholas Rowe's (1674–1718) tragedy of 1714 *Jane Shore* – one of her signature parts. For her benefit performance Mrs Siddons took the title role in Garrick's version of Southerne's *Isabella; or, the Fatal Marriage*. This was the part in which she had triumphed at Drury Lane in 1782.

Dorothy Jordan came to Margate the following year, from 25 to 31 August 1801. Much loved as a comedienne, she was also notorious for her liaison with the Duke of Clarence (later King William IV), by whom she had ten children. Mrs Jordan, too, played several roles from the repertoire in which she had made her name. For her second night, she was first advertised in the title role of Garrick's *The Country Girl* – his adaptation of *The Country Wife* by William Wycherley (1640–1716). This was changed 'At the Particular Request of Many Ladies & Gentlemen' to Rosalind in Shakespeare's *As You Like It*. Perhaps the request was made by the gentlemen rather than the ladies, as the part required Mrs Jordan to appear in breeches for most of the play.

For her benefit performance Mrs Jordan played Bisarre, a 'whimsical lady' in *The Inconstant* by George Farquhar (1677?–1707), a play that had held the stage for nearly a century. She also played Lady Conquest in *The Wedding Day*, a comedy by Elizabeth Inchbald (1753–1821) which had been specially written for her. This included a performance by Jordan of the song 'In the Dead of Night', which had achieved its own success. Mrs Jordan's popularity was such that the playbill announced 'Part of the Pit will be laid into the Boxes', a practice in London's theatres for celebrity players.

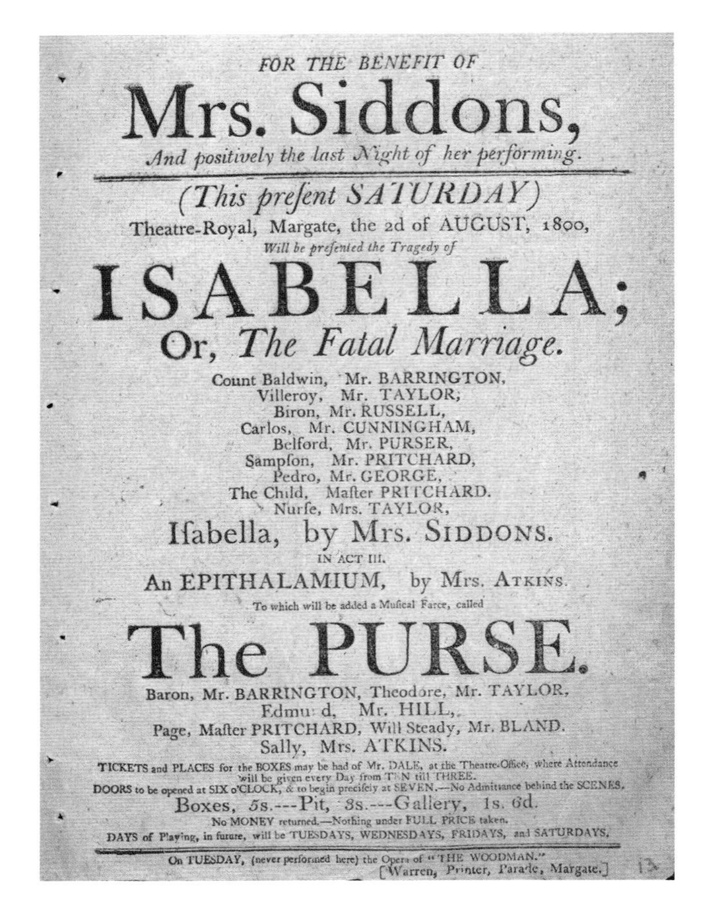

FOR THE BENEFIT OF

Mrs. Siddons,

And positively the last Night of her performing.

(This prefent SATURDAY)

Theatre-Royal, Margate, the 2d of AUGUST, 1800,

Will be prefented the Tragedy of

ISABELLA;

Or, *The Fatal Marriage.*

Count Baldwin, Mr. BARRINGTON,
Villeroy, Mr. TAYLOR,
Biron, Mr. RUSSELL,
Carlos, Mr. CUNNINGHAM,
Belford, Mr. PURSER,
Sampfon, Mr. PRITCHARD,
Pedro, Mr. GEORGE,
The Child, Mafter PRITCHARD,
Nurfe, Mrs. TAYLOR,

Ifabella, by Mrs. SIDDONS.

IN ACT III.

An EPITHALAMIUM, by Mrs. ATKINS.

To which will be added a Mufical Farce, called

The PURSE.

Baron, Mr. BARRINGTON, Theodore, Mr. TAYLOR,
Edmund, Mr. HILL,
Page, Mafter PRITCHARD, Will Steady, Mr. BLAND.
Sally, Mrs. ATKINS.

TICKETS and PLACES for the BOXES may be had of Mr. DALE, at the Theatre-Office, where Attendance will be given every Day from TEN till THREE.

DOORS to be opened at SIX o'CLOCK, & to begin precifely at SEVEN.—No Admittance behind the SCENES.

Boxes, 5s.---Pit, 3s.---Gallery, 1s. 6d.

No MONEY returned.—Nothing under FULL PRICE taken.

DAYS of Playing, in future, will be TUESDAYS, WEDNESDAYS, FRIDAYS, and SATURDAYS.

On TUESDAY, (never performed here) the Opera of "THE WOODMAN."

[Warren, Printer, Parade, Margate.]

13

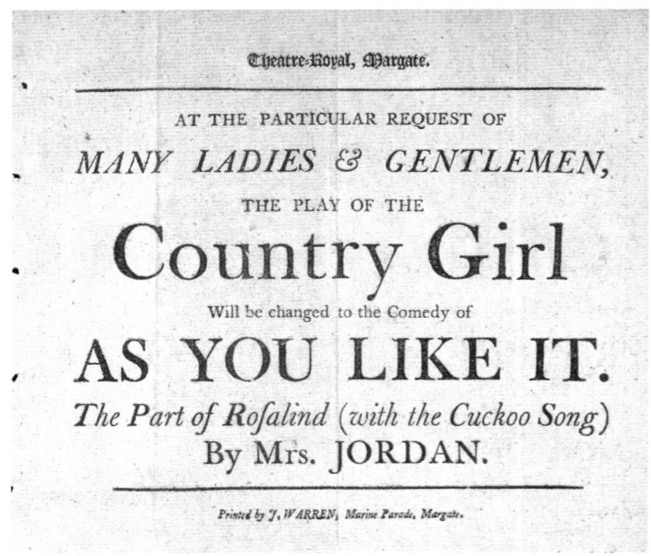

Theatre-Royal, Margate.

AT THE PARTICULAR REQUEST OF

MANY LADIES & GENTLEMEN,

THE PLAY OF THE

Country Girl

Will be changed to the Comedy of

AS YOU LIKE IT.

The Part of Rofalind (with the Cuckoo Song)

By Mrs. JORDAN.

Printed by J. WARREN, Marine Parade, Margate.

Playbills from the Theatre Royal, Margate, 1800–1 (Playbills 422, 13, 144).

Sarah Siddons as Isabella.
Thomas Stothard, engraved by
Edwin Roffe, [London, 1850–80]
(Dex. 315).

Dorothy Jordan as the Country
Girl. George Romney, engraved by
Edwin Roffe, [London, 1850–80]
(Dex. 315).

More to See and Do in Margate

Margate could offer far more than plays, comic operas and pantomimes to entertain the locals. Surviving handbills record entertainments as various as firework displays to celebrate royal birthdays at the Prospect Hotel on Hooper's Hill overlooking the town; masquerade balls (with an opportunity to gather at the Assembly Rooms before going on to dance at the Theatre Royal); public breakfasts just outside town at the manor-house and tea garden called the Dandelion; more theatrical entertainments of the polite and not-so-polite kind at local hotels and inns; an art exhibition in the form of a 'Historical Picture' showing the death of General Abercrombie at the Battle of Alexandria in 1801; a 'Royal Museum', also at the Prospect Hotel and reflecting interest in the French Revolution and the ongoing war with France (among other topics); and 'entertaining and instructive' lectures in experimental philosophy (science and its methods). The range of entertainments, and some of the individual offerings, owed as much to local aspirations as to London's influence.

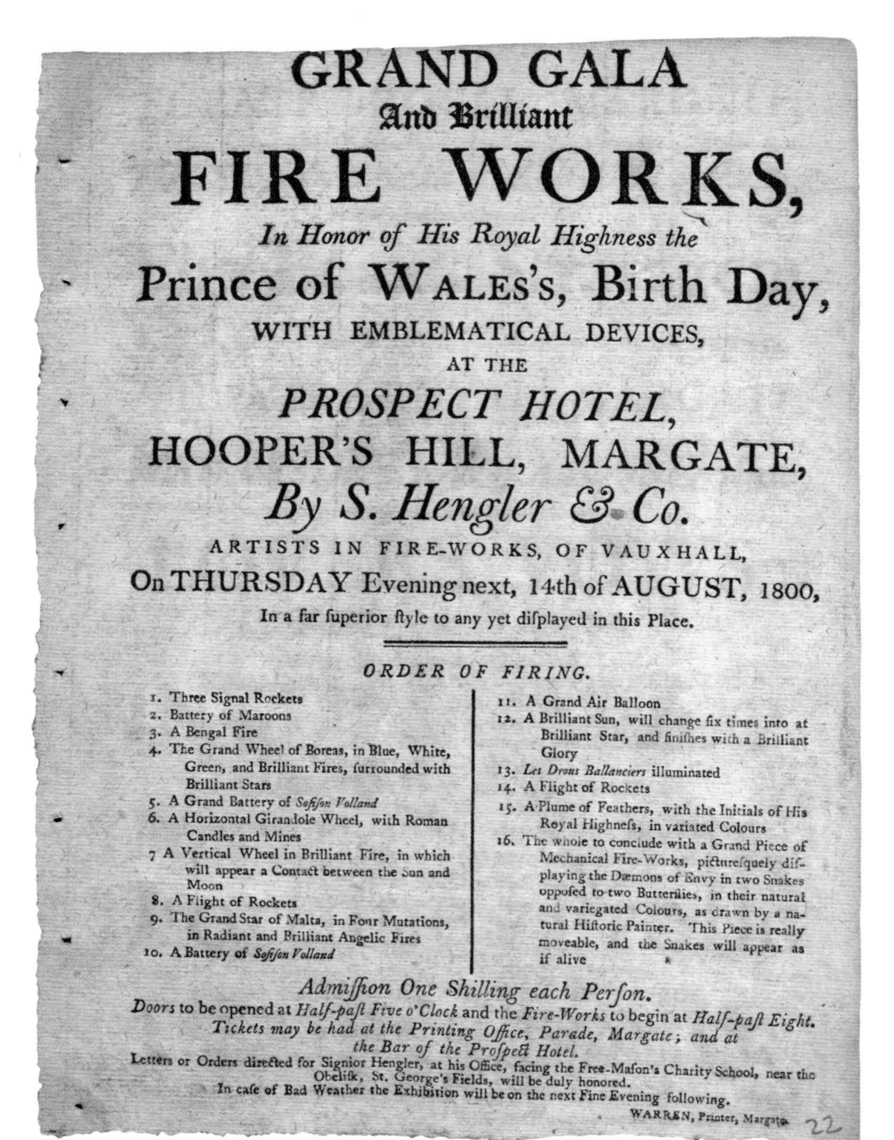

GRAND GALA

And Brilliant

FIRE WORKS,

In Honor of His Royal Highness the

Prince of WALES's, Birth Day,

WITH EMBLEMATICAL DEVICES,

AT THE

PROSPECT HOTEL,

HOOPER'S HILL, MARGATE,

By S. Hengler & Co.

ARTISTS IN FIRE-WORKS, OF VAUXHALL,

On THURSDAY Evening next, 14th of AUGUST, 1800,

In a far ſuperior ſtyle to any yet diſplayed in this Place.

ORDER OF FIRING.

1. Three Signal Rockets
2. Battery of Maroons
3. A Bengal Fire
4. The Grand Wheel of Boreas, in Blue, White, Green, and Brilliant Fires, ſurrounded with Brilliant Stars
5. A Grand Battery of *Soſiſon Volland*
6. A Horizontal Girandole Wheel, with Roman Candles and Mines
7. A Vertical Wheel in Brilliant Fire, in which will appear a Contact between the Sun and Moon
8. A Flight of Rockets
9. The Grand Star of Malta, in Four Mutations, in Radiant and Brilliant Angelic Fires
10. A Battery of *Soſiſon Volland*
11. A Grand Air Balloon
12. A Brilliant Sun, will change ſix times into at Brilliant Star, and finiſhes with a Brilliant Glory
13. *Les Drous Ballanciers* illuminated
14. A Flight of Rockets
15. A Plume of Feathers, with the Initials of His Royal Highneſs, in variated Colours
16. The whole to conclude with a Grand Piece of Mechanical Fire-Works, picturesquely diſplaying the Dæmons of Envy in two Snakes oppoſed to two Butterflies, in their natural and variegated Colours, as drawn by a natural Hiſtoric Painter. This Piece is really moveable, and the Snakes will appear as if alive

Admiſſion One Shilling each Perſon.

Doors to be opened at *Half-paſt Five o'Clock* and the *Fire-Works* to begin at *Half-paſt Eight.*
Tickets may be had at the Printing Office, Parade, Margate; and at the Bar of the Proſpect Hotel.

Letters or Orders directed for Signior Hengler, at his Office, facing the Free-Maſon's Charity School, near the Obeliſk, St. George's Fields, will be duly honored.

In caſe of Bad Weather the Exhibition will be on the next Fine Evening following.

WARREN, Printer, Margate.

22

Prospect Hotel, Grand Gala and Fireworks, 14 August 1800 (Playbills 422, 22).

Shakespeare in Pictures

During the eighteenth century Shakespeare's plays became a mainstay of London and provincial stages, while the man himself was enshrined as the nation's greatest dramatist and poet. In 1789 the engraver and printseller John Boydell (1720–1804) opened his Shakespeare Gallery in Pall Mall. The venture began as a proposal to publish a series of engravings illustrating the works of Shakespeare, taken from paintings commissioned for the purpose. The engravings were produced in both a small format, as part of a new large folio edition of the works of Shakespeare edited by the scholar George Steevens (1736–1800), and in a large format, which was sold as a set and as separate prints. The two versions of the prints were published during the period 1791 to 1805.

The paintings represent the whole of Shakespeare's dramatic output, even though not all of his plays were performed in contemporary theatres. Some paintings could plausibly relate to the actual staging of the plays, while others are creative responses to the scenes conjured by Shakespeare. Boydell's painters include Sir Joshua Reynolds (1723–92), Henry Fuseli (1741–1825), Angelica Kauffman (1741–1807) and John Opie (1760–1807). Boydell also commissioned work from some of London's best engravers although, with the exception of William Blake (1757–1827), who provided one engraving for the works of Shakespeare, none are now household names.

Reynolds contributed two paintings, the most striking being the cauldron scene from *Macbeth*. Fuseli provided eight paintings, including his phantasmagoric evocation of Titania and Bottom from *A Midsummer Night's Dream*. *Macbeth* was a favourite of the Georgian stage, but the *Dream* was yet to be rediscovered – allowing full rein to Fuseli's imagination. Angelica Kauffman's paintings were of scenes from *Love's Labour's Lost* and *Troilus and Cressida*. The former of these was not performed in the Georgian period, while the latter vanished altogether in the 1730s after only a handful of performances. The Rev. Matthew Peters (1742–1814), a Royal Academician, contributed pretty paintings of two scenes from *The Merry Wives of Windsor*, a play that had returned to the repertoire in the 1720s and proved popular because of the figure of Falstaff.

King John, surprisingly, was played regularly following its revival in 1737, perhaps because of the opportunities for pathos it offered in such scenes as the one depicted for Boydell.

A collection of prints, from pictures painted for the purpose of illustrating the dramatic works of Shakespeare, by the artists of Great Britain, London, 1805 (4.Tab.57).

Vol. 1, no. 10. Rev. Matthew Peters, engraved by Jean Pierre Simon, *The Merry Wives of Windsor*, Act III, scene iii.

Vol. 1, no. 20. Henry Fuseli, engraved by Jean Pierre Simon, *A Midsummer-Night's Dream*, Act IV, scene i.

Vol. 1, no. 39. Sir Joshua Reynolds, engraved by Robert Thew, *Macbeth*, Act IV, scene i.

Vol. 2, no. 1. James Northcote, engraved by Robert Thew, *King John*, Act IV, scene i.

James Northcote (1746–1831), another Royal Academician, was a pupil and assistant of Sir Joshua Reynolds; he later wrote a biography of the artist. Although the *Henry the Sixth* plays had to wait for their revival until a later age, Opie's depiction of a scene from *The First Part of King Henry the Sixth* has all the drama and impact of the stage.

Boydell's *Collection of Prints* was intended to be a money-spinner, but the French Revolutionary and Napoleonic wars disrupted the contintental print market (where most money was to be made), leading to Boydell's bankruptcy. In 1805 the Shakespeare Gallery was closed and its contents dispersed. The copy of the *Collection of Prints* from which these illustrations are taken is from the library of King George III. His portrait forms the frontispiece of Volume 1, with Queen Charlotte portrayed in Volume 2. The king also had a copy of Boydell's fine printing of Steevens's edition of the works of Shakespeare.

Vol. 2, no. 13. John Opie, engraved by Robert Thew, *The First Part of King Henry the Sixth*, Act II, scene iii.

Vol. 2, no. 35. Angelica Kauffmann, engraved by Luigi Schiavonetti, *Troilus and Cressida*, Act. V, scene ii.

Georgian Escapologist

Jack Sheppard (1702–1724) began life honestly enough. Apprenticed in 1717 to a carpenter in Drury Lane, he showed promise until he fell in with the wrong crowd and took to theft and burglary. The young Sheppard was arrested and imprisoned, but he escaped from jail to resume his short career as a criminal. Sheppard's activities soon reached the ears of Jonathan Wild (1683–1725), the celebrated 'thief-taker' who was a receiver of stolen goods but covered his activities by bringing criminals to justice. When Sheppard refused Wild's services as a receiver, the thief-taker made sure of his arrest and committal to the notorious Newgate prison.

Over a period of some months, Jack Sheppard succeeded in escaping from Newgate twice (a third attempt was foiled). These daring and ingenious exploits were repeatedly reported in the newspapers, and by the time of his final return to Newgate Sheppard had become a celebrity. He was visited by crowds of people while he waited to be taken for public execution at Tyburn on 16 November 1724. A detailed account of his methods of escape was quickly published as an illustrated broadsheet by the engraver Thomas Bowles (1689/90? –1767). Sheppard also inspired a short-lived pantomime, *Harlequin Sheppard*, which was performed at Drury Lane shortly after his death. Far more successful, and much longer lasting, was *The Beggar's Opera* of 1728. The theme of John Gay's work (if not its highwayman hero, Macheath) was inspired by Sheppard's life of crime, but Macheath manages to escape the gallows.

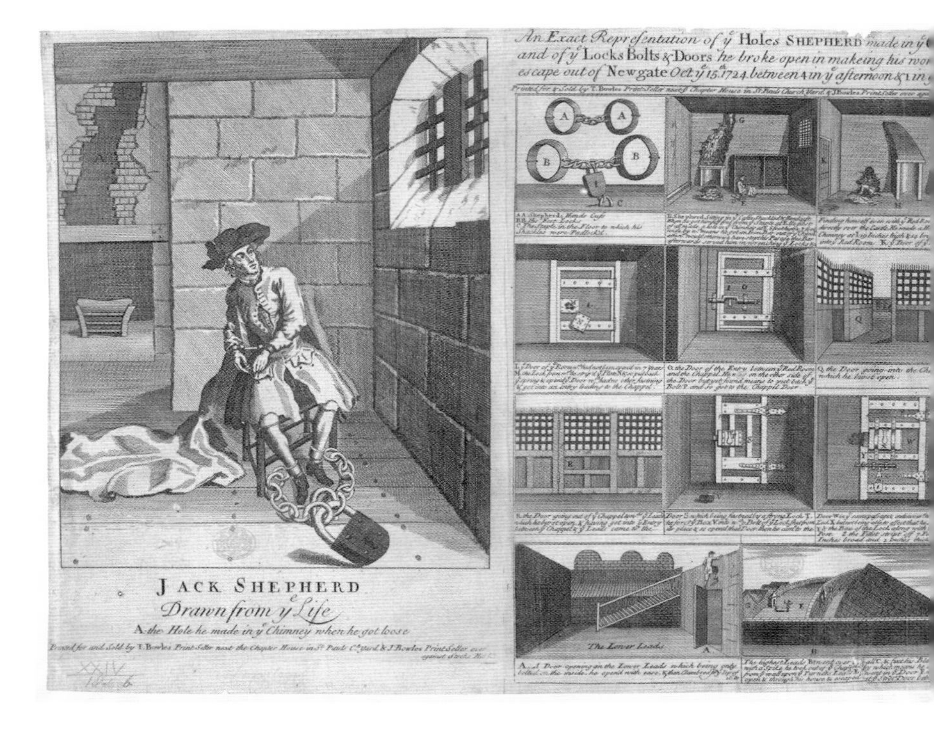

Portrait of Jack Shepherd, with a representation of the manner in which he made his escape from Newgate, Oct. 15th. 1724, London, [1724?] (K.Top.24.18.b).

John Thurmond, *Harlequin Sheppard*, London, 1724. Frontispiece (11779.e.2).

James Macleane, the Gentleman Highwayman at the Bar.

Printed for T. Fox in the Old Baily. *Publish'd according to Act of Parliament Sept 29 1750.* *Price 6d.*

WHEN Mr. *Maclean* was aſk'd by the Judge (according to the uſual Form) what he had to urge, why Sentence ſhould not be paſſed upon him, he attempted to ſpeak, but his exceſſive Grief prevented his delivering a Speech he had formed for that Purpoſe. His Countenance plainly wore the Appearance of real Contrition for his paſt Crimes, and he behaved with very becoming Penitence. The following is a Copy of what he intended to ſay, if Sorrow had not deny'd him Utterance; taken from his own Hand-writing.

'My Lord, I ſhall not preſume to trouble your Lordſhip with 'many Profeſſions of Sorrow and Penitence; ſuch, from Men in my 'unhappy Condition, are too often conſidered to proceed more from 'Fear and Shame, than from a Heart juſtly touched with a deep 'Senſe and Abhorrence of paſt inexcuſable Conduct —— Were the 'Sentiments of my Soul this Moment diſcloſed to the World in their 'true Light, I ſhould have no Occaſion to uſe any Expreſſions to 'move Compaſſion —— For the beſt of Men are the readieſt to pity 'the Anguiſh of their Fellow Creatures not hardened in Guilt —— 'I might perhaps collect ſome Circumſtances to mitigate the Execu'tion of a Sentence I am now going to receive —— But as I am 'ſenſible that nothing of that Sort on my Trial eſcaped the Penetra'tion of the Court, ſo I am equally aſſured, that if there is room for 'Mercy, it will be recommended.'

'My Lord, it is for my Offences againſt Heaven and the Publick; 'it is for my Family diſgraced, for a helpleſs Infant Daughter, that my 'Heart is weighed down with contrite Anguiſh, and dares not with 'Confidence apply to the Great and Good —— And yet, my Lord, 'permit me to implore ſo much Mercy, as will for ever remove me 'from being a Diſgrace to thoſe who once knew me worthy of a 'better Fate, and will enable me to paſs the Remainder of my Days 'in Penitence and ſorrowful Obſcurity.

Mr. Maclean's *Defence on his Tryal, as he read it before the Court.*

My Lord,

I am perſuaded from the Candour and Indulgence ſhewn to me in the Courſe of my Trial, that your Lordſhip will hear me with Patience, and make Allowance for the Confuſion I may ſhew before an awful Aſſembly, upon ſo ſolemn an Occaſion.

Your Lordſhip will not conſtrue it Vanity in me, at this Time, to ſay, that I am the Son of a Divine of the Kingdom of *Ireland*, well known for his Zeal and Affection to the preſent Royal Family and happy Government; who beſtowed an Education upon me, becoming his Character, of which I have in my Hand, a Certificate from a noble Lord, four Members of Parliament, and ſeveral Juſtices of the Peace for the County where I was Born and received my Education.

About the Beginning of the late *French* War, My Lord, I came to *London*, with a Deſign to enter into the military Service of my King and Country; but unexpected Diſappointments obliged me to change my Reſolution; and having married the Daughter of a reputable Tradeſman, to his Fortune I added what little I had of my own, and entered into Trade in the Grocery Way, and continued therein till my Wife died. I was quickly after her Death found a Decay in Trade, ariſing from an unavoidable Truſt repoſed in Servants; and fearing the Conſequence, I candidly conſulted ſome Friends, and by their Advice, ſold off my Stock, and in the firſt Place honeſtly diſcharged my Debts, and propoſed to apply the Remains of my Fortune in the Purchaſe of ſome military Employment, agreeable to my firſt Deſign.

During my Application to Trade, my Lord, I unhappily became acquainted with one *Plunket*, an Apothecary, who by his Account of himſelf, induced me to believe, he had travell'd abroad, and was poſſeſſed of Cloaths and other Things ſuitable thereto, and prevailed on me to employ him in attending on my Family, and to lend him Money to the Amount of 100*l.* and upwards.

When I left off Trade, I preſs'd *Plunket* for Payment, and after receiving by Degrees, ſeveral Sums, he propoſed, on my earneſtly inſiſting that I muſt call in all Debts owing to me, to pay me Part in Goods and Part in Money.

Theſe very Cloaths with which I am now charged, my Lord, were Cloaths he brought to me to make Sale off, towards Payment of my Debt, and accordingly, my Lord, I did ſell them, very unfortunately as it now appears; little thinking they were come by in the Manner Mr. *Higden* hath been pleaſed to expreſs, whoſe Word and Honour are too well known to doubt the Truth.

My Lord, as the contracting this Debt between *Plunket* and myſelf was a Matter of a private Nature, ſo was the Payment of it; and therefore, it is impoſſible for me to have the Teſtimony of any one ſingle Witneſs to theſe Facts, which (as it is an unavoidable Misfortune) I hope, and doubt not, my Lord, that your Lordſhip and the Gentlemen of the Jury will duly weigh.

My Lord, I cannot avoid obſerving to your Lordſhip, Is it probable, nay, is it poſſible, that if I had come by thoſe Cloaths by diſhoneſt Means, I ſhould be ſo imprudent as to bring a Man to my Lodgings at Noon day to buy them, and give him my Name and Place of Reſidence, and even write that Name and Reſidence my ſelf in the Saleſman's Book? It ſeems to me, and I think muſt to every Man, a Madneſs that no one, with the leaſt Share of Senſe, could be capable of.

My Lord, I have obſerved in the Courſe of Mr. *Higden*'s Evidence, he hath declared, he could not be poſitive either to my Face or Perſon, the Defect of which, I humbly preſume, leaves a Doubt of the Certainty of my being one of the two Perſons.

My Lord, it is very true, when I was firſt apprehended, the Surpriſe confounded me, and gave me the moſt extraordinary Shock; it cauſed a Delirium and Confuſion in my Brain, which rendered me incapable of being my ſelf, or knowing what I ſaid or did; I talked of Robberies as another Man would do in talking of Stories; but my Lord, after my Friends had viſited me in the Gate-houſe, and had given me ſome new Spirits, and when I came to be re-examined before Juſtice *Lediard*, and then aſked, if I could make any Diſcovery of the Robbery, I then alledged that I had recovered my Surpriſe, that what I had talked of before concerning Robberies was falſe and wrong, but it was entirely owing to a confuſed Head and Brain.

This, my Lord, being my unhappy Fate; but unhappy as it is, as your Lordſhip is my Judge and preſumptive Council, I ſubmit it, whether there is any other Evidence againſt me than circumſtantial.

Firſt, The Selling of the Lace and Cloaths, which I agree I did; for which I account.

Secondly, The verbal Confeſſion of a confuſed Brain; for which I account.

All this Evidence I humbly apprehend is but circumſtantial Evidence.

It might be ſaid, my Lord, that I ought to ſhew where I was at this Time.

To which, my Lord, I anſwer, that I never heard the Time, nor the Day of the Month, that Mr. *Higden* was robbed; and, my Lord, it is impoſſible for me, at this Juncture, to recollect where I was, and much more to bring any Teſtimony of it.

My Lord, in Caſes where a Priſoner lies under theſe Impoſſibilities of Proof, it is hard, nay, it is very hard, if Preſumption and Intendment may not have ſome Weight on the Side of the Priſoner. I humbly hope, and doubt not, but that Doctrine will not eſcape your Lordſhip's Memory to the Jury.

My Lord, I have lived in Credit, and have had Dealings with Mankind, and therefore humbly beg leave, my Lord, to call about a Score to my Character, or more, if your Lordſhip pleaſes; and then, my Lord, if in your Lordſhip's Opinion the Evidence againſt me ſhould be by Law only circumſtantial, and the Character given of me by my Witneſſes ſhould be ſo far ſatisfactory, as to have equal Weight, I ſhall moſt willingly and readily ſubmit to the Jury's Verdict.

On the 27th of *July James Maclean* was apprehended, and committed to the *Gatehouſe*, *Weſtminſter*, for robbing the *Saliſbury* Coach, in Company with another Perſon not yet taken, on *June* 26. They had both *Venetian* Maſks on, and the ſame Morning robbed Lord *Eglington* in a Poſt Chaiſe, and carried off a conſiderable Booty. He is a handſome tall well-made Man, dreſſes extremely gay, and was diſcovered by offering ſome Gold Lace to Sale, which he had ript from the rich Cloaths found in a Portmanteau taken from the *Saliſbury* Coach, to the very Laceman of whom it was firſt bought. At his Lodgings a Coat of Lord *Eglington*'s was found, and his Blunderbuſs: a Whip of *Thomas Lockyer*, Eſq; with his Name on it; and a Clergyman's Whip, *&c.* with ſeveral rich Suits of his own, and in the Pockets of a Frock a pair of Piſtols loaded; in ſearching his Drawers 21 Purſes of various Kinds were found all crammed into one, and a great Variety of Rings and other Effects, to the Value of 200*l.* A few Days after, there were a great Number of Perſons of Diſtinction at Juſtice *Lediard*'s Houſe, to hear the Examination of this *Maclean*, which laſted about an Hour and a half, when he confeſſed ſeveral Robberies, and frequently ſhed Tears. He likewiſe confeſs'd he was one of the Perſons who robbed the Hon. *Horatio Walpole* ſome Time ſince about *Knightſbridge* of his Gold Watch, which he advertiſed, and upon paying the Reward had it again. He was conducted back to the *Gatehouſe* by a Serjeant's Guard for fear of a Reſcue.

James Macleane, the Gentleman Highwayman at the Bar, [London], 1750 (Cup.21.g.39/64).

A Rogue and a Gentleman

The highwayman James Maclaine also caught the imagination of the public, during his trial for robbery in 1750. Maclaine cut a pathetic figure in court, shedding tears and drawing the sympathy of the ladies present who, according to one newspaper account, 'presented him with a purse of gold'. He had a reputation as a ladies' man.

Found guilty, Maclaine was sentenced to death. Like Jack Sheppard, he received crowds of visitors curious to see the 'gentleman highwayman', who dressed finely and behaved politely. Printers and booksellers responded to public interest with broadsides like this illustrated one, as well as pamphlets and numerous newspaper reports. At the time, London must have been abuzz with the story, which culminated in Maclaine's public execution at Tyburn on 3 October 1750.

Clowning for a Living

The clown Joseph Grimaldi (1778–1837) was one of Georgian Britain's best-loved performers. Joseph, or Joey, came from a dynasty of performers and began his stage career as a small child. According to an anecdote recorded in Charles Dickens's *Memoirs of Joseph Grimaldi*, published in 1838, one of his earliest roles was as a monkey alongside his father, who swung him around on a chain. George Cruikshank provided an imaginative depiction of the moment the chain broke and Joey flew off the stage to land among the audience.

Joey Grimaldi's true vocation as a pantomime clown was not apparent until the late 1790s, when he began to appear in a series of productions that made his name. He devised new make-up and developed a performance style with extraordinarily skilful and energetic physical comedy. Audiences could not help but laugh at his antics, and Grimaldi was acknowledged as a new type of clown – one that would be exceptionally influential with his successors. Among his successful pantomime appearances were roles in *Harlequin and Mother Goose* (1806), the most famous Christmas pantomime in the history of the entertainment, *Harlequin and Padmanaba, or, The Golden Fish* (1811) and *Harlequin and the Red Dwarf* (1812).

Grimaldi's comic turns lent themselves to illustration and there are many colour prints showing him in scenes from pantomimes. In one, taken from *Harlequin and Padmanaba*, he plays leap-frog, by turns, with a frog – presumably a fellow dancer-acrobat. A little more of his comic business is revealed in the cartoon from *Harlequin and the Red Dwarf*, entitled *Grimaldi & the Nondescript*, in which he is faced with a newly created mythical beast, with 'the head of an ass eagles wings cat feet & a fishes tail'. The image shows the mixture of fantasy and foolery which must have attracted audiences to pantomimes featuring Grimaldi. He could have become rich as well as famous, but he spent money as fast as he made it. Over time, the extreme demands of Grimaldi's comic business began to affect his health. He was ultimately forced to retire from the stage in 1828, by which time he was too crippled to perform.

Joseph Grimaldi, engraved portrait by H. Brown (Dex.315).

George Cruikshank, *Master Joe's unexpected visit to the pit*, engraving for Charles Dickens, *Memoirs of Joseph Grimaldi*, London, 1838 (Dex. 315).

William Heath, *Grimaldi & the Nondescript*, coloured engraving (Dex. 315).

William Heath, *Grimaldi's Leap-Frog*, coloured engraving (Dex. 315).

Naked Beauty

Elizabeth Chudleigh (*c.* 1720–1788) came from an upper-class but impoverished background. In 1743 she entered court circles as a maid of honour to Augusta, the young Princess of Wales (1719–1772). She married the Hon. Augustus John Hervey (1724–1779, later Third Earl of Bristol) the following year, but by 1749 the couple had parted because of her infidelity. In spring 1749 Chudleigh made a notorious appearance at a Ranelagh masquerade, flimsily costumed (she was apparently near-naked) as Iphigenia – an exploit that was long remembered.

Soon afterwards, she became the mistress of Evelyn Pierrepont, Second Duke of Kingston upon Hull (1712–1773). She married him in 1769, after a court ruling that her first marriage had not taken place. When the duke died, a widely publicised dispute over his will led to questions about the marital status of the 'Duchess of Kingston'. *The Matrimonial Magazine* was among the publications to join in the debate. It provided an engraving depicting all three parties alongside a brief (and none too sympathetic) biography of Chudleigh. She was tried in 1776 and found guilty, whereupon she fled Britain, never to return. The trial was much reported in pamphlets as well as in the newspapers.

Interest was renewed after the disgraced 'duchess' died in Paris in 1788. Several accounts of her colourful life were published, including the suitably illustrated *Life and Memoirs*, which featured an imagined portrait of her as Iphigenia.

Elizabeth Chudleigh with both of her 'husbands', from *The Matrimonial Magazine*, London, January 1775 (C.127.d.2).

Elizabeth Chudleigh as Iphigenia, from *The Life and Memoirs of Elizabeth Chudleigh*, London, [1788?] (RB.23.b.4109).

A Careless Maid

Fanny Murray (1729–1778) was one of the more celebrated courtesans of the Georgian age. She plied her trade in Covent Garden and is said to have earned a place in *Harris's List of Covent-Garden Ladies*, a directory of prostitutes working in London. During the 1750s she apparently married the leading actor David Ross (1728–90), and in 1758 the *Memoirs of the celebrated Miss Fanny M---* appeared, followed by several fresh editions in 1759.

There are also several portraits purporting to be Murray, underlining her celebrity status. The two woodcuts of her with accompanying texts, printed on a single sheet of paper, also assume her fame. Together they hint at the narrative behind the famous set of prints by William Hogarth (1697–1764) published in 1732 and entitled *The Harlot's Progress*. On the left Fanny Murray is shown dressed demurely 'in her primitive innocence', although the verses beneath tell of lost virtue and faded looks. The right-hand woodcut shows her as a lady of the town, publicly adjusting her garter. The accompanying text praises English female figures and dress, while satirically recommending rather looser French manners.

Miss Fanny Murray, the Fair and Reigning Toast, in her primitive Innocence, London, [1764?].

Ballet and Mute Eloquence

Although the origins of ballet go back beyond the seventeenth century, only in the early eighteenth century did it become a recognisably modern form in the theatre. One stage work with a fair claim to be the first modern ballet is *The Loves of Mars and Venus* by John Weaver (1673–1760), performed at the Drury Lane Theatre in 1717. Weaver was that rare phenomenon, a dancer and a choreographer who also thought and wrote about dancing. As a creative performer and a theorist, he wanted dancing to be expressive of human emotions. *The Loves of Mars and Venus* was intended to be a danced drama, equal to the plays seen on London's stages. The ballet's story was the age-old love affair between Venus, goddess of love, and Mars, god of war – and how Vulcan, husband to Venus, took his revenge on them both.

In *The Loves of Mars and Venus* Weaver declared that he was attempting to revive the dramatic performances of classical antiquity. In fact what he created was closer to a mute Restoration comedy of manners. The action of his ballet included a quarrel between Venus and Vulcan in a dance 'altogether of the *Pantomimic* kind', a love-tryst between Venus and Mars and Vulcan's triumphant snaring of the lovers. All of the action was conveyed in dance and mime alone, setting a pattern for future ballets.

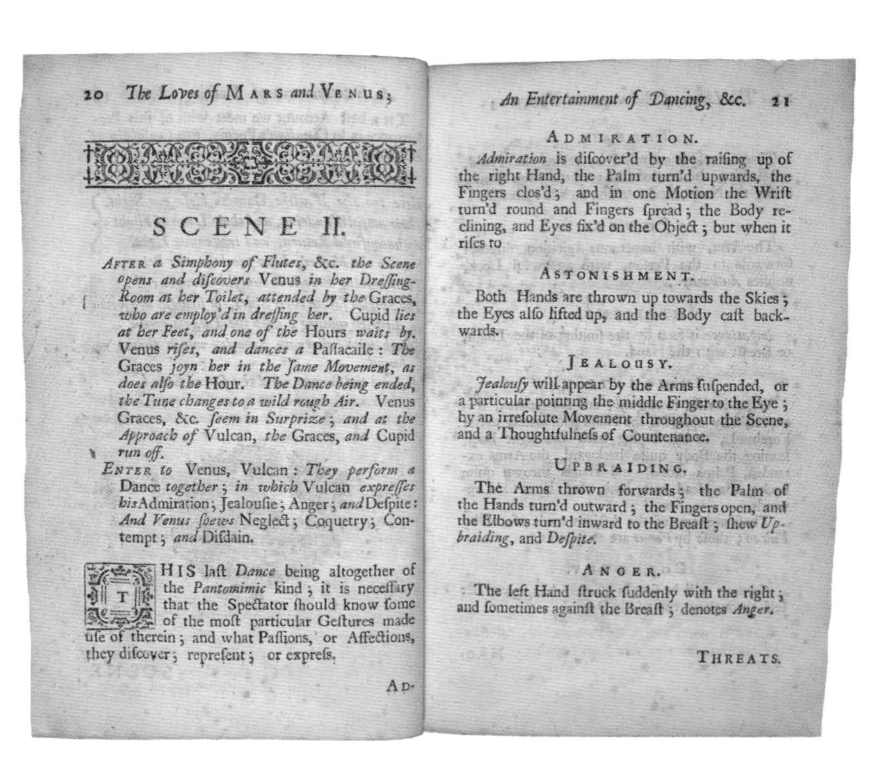

20 *The Loves of* MARS *and* VENUS;

SCENE II.

After a Simphony of Flutes, &c. the Scene opens and discovers Venus *in her Dressing-Room at her Toilet, attended by the* Graces, *who are employ'd in dressing her.* Cupid *lies at her Feet, and one of the* Hours *waits by.* Venus *rises, and dances a* Passacaile: *The* Graces *joyn her in the same Movement, as does also the* Hour. *The Dance being ended, the Tune changes to a wild rough Air.* Venus Graces, &c. *seem in Surprize; and at the Approach of* Vulcan, *the* Graces, *and* Cupid *run off.*

Enter to Venus, Vulcan: *They perform a* Dance *together; in which* Vulcan *expresses his* Admiration; Jealousie; Anger; *and* Despite: *And* Venus *shews* Neglect; Coquetry; Contempt; *and* Disdain.

THIS last *Dance* being altogether of the *Pantomimic* kind; it is necessary that the Spectator should know some of the most particular Gestures made use of therein; and what Passions, or Affections, they discover; represent; or express.

AD-

An Entertainment of Dancing, &c. 21

ADMIRATION.

Admiration is discover'd by the raising up of the right Hand, the Palm turn'd upwards, the Fingers clos'd; and in one Motion the Wrist turn'd round and Fingers spread; the Body reclining, and Eyes fix'd on the Object; but when it rises to

ASTONISHMENT.

Both Hands are thrown up towards the Skies; the Eyes also lifted up, and the Body cast backwards.

JEALOUSY.

Jealousy will appear by the Arms suspended, or a particular pointing the middle Finger to the Eye; by an irresolute Movement throughout the Scene, and a Thoughtfulness of Countenance.

UPBRAIDING.

The Arms thrown forwards; the Palm of the Hands turn'd outward; the Fingers open, and the Elbows turn'd inward to the Breast; shew *Upbraiding*, and *Despite*.

ANGER.

The left Hand struck suddenly with the right; and sometimes against the Breast; denotes *Anger*.

THREATS.

John Weaver, *The Loves of Mars and Venus*, London, 1717, pages 20–1 (C.121.c.19).

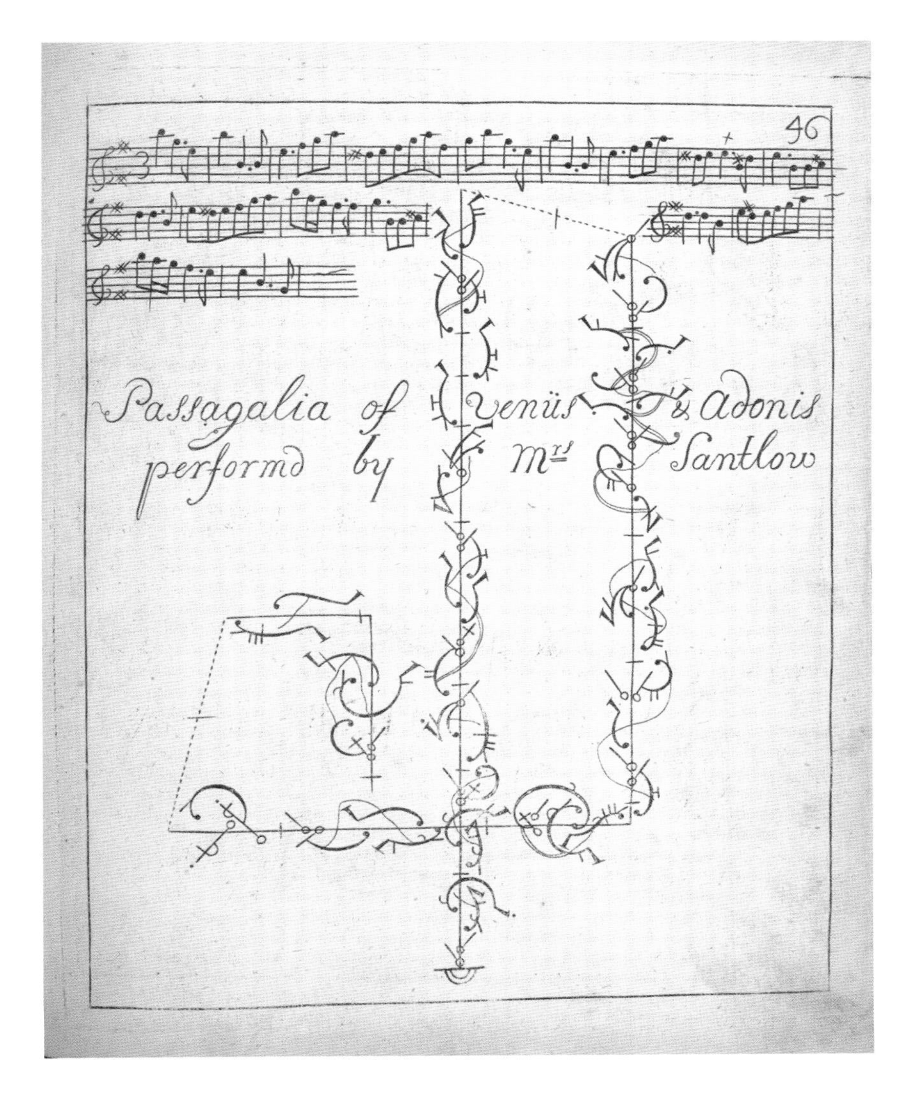

Anthony L'Abbé,
A New Collection of Dances
[London, 1725?], first
plate of the 'Passagalia of
Venus & Adonis' (K.11.c.5).

Incomparable Dancing

Neither music nor choreography for Weaver's *The Loves of Mars and Venus* survive, yet we can get a glimpse of the dancing within it. In 1700 the first form of dance notation was published, and it was subsequently used to record hundreds of stage and ballroom dances. These dances can be reconstructed and performed by dancers versed in the style and technique of baroque dance, and use many steps that can still be recognised in ballet today.

Among the notated stage dances are several choreographies performed by Hester Santlow (*c.* 1693–1773), the English dancer-actress who took the role of Venus in Weaver's ballet. As a dancer, she was described as 'incomparable' by contemporaries. On her first appearance in *The Loves of Mars and Venus*, Venus 'rises and dances a Passacaille', a long dance to a complex composition in the musical genre known as *passacaglia* or *passacaille*. The 'Passagalia of Venus & Adonis', created for Mrs Santlow by Anthony L'Abbé around 1717, reveals not only her strong technique, but also her considerable expressive abilities. This solo, which takes nearly six minutes to dance, is a miniature ballet in itself. It hints at Hester Santlow's alluring performance as Weaver's Venus.

Passions, Actions and Ballet

Like John Weaver, the French choreographer Jean-Georges Noverre (1727–1810) had ambitions for ballet as an important and expressive theatre art. Noverre set his ideas down in his *Lettres sur la danse et les ballets*, written while he was in London staying with the actor David Garrick (1717–1779) and first published in Lyon in 1760. Although he could have had no direct links to Weaver or his works, Noverre also crafted ballets that were danced dramas.

Among his most important works for the stage was *Medea and Jason*, first performed in Stuttgart in 1763. The ballet was brought to London in 1781 by the dancer Gaetan Vestris (1729–1808), who took the role of Jason; it was performed at the King's Theatre in the Haymarket. The choreography does not survive, but a flavour of the performance can be found in the published scenario and a satirical print made at the time. Noverre's ballets were full of passion and *Medea and Jason* is no exception. Jason intends to marry Creusa, daughter of the king of Corinth, and ascend the throne, but his abandoned lover Medea exacts a terrible revenge on them both. The London production of 1781 was lavish in its special effects, culminating in Medea's flying departure 'in a car drawn by fiery dragons', having caused the deaths of Creusa and Jason and murdered her own children. For some, the whole ballet and the performances by the leading dancers were overblown. This print shows Jason gazing skyward in an attitude of amazement, while Medea clutches a dagger and Creusa recoils in terror. All the dancers are elaborately dressed in contemporary style. After *Medea and Jason*, ballet in London was never the same again.

Jean-Georges Noverre, *Lettres sur la danse et les ballets*, 2nd edition, Londres [Paris], 1783. Frontispiece (Hirsch.I.439).

Nathaniel Dance, engraved by Francesco Bartolozzi, *Jason et Medée ballet tragique*, London, 1781 (British Museum, Prints and Drawings, BM Satires 5910).

A Taste for the Heroic

Although Gaetan Vestris was an established star at the Paris Opéra and danced leading roles during his visit to London in 1781, the public's adulation went to his son Auguste (1760–1842). The satirical poem *An Heroic Epistle* masquerades as a letter from Gaetan to his mistress and dancing partner in Paris. He tells her of his great success in London, where audiences are eager for anything 'that is absurd or new' and 'novelty is taste'. The anonymous author, John Nott (1751–1865), a classical scholar, even manages to work in a reference to Edmund Burke and the sublime.

The poem also dwells on the astounding success of Auguste, whose virtuosity, *brio* and charm brought an entirely new style of dancing to the London stage. Auguste's popularity owed a lot to his physical charms, not least his 'delicious thighs' – openly ogled by 'hot matrons', while the younger unmarried women peeped from behind their fans. Gaetan finishes with a call to his mistress to come to London and share 'this *Goose* with *golden eggs*', a sentiment echoed in the print of Auguste published the same year as the poem. It shows the young dancer in a pose immediately recognisable from ballet today.

Nathaniel Dance, engraved by Francesco Bortolozzi, *Auguste Vestris*, London, 1781 (British Museum, Prints and Drawings, J,2.84).

(12)

Theſe toys ſo frequent broke, I can foreſee,
Will make *, O *Poggi!* a rare trade for thee.

Before the *Opera*'s delights begin, 95
Juſt as the *mob of quality* flock in;
Perch'd on a bench that is conſpicuous moſt,
And leaning eaſy 'gainſt a ſide-box poſt,
Full in the pit my young *Adonis* ſtands,
To lend the ladies his officious hands, 100
To catch their glances as they're paſſing by,
To watch their ogle, or to mark their ſigh,
In ſhort to be admir'd—One cries, "Sweet boy!
"Our public favorite, our private joy:
"Obſerve, my lady, what a *charming ſize!*
"Then what firm legs, and what delicious thighs!"

* *Anthony Poggi*, of Orchard-Sreet, Oxford-Road, has brought the art of fan-painting, and fan-making, to a degree of excellence, hitherto unknown in this or any other country; the preſent *epocha in fans* (to uſe Mr. P's own expreſſion) will be regarded with wonder by poſterity. See a curious advertiſement of his in the *Morning Herald*, for *Jan.* 12, ſaid to be wrote by a famous *knighted magician of the bruſh*.

Broad

(13)

Broad ſtare hot matrons whó no meaſures keep,
And through their pin-prick'd fans young miſſes peep.

Is there a drum, a card-rout, or what not
In higher life, in theſe I'm ne'er forgot; 110
For every party, thinks each titled fool,
Without the *Veſtris* would be horrid dull;
While I at cards cajole the gambling race,
My amorous ſon coquets it with *her Grace*;
By love and fraud, determin'd to lay hold 115
Of *Britiſh* beauty, and of *Britiſh* gold.

On that fair day when *Albion*'s *Queen* was born,
Whoſe virtues e'en her diadem adorn,
Whoſe native worth is pictur'd in her ſmile,
The brighteſt boaſt, the glory of this iſle! 120
When peers and peereſſes, in rich array,
To this lov'd *Queen* congratulations pay;

D When

An Heroic Epistle, from Monsieur Vestris, sen, London, 1781, pages 12–13 (RB.23.b.914).

Eve of the Romantic Ballet

Towards the end of the Georgian period, ballet began to take on the form that is familiar today, with ballerinas dancing *en pointe* and ballets adapting stories from fairy tales. E. A. Théleur's attractive treatise on theatrical dance technique was published just as the Romantic ballet began to emerge. The first technical treatise to illustrate female dancers poised on the tips of their toes, it also has plates which show dancers grouped in recognisably balletic poses.

Just a few years before Théleur's *Letters on Dancing* appeared, the first Cinderella ballet was given in London. *Cendrillon*, with music by the Spanish composer Fernando Sor (1778–1839) and choreography by the French dancing master Monsieur Albert (François Decombe, 1787–1865), was performed at the King's Theatre in 1822. The published score has a pretty title-page vignette showing Cinderella departing for the ball, a scene which remains a particular feature in traditional productions today. Although the 1822 *Cendrillon* did not last as long as other Romantic ballets, its story proved to be popular with many later composers and choreographers.

TOP AND ABOVE
E. A. Théleur, *Letters on Dancing*, London, 1831 (558*.c.41).

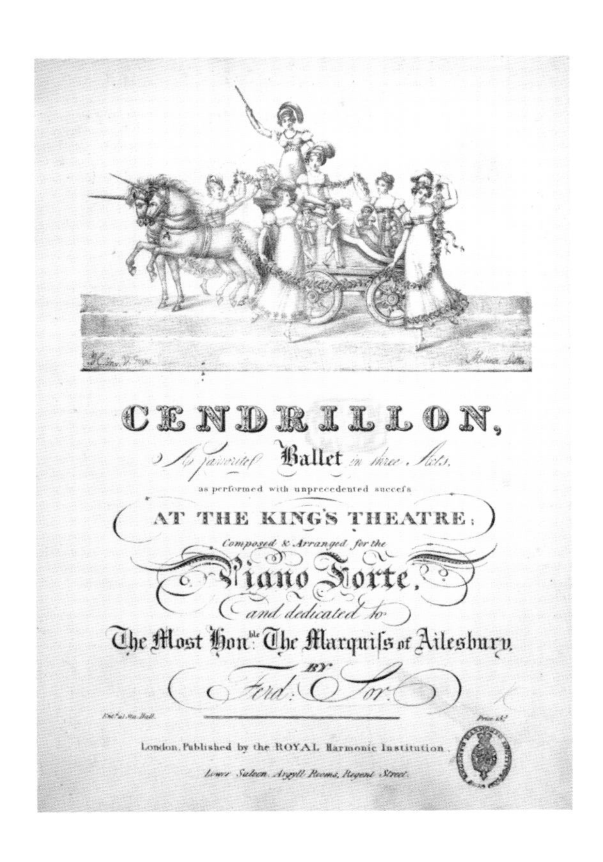

CENDRILLON,
A favorite Ballet in three Acts,
as performed with unprecedented succefs
AT THE KING'S THEATRE;
Composed & Arranged for the
Piano Forte,
and dedicated to
The Most Honble The Marquifs of Ailesbury,
BY
Ferd: Sor.

London, Published by the ROYAL Harmonic Institution,
Lower Saloon, Argyll Rooms, Regent Street.

Fernando Sor, *Cendrillon*, London, 1822, title page (h.804).

Pantomime Takes Off

The origins of the English pantomime can be found in Italy and the *commedia dell'arte*. French exponents of the genre visited London from the seventeenth century, and by the early eighteenth century they were being billed occasionally in 'Night Scenes'. These were short pieces of slapstick comedy that took place between the acts of the plays that were London's main dramatic fare. They must have looked very like the scene of Scaramouch (carrying a lantern) and Harlequin in Gregorio Lambranzi's *Nuova e curiosa scuola de' balli theatrali*. During the 1710s, against a background of rivalry between the theatres in Drury Lane and Lincoln's Inn Fields, these scenes were incorporated into longer stage pieces, and in 1723 the pantomime suddenly took off.

Drury Lane began the craze with *Harlequin Doctor Faustus*, but it was *The Necromancer; or, Harlequin, Doctor Faustus* at Lincoln's Inn Fields that ensured its lasting popularity. *The Necromancer* had dancing, singing, spectacular scenery and amazing special effects. The title role was played by John Rich (1692–1761), the manager of the theatre and London's first great Harlequin. Audiences flocked to see his antics and to enjoy the action as Helen of Troy rises and sings, the miller gets caught in the revolving sails of his own windmill and, best of all, the monstrous dragon swallows Harlequin Doctor Faustus, all the while roaring and belching out flames.

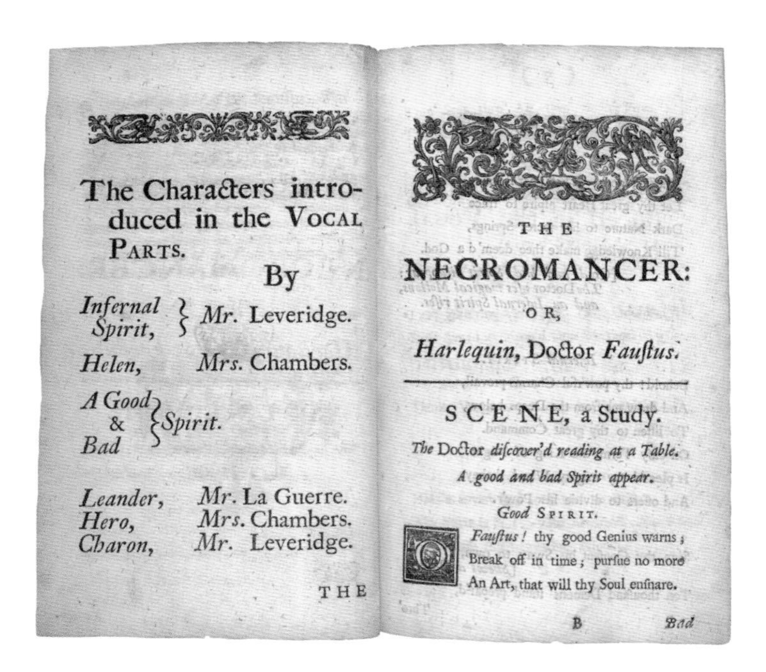

The Characters introduced in the VOCAL PARTS.

By

Infernal Spirit, } *Mr.* Leveridge.

Helen, *Mrs.* Chambers.

A Good & Bad } *Spirit.*

Leander, *Mr.* La Guerre.

Hero, *Mrs.* Chambers.

Charon, *Mr.* Leveridge.

THE

THE NECROMANCER: OR, *Harlequin,* Doctor *Faustus.*

SCENE, a Study.

The Doctor *discover'd reading at a Table.*

A good and bad Spirit appear.

Good SPIRIT.

Faustus! thy good Genius warns;
Break off in time; pursue no more
An Art, that will thy Soul ensnare.

B *Bad*

ABOVE
John Rich, *The vocal parts of an entertainment, called The Necromancer; or, Harlequin, Doctor Faustus*, London, [1723]. Dramatis personae and opening of scene 1 (11775.c.38).

BELOW
Drawing of the opening scene of *The Necromancer*, showing Mephostophilus with Harlequin Doctor Faustus, *c.* 1724 (British Museum, Prints and Drawings, 1972, U.517).

'Scaramouch and Harlequin', from Gregorio Lambranzi, *Deliciae theatrales. Nuova e curiosa scuola de' balli theatrali*, 2 parts, Nuremberg, 1716, vol. 1, plate 29 (Hirsch.I.298).

'Helen Charms Dr Faustus', from George Bickham Sr and George Bickham Jr, *The Musical Entertainer*, 2nd edition, London, 1740, vol. 2, plate 44 (K.10.b.12).

Christmas Pantomimes

Pantomimes began to be associated with Christmas in the 1750s, thanks largely to David Garrick. He disliked the genre, but was happy to exploit its popularity to make money, regularly mounting new pantomimes during the Christmas season. By the early 1800s pantomimes had acquired most of their familiar features. *Harlequin and Mother Goose; or, the Golden Egg* opened at the Covent Garden Theatre on 29 December 1806. It was an immediate success, and is still regarded as the most famous pantomime of all.

Harlequin and Mother Goose drew on a fairy tale for its story. It featured lavish scenes, costumes and a variety of special effects, with comic routines incorporating singing, dancing and slapstick comedy. Mother Goose herself was a pantomime dame, played by the actor, dancer and singer Samuel Simmons (*c.* 1773–1819), who was depicted appropriately costumed with his goose and her golden egg. The stars of the show were Joseph Grimaldi (1778–1837) as Clown and John Bologna (1775–1846) as Harlequin. Their comic duet, with Bologna disguised as a girl, became one of the show's favourite numbers, not least because it poked fun at the serious ballets performed at the King's Theatre over in the Haymarket. The eye-catching print of the dance shows Grimaldi in his characteristic clown's costume and make-up, while Bologna's Harlequin costume can just be seen beneath his skirt.

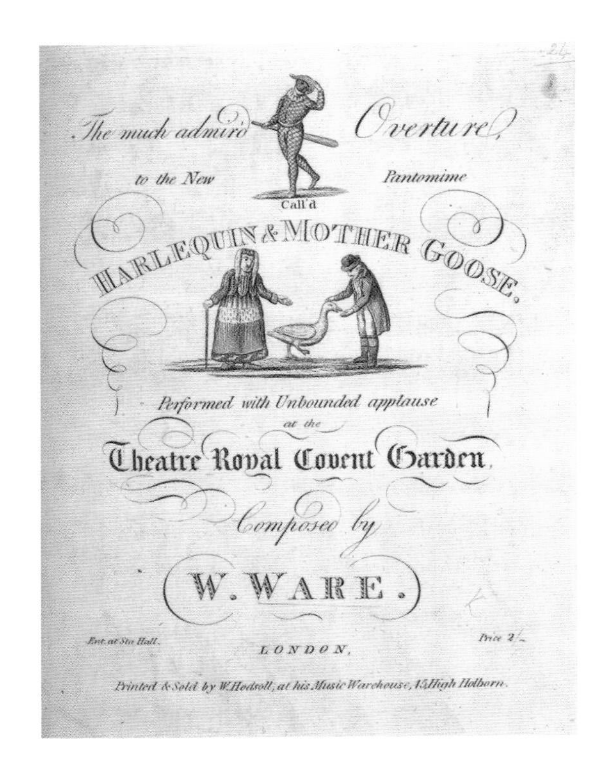

The much admired overture in the new pantomime call'd Harlequin & Mother Goose, London, [1806] (h.271.(24)).

The Favourite Comic Dance, London, 1807 (Dex.315).

OPPOSITE
After Samuel De Wilde, *Mr Simmons as Mother Goose*, London, 1807 (Dex.315).

Circus Horses

Philip Astley (1742–1814) is widely regarded as the originator of the modern circus. Both Astley and his wife, Patty (1740/41–1803), were talented riders, and in 1768 they opened a riding school south of Westminster Bridge in London. Here they held equestrian entertainments, and their son John Astley also became a popular horseback performer. As the handbill advertisements of the early 1770s indicate, the horse-riding included daring acrobatic feats; the shows also had additional speciality and comic acts for variety.

In 1795 Philip Astley opened his new 'Royal Amphitheatre', which burned down in 1803 and was rebuilt the following year. Astley's new building was as spacious as any of London's theatres, with a custom-built arena for his elaborate equestrian acts and a stage for the other entertainments. In 1801 he published *Astley's System of Equestrian Education*, which includes descriptions of the jumps and other feats that horses could be taught to perform. The treatise links Astley not only to horse acts in the circus, but also to the aristocratic tradition behind modern competitive horsemanship.

RIGHT
'Astley's Amphitheatre', from R. Ackermann, *The Microcosm of London*, London, 1808–11, vol. 1, plate 4 (190.e.1).

FAR RIGHT
Astley's performance', or 'Young Astley Vaulting' (L.R.301.h.3).

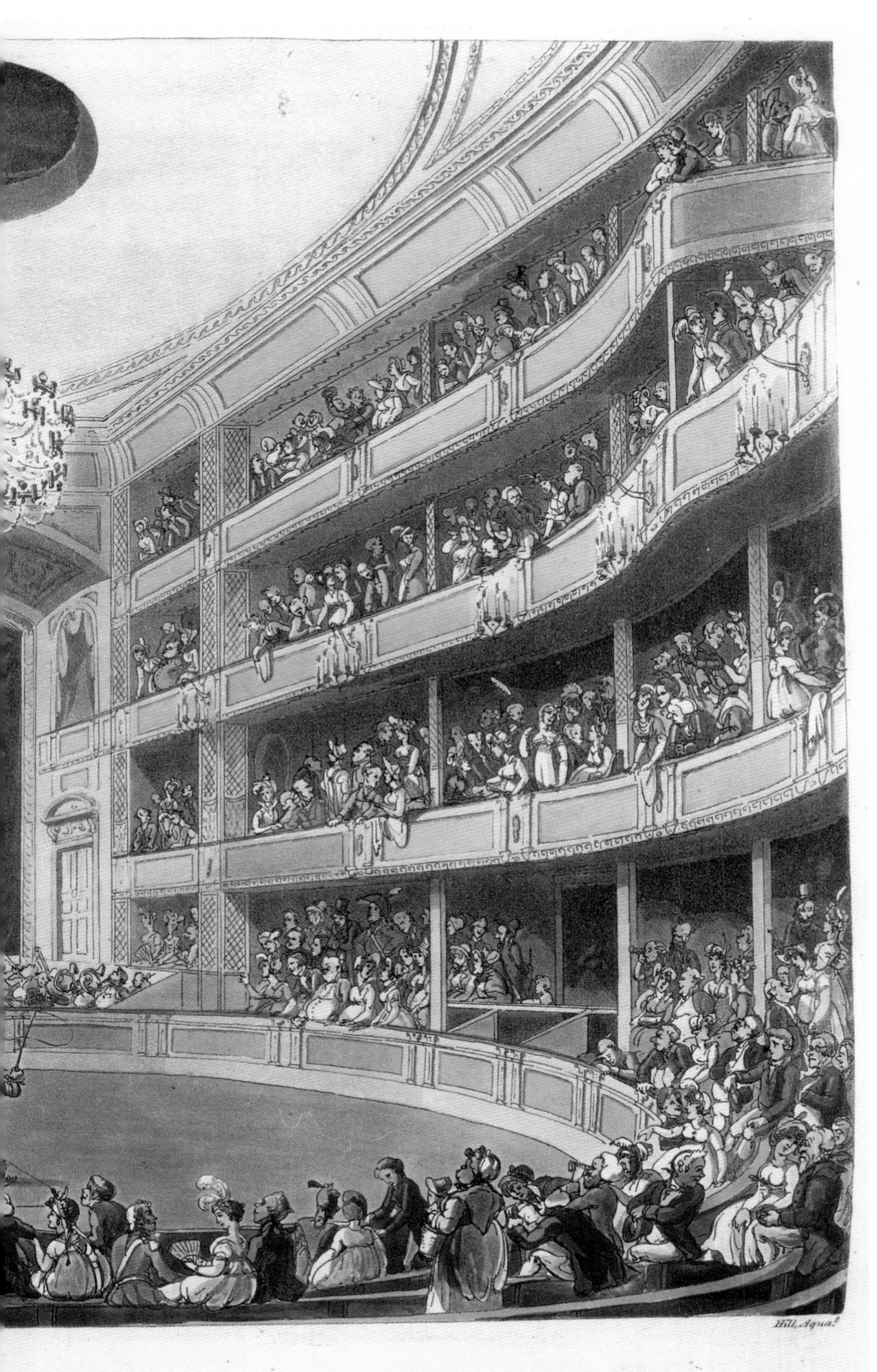

Juſt arrived from Abroad, Young ASTLEY

Moſt aſſuredly for a few Nights only.

This preſent *E V E N I N G,*

At the AMPHITHEATRE, *Weſtminſter - Bridge,*

Will be preſented, for the firſt Time this Seaſon,

A great Variety of Manly Feats of HORSEMANSHIP,

Intermixed with various Exerciſes of the *Manage*, in a Stile quite New, and never exhibited in *London*,

By Young *ASTLEY*, and his *TROOP*,

Arrived Expreſs from *France*, to conclude the preſent Seaſon. The MANLY EXERCISES are arranged in Two diſtinct *Equeſtrian Performances*, which, from their uncommon Variety and Utility, ſeem in a peculiar Manner to claim Attention. Firſt

(For the firſt Time) and never performed in *England*, an Exerciſe, called,

STILL VAULTING,

Invented by Young *Aſtley*, and performed by himſelf, demonſtrating what ought to be practiſed by every Horſeman, in order to familiarize more effectually the Body to the various Actions of the Horſe. Second

EQUESTRIAN EXERCISES,

(For the firſt Time this Seaſon) on 1, 2, 3 and 4 Horſes, *viz.* DANCING on full Speed, in *Serious*, *Comic* and *demi-Characters*, and never attempted by any other Perſon, except Young *Aſtley* and his Pupils; likewiſe a Young *Lady*, Pupil of Mr. *Aſtley's*, ſen. will aſſiſt in the above Exerciſes; after which, The Two CELEBRATED CLOWNS, will diſplay a variety of *Comic Manœuvres*, for the firſt Time, and never exhibited in *England*.

A Muſical Piece, never exhibited, called,

The LAPLANDERS,

The Scenery, Dreſſes, Machinery, Muſic, &c. entirely new, the Whole forming a ſtriking View of that Country in Winter.——Likewiſe a Muſical Piece (for the 10th Time) called,

The LOTTERY TICKET; or, *Poor Cobler.*

A new DANCE (for the firſt Time this Seaſon) called,

WHO STOLE THE SHEEP?

After which, various Experiments on

The MAGIC TABLE; or, *The little Horſe turned Conjurer*;

Experiment 1ſt. The *little Horſe* will transform a Gold Watch to an Orange, and the Orange to a living Bird, which will fly away.
Exp. 2d. The *little Horſe* will cauſe a Clock to ſtrike any Number privately appointed by the Company.
Exp. 3d. The *little Horſe* will convey Ten Diamond Rings from a ſmall Box into the Beak of a Pigeon; the Pigeon will be found in a Tea-Cheſt, at a great Diſtance from the Box.
Exp. 4th. The *little Horſe* will cauſe to be cut a Lady's Handkerchief in Twenty Pieces, and will immediately reinſtate it, and give it to the Owner.

Between the above new Exerciſes, &c. will be added,

The DANCING DOGS. | The ENGLISH ROSSIGNOL
The MUSICAL CHILD. | GENERAL JACKOO

A MINUET by Two HORSES, rode by the Two *Aſtleys*, Father and Son.
An ENTRE of HORSES in various Attitudes, the whole forming the greateſt Variety of Amuſements ever exhibited in *London*.

By Deſire, that much admired Pantomime (for the Firſt Time this Seaſon) called,

HARLEQUIN EMPEROR of the MOON.

With various Alteratinas and Additions, and a grand Proceſſion of the Inhabitants of the MOON.

The Whole to conclude (by way of concluding the Seaſon)

With a GRAND TEMPLE of Metamorphoſes; or, *La Fin couronne tout.*

Doors to be opened at half paſt FIVE, to begin preciſely at half paſt SIX o'Clock.
BOXES 3s.—PIT 2s.—GALL. 1s.—Side GALL. 6d.

Places for the BOXES to be taken at the *Amphitheatre*.

Printed by H. PACE, Nº 56, *High-ſtreet, Borough.*

Museums and Art Galleries

The widening of access to culture is an important feature of the Georgian age. Previously, access to collections of art and antiquities had been largely confined to the wealthy, privileged and well connected, but all was to change. Sir Hans Sloane, one of the most prodigious collectors of his time, had filled his house in Chelsea with paintings and sculpture, but principally with books, manuscripts, prints, drawings, coins and medals, an extensive herbarium, preserved birds, animals, insects and geological specimens. He also possessed arms and armour, and archaeological and ethnographic materials. Sloane contrived to keep all of this intact after his death by bequeathing his collections to the nation, in return for a payment of £20,000 to his daughters.

Faced with the risk of it all leaving the country, an Act of Parliament in 1753 established a British Museum to take over the collections. The new museum was also to incorporate the existing Cotton and Harleian Libraries (private collections that had been respectively bequeathed to the nation and purchased by the government). It was to be controlled by a Board of Trustees and the costs (including the payment to Sloane's daughters) were to be met from a lottery; this was also to fund the acquisition of further collections, and to purchase a home for the new museum. Support for the project was encouraged by George II's donation of the Old Royal Library, which dated back to the time of Edward IV.

In 1754 Montagu House, a seventeenth-century house in Bloomsbury, was acquired, and the business of fitting it out and moving the collections began. By 1759 all was ready, and the British Museum was opened to the public. Access was by guided tour, for which ticket applications had to be made in advance, and it proved a huge success; 10,000 tickets a year were being issued by 1761. Despite the Trustees' early apprehension

External and internal views of the British Museum, *c.* 1760 (C.55.i.1).

about the kinds of person who should be admitted, overseas visitors in particular commented on the wide social mix they encountered on the tours; and the Trustees were to reject the idea of admission charges in 1784 on the grounds that this would place the museum beyond the reach of many of its current visitors. Nonetheless, it was not until 1810 that general admission, rather than an escorted tour, was introduced.

Georgian Britain saw a flourishing of voluntary societies. A year after the founding of the British Museum in 1754, the Society of Arts (known today as the Royal Society of Arts) was established. This was not only a club for like-minded and convivial members; it also aimed to find practical and commercial applications for the growing world of knowledge, yet without losing the notion of ideas for their own sake – and indeed art for art's sake. Britain's artists had very much felt the need for an institution on the lines of the Académie des Beaux-Arts in Paris, and for a while the Society of Arts fulfilled this role, holding the first public exhibition of contemporary art in London in 1760.

However, the artist members grew increasingly uncomfortable with the practical side of the Society. They took the initiative and in 1768, led by Joshua Reynolds, established their own society under the patronage of George III, the Royal Academy of Arts. The Academy mounted an annual exhibition of modern art (which continues to this day), together with public lectures; it also organised training for students under the leadership of the outstanding practitioners of the day. Demand was high, with nearly eighty students being enrolled in the first year. By 1780 the exhibitions were being held in galleries at Somerset House, specially designed for the purpose by Sir William Chambers (and occupied by the Courtauld Institute today).

Thomas Rowlandson, 'Exhibition Stare Case', London, [1811?]. (British Museum, Prints and Drawings, 1876,0311.66).

ABOVE
'Tom and Jerry at the Exhibition of Pictures at the Royal Academy', from Pierce Egan, *Life in London*, London, 1823 (838.i.2).

RIGHT
'Drawing from Life at the Royal Academy, Somerset House', from R. Ackermann, *Microcosm of London*, London, 1808–11 (C.194.b.305).

Philanthropy and Charity

The changing social mores of the eighteenth century led to much growth in the establishment of philanthropic and charitable institutions such as schools, hospitals and orphanages.

Schooling was adapting itself to the new needs of the age, and of the growing middle class for whom the traditional public schools were not adequate or seen as appropriate. For the poorer classes, although it was still argued from time to time that society was best preserved by keeping the poor in ignorance, hundreds of charitable schools were founded. They offered education to working-class children to equip them with the skills required for the Georgian workplace; these children could thus be absorbed into Britain's expanding economy and avoid becoming a further drain on society.

Supporting such philanthropy provided patrons and supporters with evidence of their concern for their less fortunate fellows and of their practical Christianity. Religious organisations such as the Society for the Promotion of Christian Knowledge and the Methodist Church were active in promoting schooling, both to improve the understanding of Christianity and to inculcate the notion of the supposed benefits of hard work and temperance. Such schools were often very closely focused on producing compliant and useful workers, and there were always concerns that education should not give children ideas inappropriate to their social station: writing, for example, was not always taught. How successful they were is open to question; schools promoted by churches seem to have had little effect on the size of the congregations.

ABOVE
Statues of children, from Farringdon Ward School (Museum of London, 7208, 7209).

BELOW
View of St George's Hospital, Hyde Park Corner (K.Top 22.6a)

There was also a wave of hospital foundations. Five were opened in London before 1750, and others were created in the provinces. Dispensaries too were founded, providing relief to many: medical science was helping to prolong and protect lives, and the growth of secular institutions helped to place emphasis on saving lives, rather than souls. St George's Hospital was one of the new foundations. Based on an initial foundation in Westminster in 1724, it was re-established at Lanesborough House on Hyde Park Corner in 1733, and by 1744 was able to accommodate over 250 patients. Formal training of student doctors began in 1751, and the hospital, now located at Tooting in south London, is still one of London's major teaching hospitals. Edward Jenner, who was to develop the first successful smallpox vaccination, studied there, and the hide of a cow said to have supplied material for his first vaccination in 1796 is preserved at the hospital. The original site was closed in 1980.

Perhaps the best known of the charitable foundations of the Georgian era is the Foundling Hospital in London. It was established by a retired sea captain, Thomas Coram, in 1739 after many years spent trying to raise support. Such institutions were not universally welcomed: having somewhere where an unwanted newborn could be handed in was seen by some as encouraging immorality. However, Coram's efforts succeeded in establishing a foundation that still supports children today. His courting of celebrity patrons helped to ensure that charity became viewed as a fashionable pastime, while the organisation of the famous exhibitions by the artist (and founder governor) William Hogarth provided events for the social calendar.

Charity concerts became a regular feature at the hospital, especially the annual benefit performance of *Messiah*, organised by the composer George Frideric Handel, that took place between 1750 and his death in 1759. As with the charity schools, the practical side of the Foundling Hospital showed in the way the children were prepared for lives of useful work: boys were intended to follow the example of the founder and go to sea, while girls were prepared for domestic service. Tokens were left with the children by their mothers in the hope that they might one day be reunited, although in practice the foundation did little to encourage later contact.

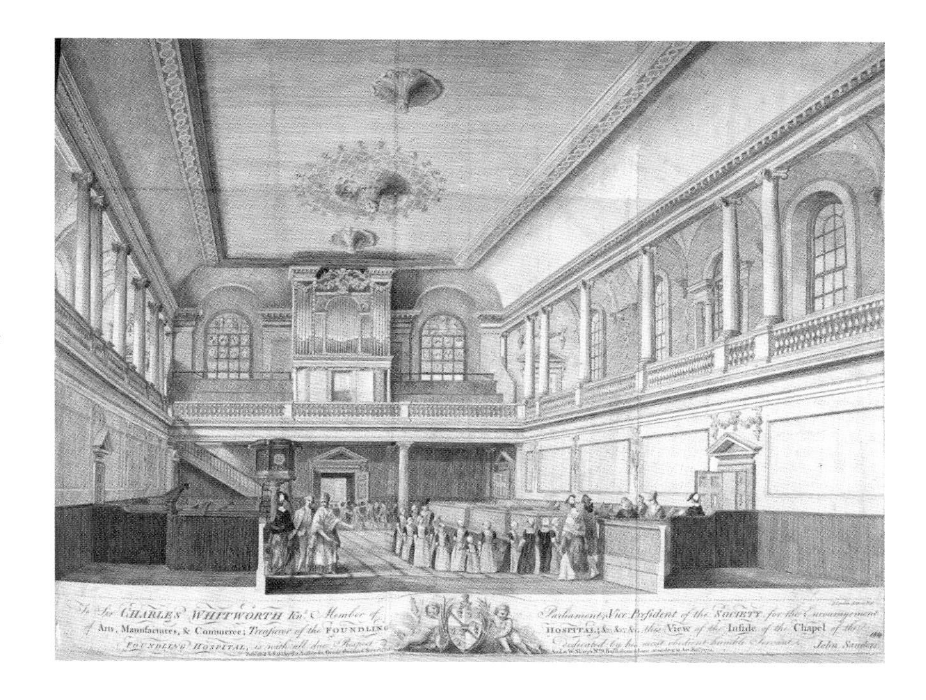

View of the Foundling Hospital (interior), Coram's Fields, [London, between 1753 and 1770] (Crach.1.Tab.4.b.3).

Part of the Hallelujah Chorus from G. F. Handel's *Messiah*. Autograph manuscript, 1741 (R.M.20.f.2).

4 Leisure and Pleasure

The prestigious arbiter of Georgian taste and politeness, Philip Stanhope, Fourth Earl of Chesterfield (1694–1773), became celebrated for his *Letters to His Son*, published in 1774. The *Letters* set standards for behaviour in polite society, although Chesterfield was also criticised for placing manners above morals. The *Letters* went through numerous editions and adaptations in succeeding years. Chesterfield had a low opinion of dancing, but he nevertheless wrote that 'to dance well, is absolutely necessary in order to sit, stand and walk well'. There was a great deal of dancing in Georgian Britain.

Assemblies, occasions for the public display of taste and politeness, frequently included a ball among the entertainments. Every provincial city of note had its assembly rooms. Pleasure gardens were not invented by the Georgians, but they took them to a higher degree of sophistication than before. Masquerades were much enjoyed, for they gave participants the chance to perform in a drama of their own creation as a stage character or in disguise.

Sports became ever more popular, drawing crowds of spectators who were likely to place bets on the outcome as they watched. This was the era when rules were set down and players started to become professionals. Events were advertised in advance and results were reported afterwards in newspapers and handbills. The welfare of animals became a concern, and some older sports were criticised for their cruelty.

As road networks improved and stagecoaches ran to regular timetables, people travelled further afield for interest and entertainment. Visits to the seaside for relaxation and sea-bathing were new, and became a regular diversion for many. The Grand Tour to France and Italy was confined to the wealthiest young men, but the middle classes could enjoy awe-inspiring scenery in the British Isles. Later in the eighteenth century, during times of peace with France, they ventured to Paris among other continental cities. Tourism had arrived.

Assembling Polite Society

Georgian polite society enjoyed assemblies – gatherings where the great, the established and the aspiring could dance, gamble and take supper together. In London, and particularly in the provinces, assembly rooms were purpose-built to provide elegant and convenient venues for the subscribers who met at these fashionable events. Bath acquired new assembly rooms as early as 1708. York's much admired building, designed by Lord Burlington, went up in the early 1730s. Newcastle-upon-Tyne's assembly rooms, built by William Newton (1730–1798) and opened in 1776, were considered to be very fine and are still in use today.

An assembly was a formal occasion where local society could see and be seen. It combined a ball, or a promenade if the crush was too great, with card-playing in side rooms off the ballroom. Refreshments (tea followed by supper) were provided in another room, set aside for the purpose. The event might begin at any time between 8 pm and 11 pm, and dancing could continue until dawn if the company so wished. Such an occasion had to be carefully regulated if it was not to degenerate into a free-for-all, and each assembly house had its master of ceremonies. The most famous was Richard 'Beau' Nash (1674–1762), who presided at

Ralph Beilby, engraved by James Fittler, *View of the Assembly House … in Newcastle Upon Tyne* (K.Top.32.57.p).

Bath. He set the tone and provided rules for correct behaviour, for example declaring that 'gentlemen crowding before the ladies at the ball, shew ill manners' and ordering that they were not to do so. Nash's strictures, as relayed by Oliver Goldsmith (1728–1774) in his *Life*, were not altogether serious.

Assemblies were not simply social events. They were also places where business contacts were to be made and alliances contracted. The master of ceremonies might act, quietly, as a marriage broker, as this print by Thomas Rowlandson (1756–1827) gleefully acknowledges.

Oliver Goldsmith,
The Life of Richard Nash, of Bath, Esq., London, 1762
(C.107.df.5).

Thomas Rowlandson,
A Master of the Ceremonies Introducing a Partner,
London, 1795
(British Museum,
BM Satires 8737).

'Characteristic Dancing'

Of the relatively few depictions of dancing from the Georgian period, the most vivid are satirical. They may reflect the reality of dancing at the time – then, as now, enthusiastic bad dancers were rather more numerous than good ones. More probably, however, such images reflect the age-old suspicion of the sheer physical pleasure displayed when people dance.

La Belle Assemblée or Sketches of Characteristic Dancing, a hand-coloured etching by George Cruikshank (1792–1878), was published in 1817. It pokes fun at both social and theatrical dancing. Cruikshank's dancers range from the stock figure of the dancing master with his fiddle and his turned-out toes, on the far left, to the near-contortion of the professional dancers in the 'Ballet Italienne' on the far right. In between are a variety of dancers showing off their paces, some of whom are obviously enjoying themselves.

Cruikshank has a sharp eye for current fashions in dance and its well-worn conventions, while his dancers come in all shapes and sizes. From left to right, one group enjoys a traditional country dance, and the next three step through the newly popular

George Cruikshank, *La Belle Assemblée or Sketches of Characteristic Dancing*, London, 1817, vol. 1, 258 (Crach.1.Tab.4.b.4).

Scots reel, with arms as well as feet in action. Beside them three more dancers get into the spirit of an Irish jig, aided by some liquid refreshment, in contrast to the next, very slender couple who are striving for authentic elegance in an overly refined minuet. They, in turn, contrast with two tubby dancers grappling with the ultra-fashionable waltz and an over-dressed group battling through the figures of a 'French' quadrille.

Before the 'Ballet Italienne', Cruikshank throws in a couple dancing a 'Spanish Boliero'. He may be referring to a popular duet from the ballet *Don Quichotte* by James Harvey D'Egville (*c.* 1770–*c.* 1836); a performance was given at the King's Theatre in 1809, in which Auguste Vestris's son Armand Vestris (1788–1825) made his London debut. Cruikshank was keenly aware of dance's comic aspects, and the overall design of this caricature is reminiscent of *The Country Dance*, from Hogarth's *Analysis of Beauty*. Unlike Hogarth, however, Cruikshank has no place for truly graceful and accomplished dancers, suggesting his disapproval of dancing – even though this takes the form of mirth rather than censure.

Dancing for the King

At the English court in the early 1700s, royal birthdays were celebrated not only with a ball: a ballroom duet was especially created for a performance before the sovereign and family. This practice, well established under Queen Anne, continued in the reign of George I, initially with choreographies created for his granddaughter Anne, Princess Royal (1709–1759). These dances were regularly published in notation so that those lower down the social scale could also perform them.

Several dancing masters in London sought royal patronage, among them John Essex (d. 1744). His book *For the Further Improvement of Dancing*, translated from a French treatise on the notation of country dances, first appeared in 1710. Essex had the work reprinted as a handsome folio, dedicating it to Caroline of Ansbach, the new Princess of Wales (1683–1737) and wife of the future George II. Essex also added some extra dances, among them the Princess's Passpied. The duet, with its simple but lively choreography, may have been intended for performance by Caroline's daughter the Princess Royal, then aged six. This unique copy of the reprinted treatise with its additional dances is handsomely bound. It comes from the library of George III, and may well be the one presented by Essex to Princess Caroline.

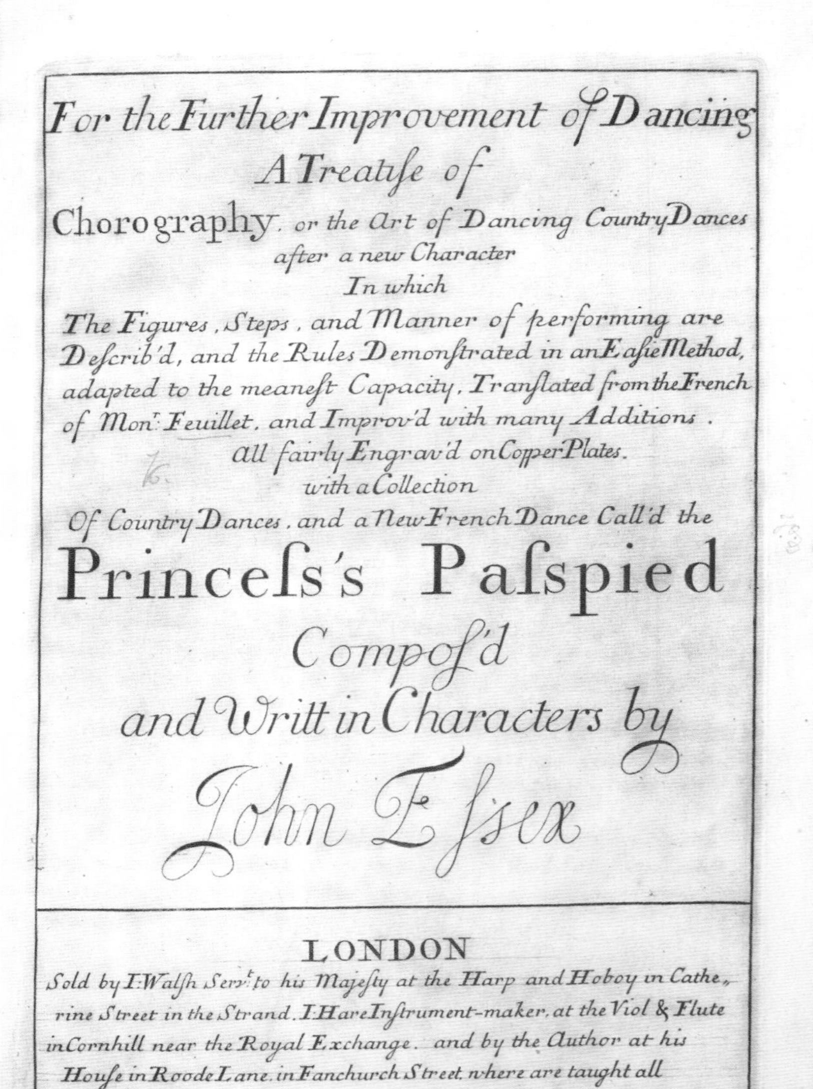

For the Further Improvement of Dancing
A Treatise of
Chorography. or the Art of Dancing Country Dances
after a new Character
In which
The Figures, Steps, and Manner of performing are
Describ'd, and the Rules Demonstrated in an Easie Method,
adapted to the meanest Capacity. Translated from the French
of Mon.r Feuillet, and Improv'd with many Additions.
all fairly Engrav'd on Copper Plates.
with a Collection
Of Country Dances, and a New French Dance Call'd the
Princess's Passpied
Compos'd
and Writt in Characters by
John Essex

LONDON
Sold by I. Walsh Serv.t to his Majesty at the Harp and Hoboy in Catherine Street in the Strand. I. Hare Instrument-maker, at the Viol & Flute in Cornhill near the Royal Exchange. and by the Author at his House in Roode Lane, in Fanchurch Street. where are taught all the Ball Dances of the English and French Court.

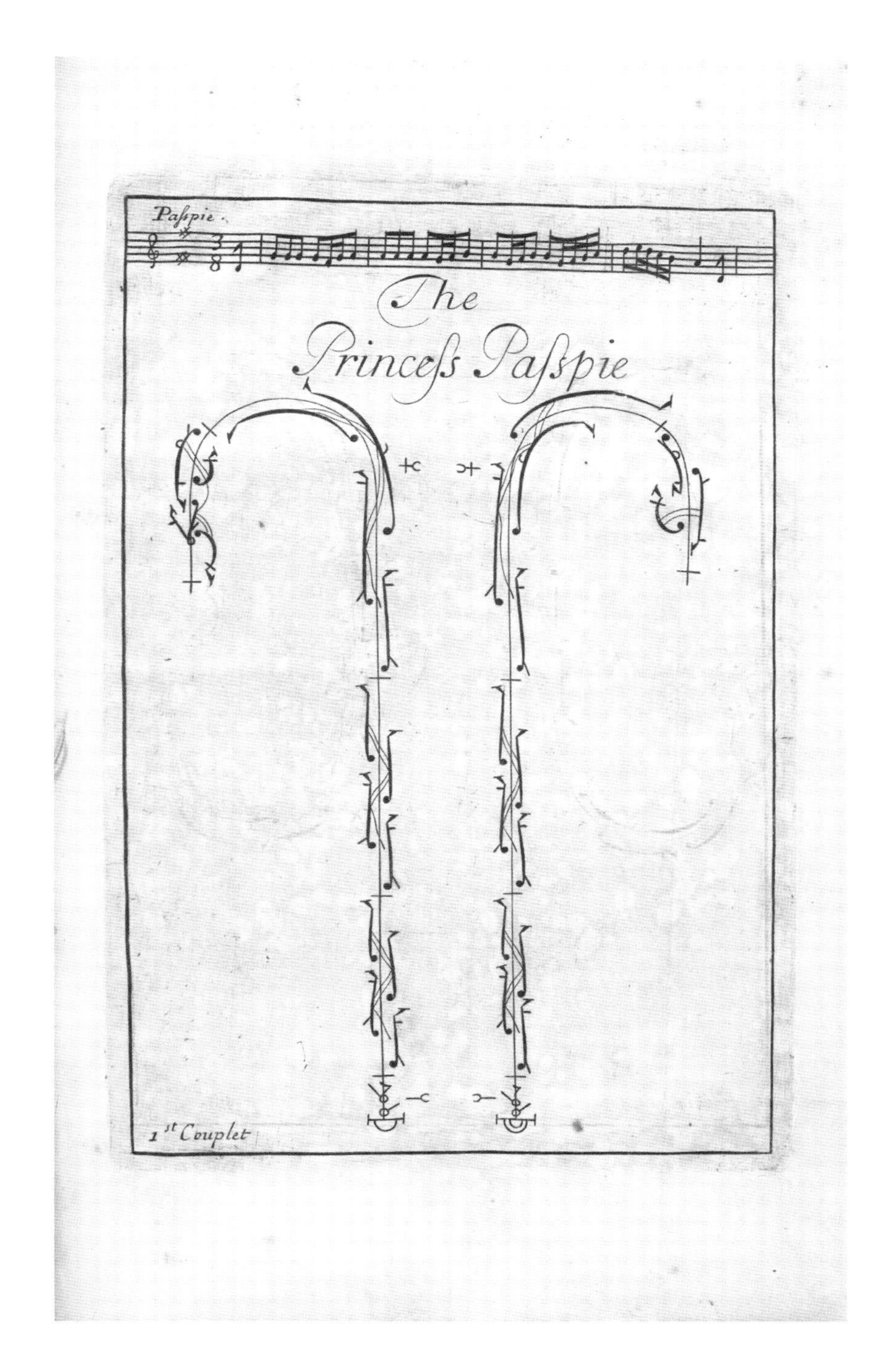

John Essex, *For the Further Improvement of Dancing*, London, [1715?]. Title page and opening plate of the 'Princess's Passpied' (60.h.28).

Ordeal by Minuet

The ballroom duets created for performance at court before members of the royal family were display pieces, danced by a single couple before the intense scrutiny of their peers. So, too, were the minuets that opened public balls and dancing at assemblies throughout Britain. The minuet was a severe test of dance style and technique, and dancing masters devoted much of their teaching to it. Kellom Tomlinson (*c.* 1688–1761) describes the minuet, its steps and figures, in detail within the second book of his treatise *The Art of Dancing*, illustrating it with several fine engravings and providing a version in notation.

Although the minuet had a series of prescribed figures, which were always performed in the same order, it was partly improvisatory. The dancing couple could start at any point in the music and were free to vary their steps within the principal figures of the dance, including substituting quite different steps from the basic minuet steps. Tomlinson's plates, each of which has its own dedicatees, show the refined deportment and subtle turns of body and head expected of dancers.

George Bickham the Younger (*c.* 1704–1771) was not a dancing master. Rather, he was an engraver and printseller, alert to any possibility of making money. *An Easy Introduction to Dancing* plagiarises other dancing manuals to produce a little book intended to make the minuet's mysteries accessible to aspirants rather lower down the social scale than Tomlinson's pupils. Bickham manages to fit all the figures of the minuet on to a single plate, without resorting to dance notation.

ABOVE
Kellom Tomlinson, *The Art of Dancing*, London, 1735. Book II, plate VI (K.8.k.7).

RIGHT
George Bickham the Younger, *An Easy Introduction to Dancing*, London, [1755?]. Final plate, showing all the figures in the minuet (K.2.d.20).

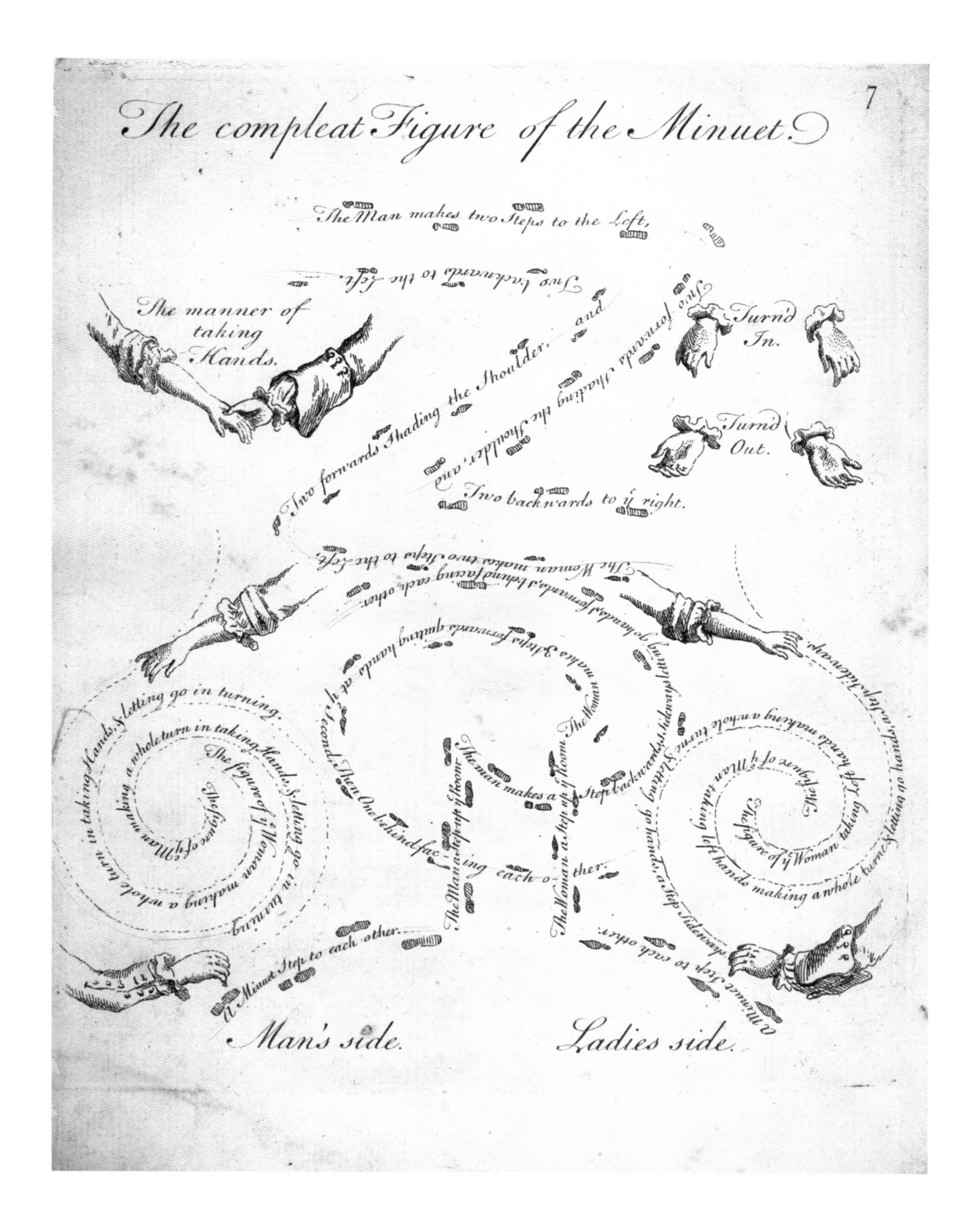

The compleat Figure of the Minuet.
7
The Man makes two Steps to the Left,
Two backwards to the Left.
The manner of taking Hands.
Two forwards shading the Shoulder, and
Turn'd In.
Turn'd Out.
Two backwards to y right.
The Woman makes two Steps to the Left,
A Minuet Step to each other.
Man's side.
Ladies side.

Le menuet, unmounted fan leaf, 1790–1811 (British Museum, Prints and Drawings, Schreiber 1891,0713.639).

The Minuet at Bath

The importance of the minuet, and the terror it inspired in would-be dancers, made it a ready object of satire. Bath balls, of course, opened with a series of minuets, a practice which continued throughout much of the eighteenth century. In 1787 the caricature *A Long Minuet as Danced at Bath* by Henry Bunbury (1750–1811) was published, and the sequence of couples was used as part of the decoration of a fan leaf a few years later. All of them are shown, in the outermost strip and the centre of the middle strip of the fan, in the same order in which they appear in Bunbury's engraving. The colouring in the fan brings out the finery of their attire and exaggerates their various *faux-pas*.

None of the couples looks entirely at ease, or indeed well-matched. They each seem to have reached a different point of the dance. The first couple, in the top left, have begun the final figure as they are tentatively taking both hands. The two couples in the top right are apparently taking right hands, a central figure in the minuet, although the arms of the gentlemen do not quite follow the elegant lines prescribed by dancing masters. The couple in the centre right, corresponding to the last couple in the *Long Minuet*, may have completed the dance – they seem to be looking at one another with relief and even pride. In between, several couples appear to be bowing or about to bow to either the onlookers or each other – though whether at the beginning or the end of the dance, it is impossible to tell. The gentleman of the centre left couple has made his bow so low that he is bent double, to the disapproval of his partner. By the late 1700s the minuet was viewed as an archaic ritual that had nevertheless to be honoured. This, at least, is how Bunbury depicted it.

The Waltz: Chaste or Lewd?

If the newspapers are to be believed, the waltz came to public notice (if it did not actually arrive) in London in 1811. In that year several letters about it appeared in the influential *Morning Post*. Correspondents were divided in opinion as to whether its continental origin, and the manner in which the lady was held by the gentleman, made the waltz a chaste or a lewd dance. The dancing master Thomas Wilson (fl. 1800–39), a prolific author of dance treatises, brought out his *Description of the Correct Method of Waltzing* in 1816, by which time the dance was well-established in fashionable circles.

Wilson, like his contemporaries, ascribes the origins of the waltz to Germany. In his treatise he distinguishes between the French Waltz, the Sauteuse Waltz and the Jetté or Quick Sauteuse Waltz, which are to be performed in succession and become progressively faster, and the German Waltz of which he thinks most highly because it is 'truly elegant'. His pretty frontispiece shows a couple ready to begin (Fig. 1), about to start the slow French Waltz (Fig. 2), the first movement of the Sauteuse Waltz (Fig. 5), the first movement of the Jetté or Quick Sauteuse Waltz (Fig. 8) and a movement in the German Waltz (Fig. 9). Contemporary fears about the lascivious possibilities of the waltz are tellingly illustrated by the engraving from Pierce Egan's *Life in London*, which shows the author's heroes, the young men-about-town, Tom and Jerry, with 'Corinthian Kate'. Neither the couple's hold nor the lady's décolletage correspond with any of Wilson's far more decorous figures.

Thomas Wilson, *A Description of the Correct Method of Waltzing*, London, 1816. Frontispiece (1042.k.35.(1)).

Pierce Egan, plate from *Life in London*, London, 1823 (838.i.2).

Windings of the Dance

The English country dance was usually performed in a longways set, in which couples faced each other in two lines, gentlemen on one side and ladies on the other. In his *Analysis of Beauty* William Hogarth records his great pleasure in watching country dances, with their winding and interweaving figures. Their visual appeal was so great that he used a country dance for one of the plates in his treatise, referring in his text to the 'composed variety of lines, chiefly serpentine' to be found within these intricate choreographies.

Hogarth's focus was, in fact, on the individuals participating in his country dance, depicting them in attitudes which are decidedly awkward and ridiculous. Although he does show an elegant and genteel couple at the head of the dance, to provide an example of his line of beauty, Hogarth features schematic sketches of dance figures in the top left corner of his engraving. One is intended to show a country dance hey (a figure in which the dancers pass each other weaving in and out until they return to place), while the other looks very like the floor pattern of the opening figures of the minuet. Hogarth may have been recalling dance notations of the time. In his notated country dance 'The Lottery', John Essex (d. 1744) provides a similar image. The dance's title may refer to the Lotteries Act, which was passed in 1710 and allowed the government to raise money by running a public lottery.

The use of notation for country dances was a short-lived phenomenon in Britain. Throughout the Georgian period country dances were usually published with their music (which would be repeated as many times as needed) and written descriptions of the steps and figures, following the conventions established as early as 1651 with the publication of *The English Dancing Master*. The music publisher and printer John Playford's first collection continued to appear in new editions, with the addition of ever more country dances, until the 1720s. The 17th edition, published in 1721, still included dances from 70 years earlier, alongside more recent additions such as The Marlborough, added in 1706, and Edinborough Castle – a new dance, although the title had been used for a different one in 1651.

William Hogarth, *The Analysis of Beauty*, London, 1753. Plate II, showing a country dance. (61.d.9).

John Essex, *For the Further Improvement of Dancing*, London, [1715?]. Opening plate of 'The Lottery' (60.h.28).

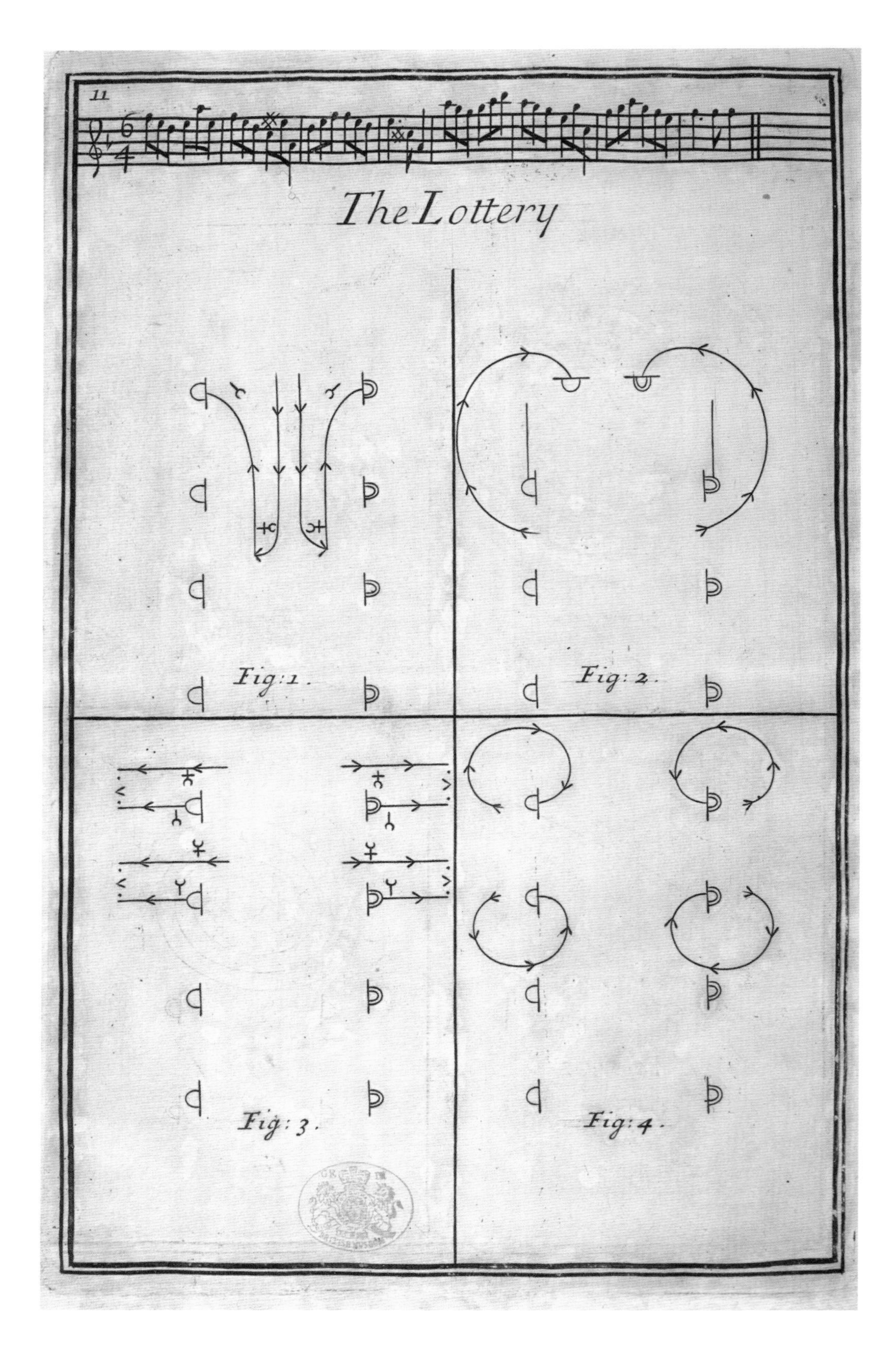

[220]

Edinborough Caſtle : *Or,* Mother *Dobney's* Trencher.

Longways for as many as will.

Note: *Each Strain is to be play'd twice over.*

The firſt and ſecond couple hands all four a-croſs and jump quite round.— Then hands a-croſs all four back again.: Then the firſt couple croſs over, and half Figure at top, then Right and Left quite round, and turn your Partner.

[345]

The *Marlborough.*

Longways for as many as will.

Note : *Each Strain is to be play'd twice over.*

The firſt Man and 2. Wo. Sett to each other, and then Figure the whole Figure round their own Partners.— The other two do the ſame.: Then 1. Man turn the 2. Wo. croſs with the Minuet Step, the other two the ſame, then Hands quite round; then turn Hands, ſides half round, and back again; the firſt couple being at the top, both caſt off and turn.

The Dancing master,
Vol. the First, 17th edition,
London (K.1.b.6).

Cotillons and Quadrilles or Square Dancing

French country dances, known as *contredanses*, were performed by four couples facing inwards around a square set, with each lady on the right of her gentleman. They used figures similar to those in English country dances, but the square formation allowed very different choreographies to develop. Cotillons, described in the newspapers as 'very elegant French country dances', became fashionable in London in the late 1760s, and cotillon balls were often advertised. The dance comprised a series of simple changes, for example all dance in a circle or turn partners with both hands, alternating with a more complex figure which might take the dancers right around the set. Cotillons were energetic and participants had to keep dancing throughout. There was no time to stand and talk as in English country dances. This print of *The Cotillion Dance* catches this liveliness, as the dancers do their best to keep up with the steps and the music. As befits a satire, they all appear to be past the first flush of youth and fitness.

The quadrille, also danced in a square set, reached London in the early 1800s and would become ever more popular as the nineteenth century advanced. It had a series of figures which brought together some of those familiar from English country dances. Each figure had its own name – 'Le Pantalon', 'L'Eté' and so on – and was danced to different music, unlike the cotillon where music was usually repeated for each change and its succeeding figure. Quadrilles were danced by two couples at a time, allowing those who were not dancing to converse. The Cruikshank plate from *Life in London* shows the elegance as well as the sociability of the quadrille when danced at Almack's, the assembly rooms that were also an exclusive club, patronised by London's highest society. Thomas Wilson (fl. 1800–39) thoughtfully provided a compendium of cotillon and quadrille figures for those enthusiasts who wished to compose their own dances.

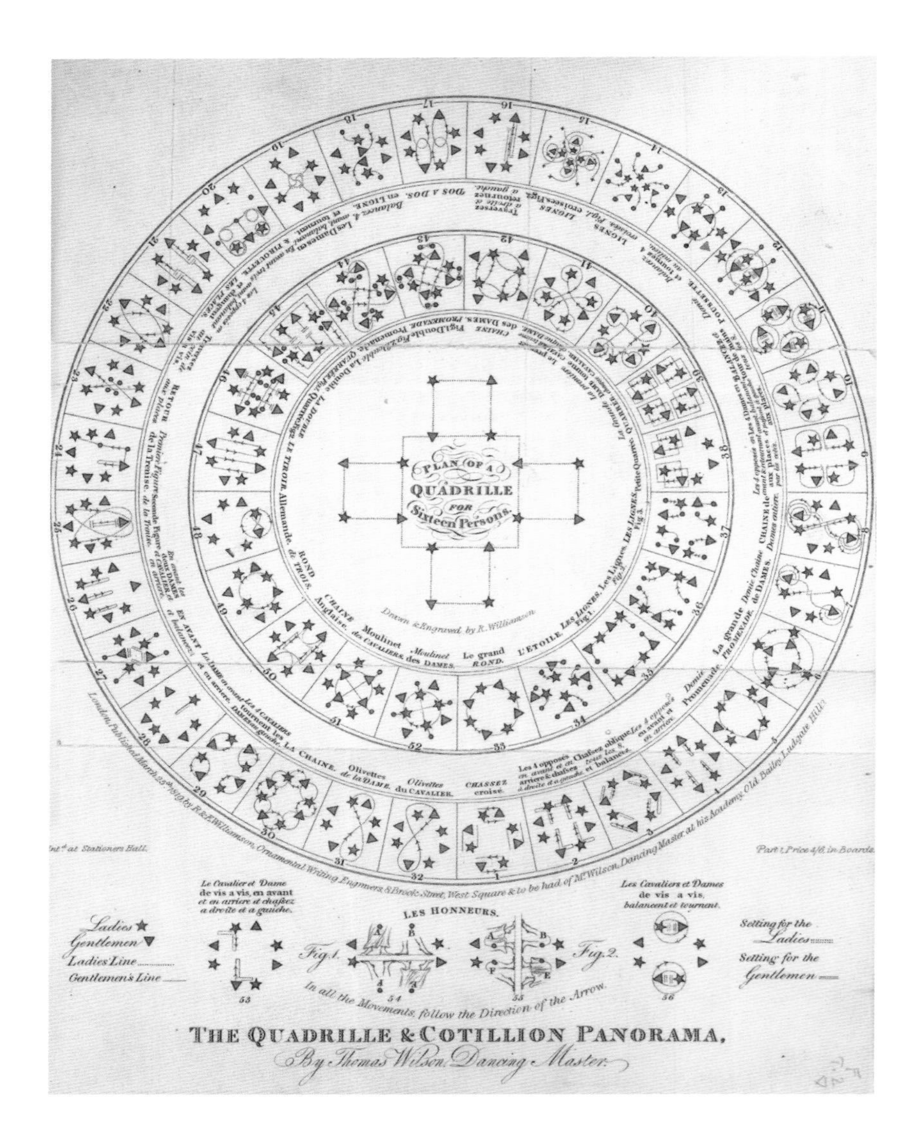

Thomas Wilson, *Quadrille & Cotillion Panorama*, London, 1822. Fold-out plate showing all the quadrille and cotillon figures (1042.l.24.(2)).

James Caldwell after John Collet, *The Cotillion Dance*, London, 1770 (British Museum, Prints and Drawings, BM Satires 4599).

Plate from Pierce Egan, *Life in London*, London, 1823 (838.i.2).

Bagnigge Wells, Lost Place of Pleasure

Many pleasure gardens existed during the Georgian period, in provincial towns as well as in London. Some, like Vauxhall Gardens, remain very well known, even though they have disappeared, while others have been entirely lost from public memory. Bagnigge House, on what is now the Kings Cross Road not far from the railway station, enters history as the summer residence of Charles II's mistress, Nell Gwyn. It later became a public garden where Londoners could enjoy the countryside and patronise a nearby pub. With the discovery around 1760 of mineral springs, the garden became known as Bagnigge Wells, offering entertainment within the house as well as outdoors.

Bagnigge Wells was never in the first rank of pleasure gardens, and it quickly gained a dubious reputation. The engraving by John Raphael Smith (1751–1812) shows a crowd of fashionably dressed visitors taking tea and socialising. The lighted chandeliers and darkened windows suggest that it is evening. The deportment of the female figure in the foreground marks her lack of respectability, probably shared by those around her. The illustration of *The Road to Ruin* appears in an extra-illustrated copy of *A Sunday Ramble*, a tour around London's places for leisure and pleasure. Here, the satire is even more direct: the venue is the garden of Bagnigge Wells and the young man stands between rival prostitutes.

The Musical Entertainer by the Bickhams, father and son, is actually a set of attractively illustrated song sheets. *The Charms of Dishabille* sings the praises of new Tunbridge Wells at Islington, another small and now forgotten pleasure garden, as a place for the informal enjoyment of life.

Engraved by John Raphael Smith, after John Sanders, *Bagnigge Wells*, 1783 (British Museum, Prints and Drawings, BM Satires 5090. 2010,7081.3808).

ABOVE
The Road to Ruin, plate from *A Sunday Ramble*, London, 1776 (578.i.10).

The Charms of Dishabille or New Tunbridge Wells at Islington, plate from George Bickham Sr. and George Bickham Jr., *The Musical Entertainer*, 2nd edition, London, 1740, vol. 1 (K.10.b.12).

The World in Masquerade

Masquerades were a very popular form of entertainment throughout the eighteenth century and beyond. They united the pleasures of the assembly to glamorous fancy dress with the added *frisson* of disguise, for participants could be cloaked and masked. Ranelagh, adjacent to the Royal Hospital Chelsea, first opened in 1742. It was more fashionable, expensive and exclusive than Vauxhall, although its popularity was such that it drew visitors from quite a wide social range. It has been credited with introducing the masquerade to the middle classes.

Hand-coloured prints of Ranelagh show the range of masquerade costumes. Figures from the *commedia dell'arte* (with Harlequin and Punch prominent among them) and the East (especially Turks and Chinese) were popular, alongside pastoral, historical and even religious characters. *A collection of the dresses of different nations*, intended to illustrate a variety of attire throughout the world, was a good source for masquerade costumes. The Hussar and the Shepherdess, besides being important characters in dramas on the London stage, were favourites with masqueraders.

A rare surviving masquerade mask shows one method of disguise, with the face obscured not only by a half-mask, but also by a silk veil. This would have been worn with a black domino, an all-enveloping cloak in light silk. The greatest fun of the masquerade was the moment of unmasking, which took place late in the evening. The dramatic possibilities of the masquerade were exploited by novelists as well as playwrights. Fanny Burney devotes an entire chapter of *Cecilia* to a masquerade, in which her heroine encounters a Devil and a Don Quixote before being rescued by an unknown gentleman in a white domino.

Ranelagh Gardens showing Masqueraders, from a collection of prints and printed matter concerning Ranelagh House and gardens, 1740–1805 (L.R.282.b.7).

THE ONLY

MASQUERADE

AT

RANELAGH

THIS SEASON.

BY PARTICULAR DESIRE

This prefent THURSDAY, April 11,

WILL BE

A Grand Mafquerade.

The Doors to be opened at Ten o'Clock.

And an Elegant Supper ferved at One,

WITH

Champagne, Burgundy, Claret, &c.

Tickets at TWO GUINEAS each, to be had at Meff. Longman and Broderip's Mufic Shops; Mrs. Richman's Mafquerade Warehoufe, Oxford-ftreet; and at Ranelagh-Houfe.

The Managers refpectfully inform the Nobility and Gentry, that the Rotunda is rendered as Warm as any Place of Public Entertainment.

The GARDENS and ROTUNDA will be Opened for the Seafon, on MONDAY next, April 15, 1793.

Tickets for Private Coach Stands for the Seafon, may be had at Ranelagh Houfe.

Mafquerade Dreffes to be had this Evening at Ranelagh Houfe.

ABOVE
[Jeffreys], *A collection of the dresses of different nations*, 4 vols, London, 1757–72. Vol. 2, Habit of Tancred in *Tancred and Sigsmunda* (Hussar costume), Perdita in *The Winter's Tale* (shepherdess costume) (144.f.11,12).

LEFT
Handbill advertising a masquerade for 11 April 1793 (937.c.11).

RIGHT
Masquerade mask, 1770–1800. Silk and tarletan (Museum of London 70-592).

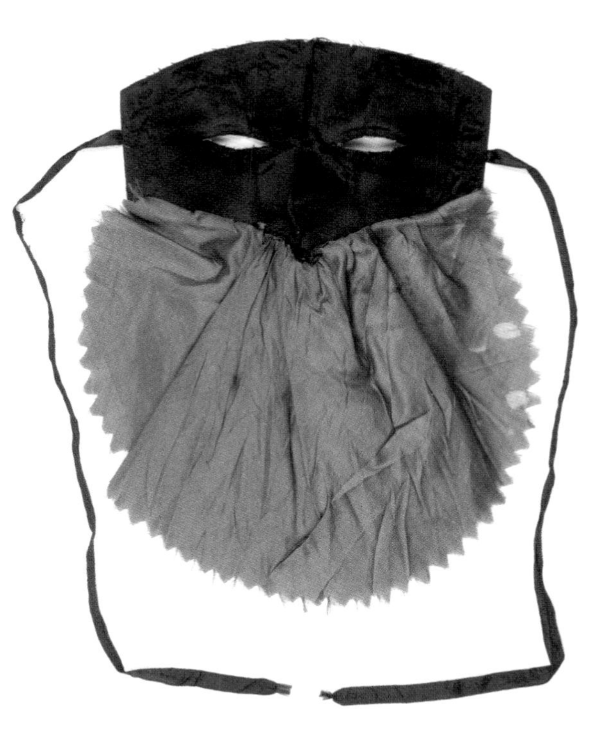

Culture in the Coffee House

If the tea table was a female domain, the coffee house belonged to men. The comforts, and the disorder, which such male-dominated places offered are nicely illustrated by the frontispiece to the fourth part of Edward Ward's satire *Vulgus Britannicus* of 1710. In the foreground some customers have got into a fight, probably over politics, while behind them others are quietly smoking and the barmaid looks on calmly.

Coffee and coffee houses had been introduced to Britain in the mid-seventeenth century. By the Georgian period they were well-established in London and elsewhere as places to take refreshments, talk, smoke and read the newspapers. One of the most famous coffee houses was King's in Covent Garden, with the redoubtable Moll King (1696–1747) as proprietor. She was the widow of Tom King (1694–1739), for whom the coffee house was named. King's Coffee House was fashionable but disreputable; it attracted theatre-goers after the show and those seeking early morning refreshment following all-night entertainment. Moll offered a range of services beyond the beverages of coffee, tea and chocolate. She was depicted in an anonymous engraved portrait around 1740, and became the subject of a colourful biography soon after her death in 1747.

Coffee houses in early nineteenth-century London offered much the same, and were not places where respectable women could or should be seen. The Cruikshanks's illustrations to *Life in London* by Pierce Egan (1772–1849) include the *Coffee Shop near the Olympic*. The patrons depicted are an unruly crowd; they include some performers still in costume, presumably from the Olympic Theatre just off Drury Lane. Egan's fashionably dressed heroes Tom and Jerry survey the scene from the centre, while around them, apart from the eating and drinking, an amorous encounter takes place and a fight is about to start. There are women as well as men in this coffee house, but it has the same mixture of calm and violence as in 1710.

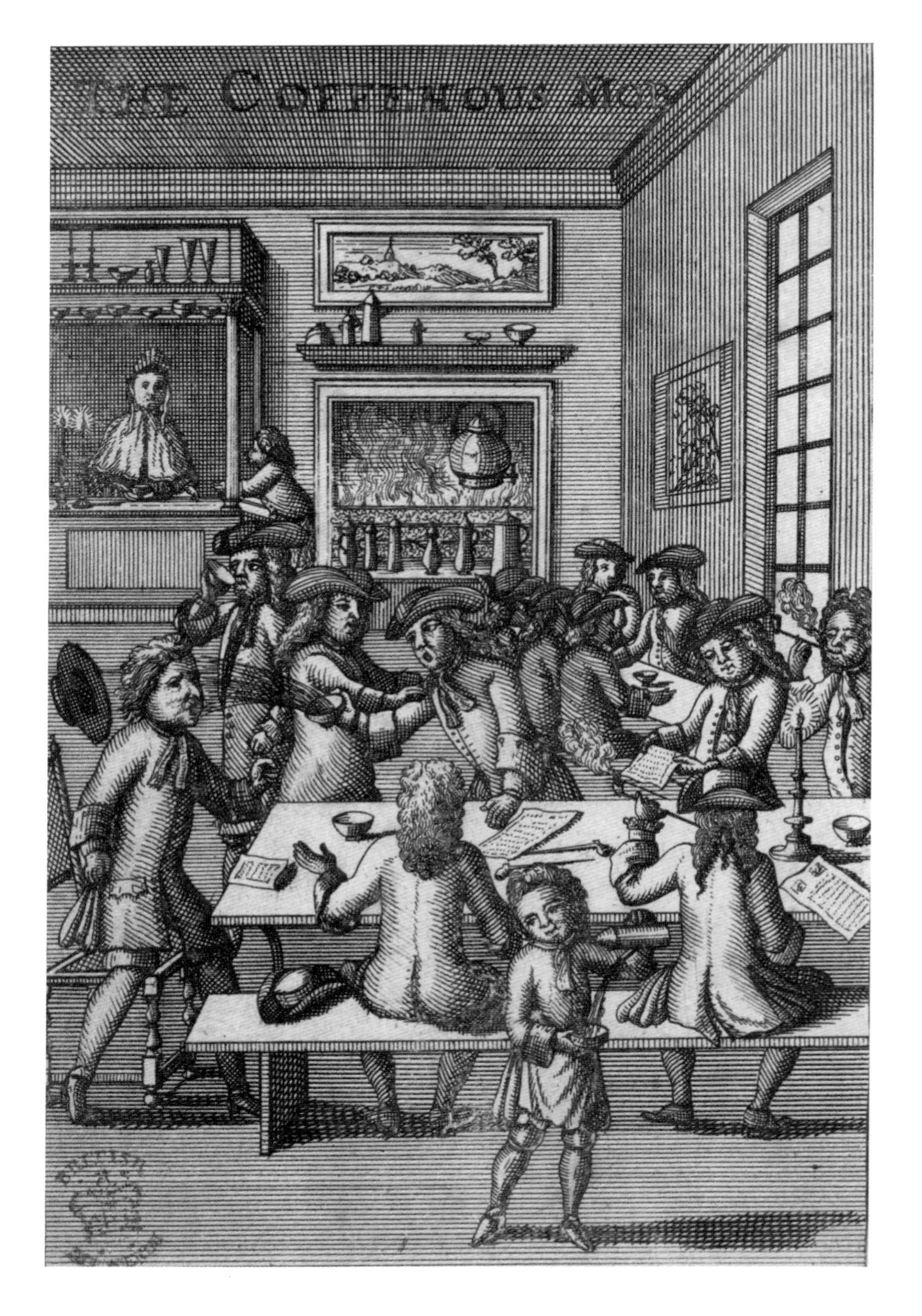

LEFT
Edward Ward, *The Fourth Part of Vulgus Britannicus: or, the British Hudibras*, London, 1710. Frontispiece (illustration from 578.i.10. An extra-illustrated copy of *A Sunday Ramble*, London, [1776?]).

Engraving of Moll King, *c.* 1740 (British Museum, Prints and Drawings, Heal, Portraits.212).

Coffee Shop near the Olympic, plate from Pierce Egan, *Life in London* (838.i.2).

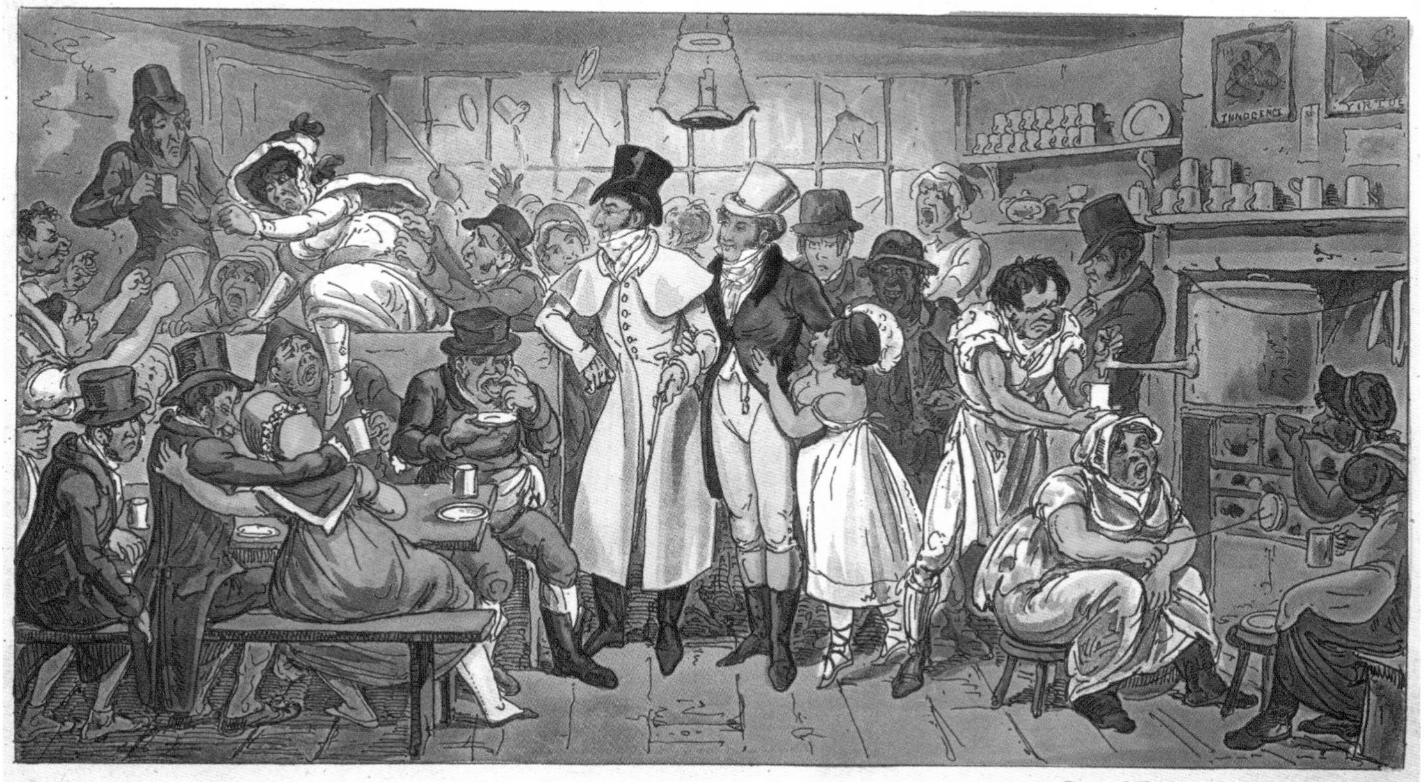

Writing the Rules

The eighteenth century saw the largely unregulated pastimes of previous eras turned into organised and increasingly professional sports. Part of this process involved the drawing-up and agreeing of rules, and the forming of authorities who could maintain and develop these rules. These changes can be seen as part of the process of developing a more stable and less unruly civil society in Britain, and many rules were introduced to ensure safer play and to reduce the risk of injury. More often than not, however, the immediate push for standardisation and codification in public sports came from the apparently limitless enthusiasm of the era for betting and gambling: the clearer the rules, the easier it is to lay bets, and there is less scope for argument both on and off the field of play.

Cricket appealed to a wide spectrum of society, and rules for the game date back to 1727. More detailed sets of rules were published from 1744, often on behalf of the Star and Garter Club, a forerunner of the Marylebone Cricket Club (or MCC), which has played the predominant role in establishing and interpreting the laws of cricket ever since. Professional cricket became a business: money was to be made from betting, and from providing food and drink for the spectators. Many leading politicians (and thus legislators) played major roles in the process, and cricket was commonly used by politicians as a way of entertaining their supporters and organising confrontation with their opponents. Ad hoc matches also satisfied the desire of gamblers to have an excuse to place bets.

Rules were drawn up for many other sports at this time, although football had to wait until the mid-nineteenth century. Yet even such small-scale games as skittles could benefit from agreed rules to save arguments between players and establish clear methods for scoring, which in turn encouraged gambling on the results.

ABOVE
New articles of the game of cricket, Maidstone, [1780?]. Frontispiece (C.106.cc.6).

BELOW
Thomas Rowlandson, *Rural Sports, or a Cricket Match Extraordinary*, 1811 (Britsh Museum, 1935,0522.10.226).

RIGHT
Rules and instructions for playing at skittles, [London,] 1786 (C.161.f.3.(40)).

A View of a SKITTLE GROUND.

Plan of a double Skittle Ground half an Inch to a Yard.

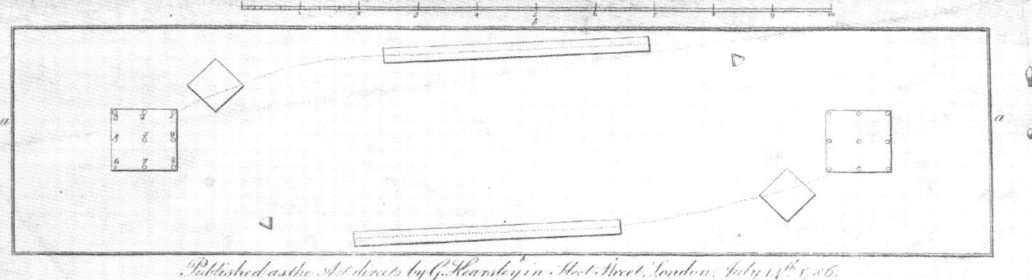

Published as the Act directs by G. Kearsley in Fleet Street, London, July 14th 1786.

RULES and INSTRUCTIONS for PLAYING at SKITTLES.

By a SOCIETY of GENTLEMEN.

As the GAME *of* SKITTLES *is now a favourite Amuſement, a general Guide to remove Doubts, and prevent Diſputes, is become neceſſary. Stimulated by theſe conſiderations, a reſpectable Society of Gentlemen (who are eſteemed good Players) have been induced to print the following Rules and Inſtructions, which they have themſelves often lamented the want of; hoping they will be found generally uſeful, but particularly to Learners.*

RULES.

I. THE Bowler muſt ſtand at the mark with one foot, and from thence deliver his Bowl fairly out of his hand; which Bowl muſt run upon the Board, fixed for that purpoſe, before it arrives at the Frame.

II. If the Bowler ſhould throw the Bowl in ſuch manner as to cauſe it to run double (as it is commonly called), and any one of the oppoſite party call out, A foul Bowl; if it has not reached the Pins, the Party muſt bowl again: but if it arrives at the Frame before the oppoſite Party called out Foul, whatever number are bowled down are fair.

III. If the Bowler does not cauſe his Bowl to run along the Board, (or touch it in ſome part), he loſes the benefit of Bowling.

IV. If a Bowl runs clearly through the Frame and knocks down any number of Pins, the Bowl being impeded in its return back again by one of the oppoſite Party, one additional Pin muſt be allowed the perſon who bowled.

V. If the Bowl paſſes through the Frame, and in its return back again ſtrikes a ſtanding Pin, and immediately after a rolling or live Pin (as it is called) runs againſt the falling Pin, it ſhall be deemed fair, becauſe it hit the Pin laſt.

VI. If a live Pin roll againſt a ſtanding Pin, and the Bowl comes on its return againſt the falling Pin, before it is down, it is deemed an unfair Pin, becauſe the Bowl ſtruck it laſt.

It has been thought neceſſary to allow the two preceding articles in the manner here given, as more diſputes have ariſen from theſe circumſtances than from any others; but, by obſerving whether the live Pin or the Bowl hits the falling Pin laſt, they may be hereafter avoided.

VII. If the Bowl runs through the Frame, and knocks at the Head-board, although it may have bowled down many Pins, none are allowed fair.

VIII. If the Bowl runs through, or on the outſide of the Frame, and knocks, and then runs round the other ſide of the Frame, without croſſing any part thereof, or touching any of the live Pins, the Bowler muſt ſtand to take his Tip with one foot upon the ſpot where the Bowl ſtopped. And in Tipping from ſuch place, he muſt take care not to ſtrike the ground with the Bowl before it hit the Pins; if it does, he loſes all the Pins he may have ſtruck down.

IX. If in Tipping the Bowl is caught or ſtopped by one of the oppoſite Party, and in ſo doing he ſtops or impedes a live Pin, he loſes a Pin; becauſe he prevented the Tipper from receiving the benefit which might ariſe from a live or rolling Pin.

X. If an oppoſite Partner takes up the Bowl in order to prevent its running amongſt the Pins, and lets it ſlip out of his hand, if it hits any of the Pins, he loſes one for ſo doing.

XI. If a perſon in Tipping gives a ſweep round with his hand, and brings down the ninth or any other Pin, by means of his hand or coat ſleeve, it is deemed unfair; and he muſt loſe one Pin.—The Bowl is to be clearly and fairly delivered from the hand, both in Bowling and Tipping.

XII. Care ſhould be taken in Tipping not to jump into the Frame immediately after, as in this caſe he is not allowed any of the Pins he Tips.

XIII. If you Bowl and Tip, for a limited number, at the cloſe of the Game, and throw down more than you want, you muſt go for Nine.

N. B. In the Ground where theſe Rules are obſerved, a diſintereſted perſon is generally appointed to Score the Game, and in diſputes, (if the caſe differs from any of thoſe herein ſtated, which is hardly poſſible) his deciſion is, or ſhould be, final.

INSTRUCTIONS.

BOWLING.

THE Art of Bowling well muſt be acquired in a great meaſure through practice, yet a little inſtruction will ſoon be found very uſeful, and a proper attention will enable a Learner to become a good Player.

Let the Player hold the Bowl in his Right Hand, with the bias-ſide from him, with his Left Foot advanced before his Right, which muſt be at the mark, his body bending towards the Frame, but in an eaſy poſition: then, with an equal motion, he muſt throw the Bowl along the Board, at the ſame time with ſufficient ſtrength to reach the Frame; the Left Hand ſide of the firſt Pin he ſhould endeavour to hit with the Bowl, which if he can accompliſh, he will be pretty certain of bringing Four or Five every time the Firſt Pin is hit in that manner.

He muſt take care not to aim at the Firſt Pin in a ſtreight direction, but cauſe the Bowl to form a curved line; by which it will loſe ſomething of its force, and ſtrike the Pins with much more certainty of ſucceſs.

TIPPING.

When the Learner is going to Tip, he ſhould hold the ſmaller circumference or oppoſite ſide of the bias in the palm of his hand, graſping it very ſtrong with his fingers; as few can be Tipped when the Bowl is looſely held; he muſt place his Left foot, quite clear of the Frame, between the Firſt and Ninth Pin; and his Right Foot behind him, in an eaſy poſition, and in ſuch direction that he may with eaſe hit his Pins in the manner following.

He muſt ſtrike his Firſt or Second Pins in the middle or largeſt part, and with the ſame motion and inſtant of time deliver his Bowl at the Fourth or Bowl-Pin. Striking them in this manner generally has the following effect.—If you hit the Firſt Pin not quite full, it forces it againſt the middle or Fifth Pin, from thence to the Seventh, and will frequently rebound to the Eight without any roll.

The Second Pin, if ſtruck well, will knock down the Third; and the Fourth, or Bowl-Pin, will ſtrike the Sixth; and, if the Pins are good, the Ninth is often brought down by ſome of the rolling ones.

When the Learner is to Tip for Four upon Game, he ſhould chuſe the Pins No. 8, 7, 6, and 4; placing his Left Foot by the ſide of the Frame, with his toe nearly in a line with the bottom of the Seventh Pin, and Right Foot behind him; he muſt ſtrike the three Side Pins at one motion, at the ſame time throwing the bowl at the Pin No. 4.

To Tip for Five, let him place his Left Foot a little to the left of the Pin No. 9, and his other foot behind. He muſt ſtrike the Ninth Pin to hit the Seventh, the Fifth to hit the Fourth, and the Bowl muſt knock down the Sixth.

When Six only are wanted, which are generally thought the moſt difficult, place the Left Foot in a line with the oppoſite angle of the Frame, and the other Foot behind at a good diſtance; he muſt ſtrike the Eighth Pin full in the middle, which will hit the Seventh and Sixth, and with the ſame motion he ſhould hit the Middle Pin againſt the Third, and the Bowl ſhould hit the Fourth; by which means he will lay the Six fairly down, and, if not ſtruck hard, without the danger of their rolling, eſpecially if they are tipped down hill; to which he muſt make the Sixth his firſt Pin.

☞ For the benefit of the Learner the Skittles are all numbered in the above Plan.

DIMENSIONS of a DOUBLE COVERED GROUND, by which, and the above PLAN, either a SINGLE or DOUBLE GROUND may be FORMED.

a a The whole length of the incloſed Ground 17 yards and an half. *b b* Breadth of the Ground, from ſide to ſide, 4 yards. The Dots ſhew the curved Line which the Bowl ſhould form. The juſt proportion of a Skittle is 15 inches round in the largeſt part, and 12 inches high.——The Bowl ſhould be 18 inches in circumference; each angle of the Frame for the Pins 3 feet 4 inches.—The proportions and diſtances of every part, as well as thoſe already deſcribed, may be aſcertained by the Scale.

PRINTED for G. KEARSLEY, at No. 46, in FLEET-STREET, 1786.——PRICE 6d. PLAIN, or 1s. COLOURED.——*Entered at Stationers-Hall.*

A Day at the Races

While cricket was at this time as much played as watched, horseracing was much more of a spectator entertainment. Increasingly elaborate stands were erected to provide better views of the racing, and illustrated race lists served to advertise these facilities at the courses; visitors knew they could expect a good day out. The sport provided ample scope for betting and gambling, which, of course, have always been thought to depend on sound information as much as chance. Attention thus became increasingly focused on the recording of races and their results, and on controlling the market in thoroughbred horses.

By far the most successful auctioneer of horses has been Tattersalls. Currently based in Newmarket (and still selling 10,000 horses a year), they were established in 1766 at Hyde Park Corner. For a while Tattersalls accommodated the Jockey Club, one of the governing bodies of racing at the time. Successful race winners became celebrities, often more so than the jockeys on their backs. Few horses were more celebrated than Eclipse who, after winning his first race as a five-year-old in 1769, went on to win seventeen more over the next two years. With people increasingly reluctant to bet against him, Eclipse was retired to stud in 1771; he is the ancestor of nearly every thoroughbred horse racing today. His anatomy was studied carefully at his death, and most of his skeleton is still preserved at the Royal Veterinary College – the first principal of which, Charles Vial de Saint-Bel, published this appreciation of Eclipse in 1797.

PLAYS
At the THEATRE in St. MARY's GATE,
Every Evening as soon as the Race is over.

ASSEMBLIES
On Tuesday and Wednesday Evenings,
At the Ladies Room, on the Low Pavement.

PRICE ONE PENNY EACH. | BURBAGE and SON's LIST | Mr. WISE's CONCERT will be on Thursday Evening.

— OF —

NOTTINGHAM RACES, 1781.

Tickets for the Stand, admitting one Gentleman or Lady during the Race Week, at One Guinea each; and Tickets for the Assembly at Five Shillings each Night, may be had at Mr. EDWARD MERREY's, Surgeon and Apothecary, near the Hen-Cross, or at Mr. W. MERREY's, next door to the Falcon, Castle-gate.
*** SILVER TICKETS to be admitted as usual.

Tuesday, *August 7th.*

His MAJESTY's PURSE of ONE HUNDRED GUINEAS for six year olds, carrying 12st. one four mile heat.

1 Mr. Fall's ch. h. Pirate, Rider, James Baker, Pink and bl. Cap — 5
2 Mr. Pratt's b. h. Somebody, Rider, John Cade, Pink and bl. Cap — 2
3 Mr. Madon's br. h. Rodney, Rider, Miles Thistlewaite, Blue — 4
4 Mr. Hutchinson's b. m. Abigail, Rider, L. Jewison, Pea Green — 3
5 Mr. Freeman's ch. h, Stand by, Rider, John Holliday, Yellow — 1
6 Mr. Ellison's b. h. Parasite, Rider, John Shaw, Crimson — dr

SAME DAY, the first year of the renewed DEVONSHIRE STAKES for 20gs. each, for horses, &c of all ages, that never won before starting for the above Stakes; four year olds, 11st. 5lb five year olds, 11st. 12lb. six year olds and aged, 12st. twice round the Course. The horses to be bona fide the property of Subscribers at the time of naming, and to be named on or before the last day of the first Spring Meeting, each year, to Mr Weatherby, Newmarket; at his office, London; or to Mr. Shore, Nottingham. This to continue for three years.

1 Lord Rockingham's br. b. h. Sextus Pompeius, aged — 2
2 Lord Grosvenor's ch. h. Knavestock, aged — 1
3 D. of Rutland's br. h. by Evergreen, bought of Mr. Cross, 4 years old — dr
4 Lord G. H. Cavendish's b. h. by Surly, aged — dr

Duke of Portland, Duke of Devonshire, Lord Ed. Bentinck, Lord Lincoln, and Lord Richard Cavendish, are Subscribers, but did not name.

SAME DAY, the COUNTY MEMBERS' PLATE of 50l. (free of all deduction) for three year olds; colts, 7st. 13lb. fillies, 7st. 11lb. the last mile and half. To pay 5gs. entrance, which will go to the winner.

1 Lord Edw. Bentinck's br. m. Fairy, Rider, John White, Pompador and Orange — 5
2 Mr. Maurice's b. c. Rider, John Price, Purple and bl. c. — 3
3 Mr. Douglas's gr. f. Grantham, Rider, Anthony Hall, Black and White — 2
4 Mr. Bethell's b. c. Cupid, Rider, John Cade, Pink and bl. c. — 1
5 Mr. Eyres's bl. f. Rider, Wm. Swainston, Bl. Waistcoat, and wh. c. — 4

Same Day A Produce SWEEPSTAKES of One Hundred Guineas each h. ft. by colts and fillies, got by untried stallions, colts 8st. 3lb. fillies, 8st. once round the course. Any of the mares not producing, or the produce not living three weeks, the owner of such to be off without forfeit.

1 Lord Grosvenor's Rarity, covered by Sweetbriar — p. f.
2 Lord E. Bentinck's Squirrel mare, covered by Pyrrhus — p. f.
3 Sir H. Harpur's Bajazet Mare, covered by Juniper — 1

Mr. Scawen is a Subscriber but did not name.

SAME DAY, a MATCH for TWO HUNDRED GUINEAS, h. f.—One four Mile heat, between
1 Lord G. H. Cavendish's gr. m. Reputation, by Pangloss, 5 yrs. old, 8st. 2lb. — 2
2 Lord Rockingham's b. c. by Tantarum, out of Floss, 5 yrs. old, 8st. 5lb. — 1

Wednesday, *August 8th.*

The fourth year of a SUBSCRIPTION of TEN GUINEAS each, to which will be added SEVENTY GUINEAS, for 4 year olds, 7st. 7lb. five year olds, 8st. 7lb. six year olds, 9st. 2lb. and aged, 9st. 8lb. twice round the course. The horses, &c. to be bona fide the property of Subscribers at the time of starting.—N. B. By the unanimous agreement of all the Subscribers, no horse, the property of a Non-subscriber will be entitled to start.

1 Marquis of Rockingham's b. h. Copperbottom, Rider, Chris. Scafe, Green — 3
2 Lord Grosvenor's b. h. Whipcord, 5 yrs old, Rider, John Pratt, Orange — 2
3 Mr. Douglas's b. m. Tetotum, 4 yrs old, Rider, Ant. Hall, Black and White — 4
4 Mr. Walsh's br. m. 4 yrs old, by Turk, Rider, John Mangle, Purple — 5
5 Sir L. Dundas's ch. h. 4 yrs old, Rider unknown — 1
6 Sir Henry Harpur's br. h. Rider, John Shaw, Blue — dr

Wednesday *Continued.*

SAME DAY, the second year of the renewed NOTTINGHAM SWEEPSTAKES of 25gs. each, for 4 yr olds; colts, 8st. 7lb. fillies 8st. 4lb. twice round the course. Made for three years, and to name on or before Christmas-day preceding the races, to Mr. Shore, Nottingham; or to Mr. Weatherby.

1 Sir F. Molyneux's ch. c. Diomed, by Florizel — 2
2 Lord Edw. Bentinck's br. c, by Match'em, out of Mr. Bethell's Laura — dr
3 Lord Grosvenor's b. c. by Herod, out of the Dam of Royal — 1
4 Mr. Sulsh's ch. f. by Sweetbriar, dam by Squirrel, out of Goldfinder's dam — dr
5 Mr. Swinfen's b. c, King William, by Herod, out of Madcap — dr
6 Lord Clermont's br. c. Occulator, by Conductor — dr
7 Mr. Vernon's c. Bay Bolton, by Match'em — 3
8 Mr. Wentworth's b. c. Prince William, by Dainty Davy — dr
9 Mr. Stapleton's ch. c. Antagonist, by Herod — dr
10 Lord J. Clinton's gr. c. by Juniper — dr
11 Sir H. Harpur's ch. c. by Juniper, dam by Cade — dr
12 Mr. Bertie's b. c. Urtica, by Marsk, dam bo the Saanah Arabian — dr
13 Mr. Tempest's gr. f. Gunilda, by Star, out of the dam of Hollandise — dr
14 Mr. Dashwood's b. c. by Goldfinder — 4
15 Mr. Bethell's b. c. Ruler, by Young Marsk — dr
16 Mr. Hebden's b. c. by Mr Joliff's Foxhunter, dam by Northumberland — dr

D. of Portland, Ld Rockingham, Mr. Musters, Lord G. H. Cavendish, Sir J. Lade, Sir L. Dundass, Mr. Eyre, D. of Devonshire, and Ld Craven did not name.

SAME DAY, FIFTY POUNDS for four year olds, colts, 8st. 7lb. fillies, 8st. 4lb. two mile heats.

1 Mr. Tempest's gr. f. Gunilda, Rider, Rob. Collins, — 1 | 2 | 2 | 3
2 Mr. Douglass's br. h. Catch, Rider, Anthony Hall, — 2 | 1 | 3 | 2
3 Sir H. Harpur's br. h. by Juniper, Rider John Shaw, — 3 | 3 | 1 | 1

Thursday, *August 9th.*

FIFTY POUNDS, for five, six years old, and aged horses, &c. five year olds 8st. 7lb. six year olds 9st and aged 9st. 5lb. A winner of a six year old King's Plate to carry 10st. four mile heats.

1 Mr. Ellison's bay h. Parasite, Rider John Shaw, Crimson — 4 | 3 | 4
2 Mr. Hutchinson's bay m. Abigail, Rider L. Jewison, Pea Green — 1 | 2 | 2
3 Lord Grosvenor's ch. h. Knavestock, aged, Orange — 3 | 4 | 3
4 Mr. Pratt's b. h. Somebody, Rider John Cade, Pink and bl. Cap — 2 | 1 | 1
5 Mr. Fall's ch. h. Pirate, Rider James Baker, Pink and bl. Cap — 5 | dr.

Orders for the Nottingham Meeting, 1781.

ALL the Horses, &c. that enter for the Plates, to stand at the house of a Subscriber of 10s. 6d. at least, and to be plated by a subscribing Smith.—To run according to the King's Plate Articles, and all disputes to be determined by the Stewards, or whom they shall appoint.—The Winner of each Match, Sweepstakes or Plate, (except that given by the Members for the County) to pay One Guinea and Half to the Judge, Mr. Shore; and each Horse, &c. Two Guineas Entrance or double at the Post.

No Persons either on Foot or on Horseback are to come on the Running Ground at any Time during the Race; and positively none, under any Pretence, are to be within the Rails.

And all Dogs seen on the Race Ground, to be driven off or destroyed.

The HORSES are to begin to start each Day exactly at Four o'Clock—Twenty Minutes to be allowed between each Sweepstake or Match, and Half an Hour between the Heats for the Plates—All the Plates, except the King's, to be run for the last on each Day.—Every Match, Sweepstakes, &c. to be run in the exact Order of this printed List.

Sir F. MOLYNEUX, Bart. / ROBERT SMITH, Esq; } Stewards,
Mr. SHORE, Judge, and
Mr. PACEY, Clerk of the Course.

A Main of Cocks will be fought at the White Lion during the Meeting, between the Gentlemen of Nottinghamshire and Derbyshire; to shew 51 Mains on each Side, to fight for 10 Guineas a Battle, and 200 the Main.

FEEDERS } DAVID SMITH, Nottinghamshire. / JOHN BESTALL, Derbyshire.

Mr. PACEY will provide a genteel ORDINARY, in the Great Room, at the White Lion Inn, on Tuesday and Thursday in the Race Week; and Mr. PREST's ORDINARY, will be at Thurland-Hall, on Wednesday and Thursday.—Likewise, Ordinaries at all the other principal Inns every Day of the Meeting.

Nottingham race list, 1781
(C.194.c.28).

The Oatlands Sweepstakes at Ascot, June 1791. Aquatint by J. W. Edy after a painting by J. N. Sartorius, 1792 (K.Top.7.52.).

Eclipse, plate from Charles Vial de Saint-Bel, *Elements of the Veterinary Art*, London, 1797 (1601/246 (1)).

Traditional 'Sports' Die Hard

The attempts to control games and sports to improve safety also saw campaigns against bloodsports seen as unnecessarily cruel. A popular pastime at fairs up and down the country, especially at Shrovetide, was cock-throwing, in which a cock would be tied down and spectators encouraged to throw sticks or stones at it until it died. The caster of the fatal throw was awarded the dead bird. Money could be made from the 'sport' by hiring out missiles and betting on the outcome.

Despite its being preached against since the 1760s at least, the longevity of cock-throwing is shown by its use in a print of 1829 to satirise the Prime Minister, the Duke of Wellington. He is depicted as the cock being subjected to the battering of his enemies in the Press and the House of Lords (the Duke of Cumberland and Lord Eldon can be seen in the foreground). Wellington was being vilified at the time for having successfully carried through legislation to free Roman Catholics from many of the restrictions that had been in place on their lives.

Shrove Tuesday all the year round – a cock wot everyone throws at, 1829 (British Museum, 1868,0808.9055).

The Royal Cock Pit, from R. Achermann, *The Microcosm of London*, London [1808–10] (190.e.1).

Boxing lessons, from Pierce Egan, *Life in London*, London, 1823 (838.i.2).

A Record of the Roads

John Ogilby (1600–1676) had a rather varied career, being successively a dancing master, courtier, theatre owner, publisher and geographer. He was responsible for a number of well-produced publications, but he is today best remembered for his *Britannia: or, The Kingdom of England and dominion of Wales, actually survey'd*. It was published in London for the first time in 1698, in a large folio with 100 plates. In this work Ogilby drew out the miles of road on strip maps – long, narrow maps showing the course of each road – and made allowances for extra miles in his measurements when roads ascended hills. The standardisation of the mile at 1,760 yards was partly due to Ogilby's work, and his technique of measuring and drawing the roads was repeatedly imitated in the eighteenth century.

Ogilby's publication was printed again in 1719 under the title *An actual survey of all the principal roads of England and Wales*. This time it took the form of an oblong quarto, a much smaller book that was wider than it was tall and was to be read in landscape format. In 1720 it was again published, this time as *Britannia Depicta or Ogilby improv'd*, in a pocket-sized quarto format. In this smaller size the book could be of practical use to travellers, accompanying and guiding them from one place to another. Each journey described in the 1720 edition has a short summary at the top, then a map of the relevant county or counties below. This is followed by a depiction of the roads as well as a step-by-step description of the route from A to B.

John Ogilby, *Britannia Depicta or Ogilby improv'd*, London, 1720 (RB.23.a.22274).

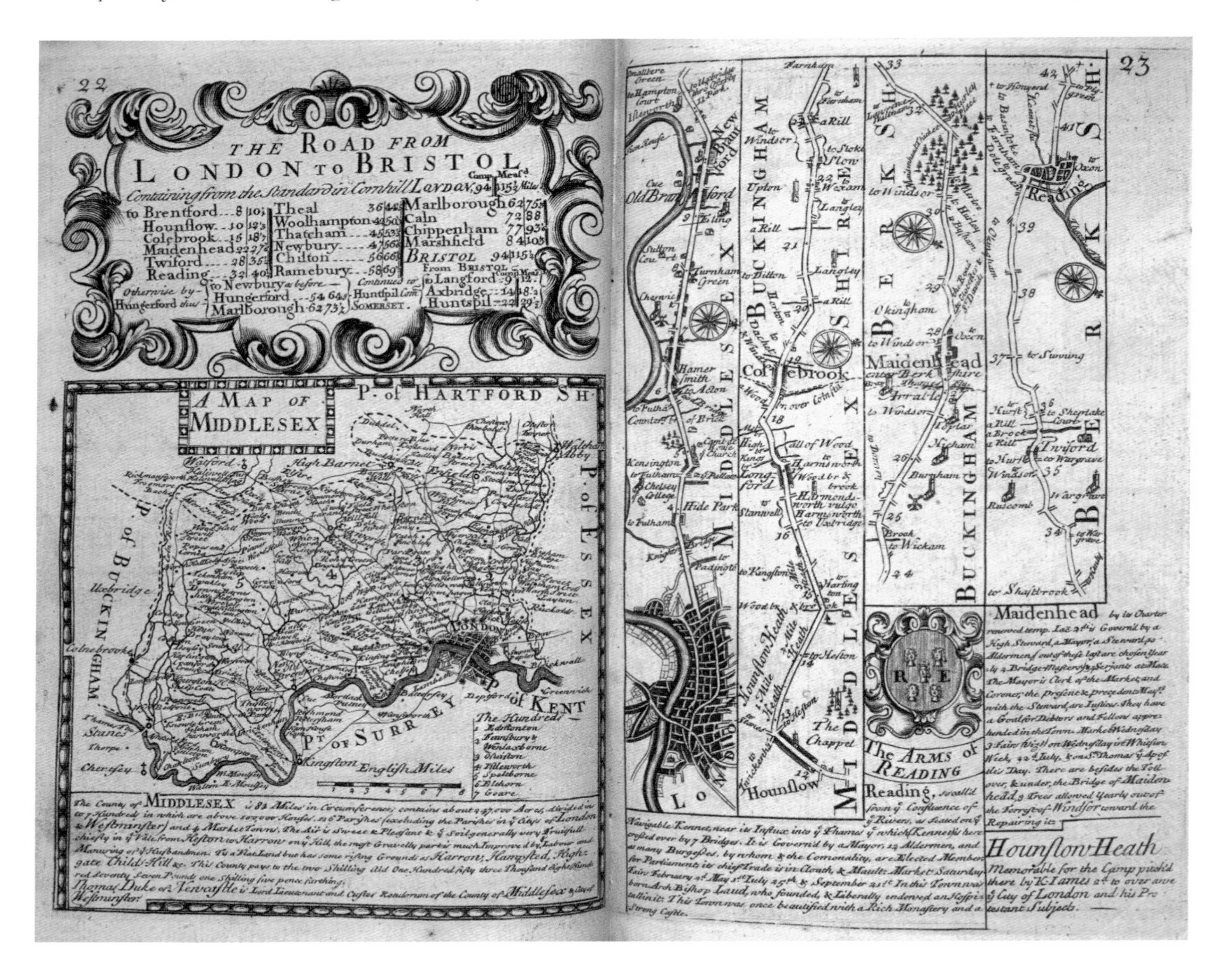

Before the pocket-sized version of Ogilby's *Britannia* was printed in 1720, its printers advertised the forthcoming work. As was common at the time, people who wished to purchase the book could subscribe to it and thereby co-finance its production. This advertisement incorporates a border made up of elements of the forthcoming publication as well as other decorative features, such as surveyors at work at the top and cherubs at the bottom.

PROPOSALS,
For Printing by Subscription,
Britannia Depicta,
Or Ogilby improv'd, and Contracted into a neat Pocket Vollume:

Wherein (beside all the direct and principall cross Roads in England, and Wales, with the several By-ways and Turnings, the Cities, Towns, Churches, Rivers, Bridges, Computed and Statute-Miles, &c. in the said Ogilby's Survey Contain'd) are Added, and Curiously Engraven,

The Arms & a Description of all the said Cities & Burroughs, their present Goverm.t When & by whom Incorporated, the Privileges, & Immunities by their respective Charters Granted.
Likewise the Arms of the Peers of this Realm, with the Titles they Derive from Places Scituate upon these Roads.
Also the Arms of all the Bishopricks & Bishops, Deanry's & Deans, Extent of each Diocess & their Yearly Value, with the N.o of Parishes therein.
Together with the Arms of both Universities & their several Colledges, an Account when & by whom the same were Founded, N.o of Fellows in each &c.
And the Arms of the Honourable Members of Parliament Subscribers to this Work (if they'll be Pleas'd to send in an Account of the same to the Undertakers) shall be Engraven near the Cities, Burroughs, &c they Severally Represent.
To which is Added a curious Draught of the River Thames from its Spring in Gloucestersh. to Sheerness shewing the Turnings & Windings of the Same, with the Names of the Towns & Villages that lye on each Side.
An Entire & Accurate Map of England & Wales.
With Exact Plans of the Cities of London York, Oxford, Cambridge, Bristol, Norwich &c.

And to Render this Work Usefull to Gentlemen in Scotland & Ireland:
Here is Added a New & Correct Map of Scotland, with the Roads, Distance of Miles &c.
And four Correct Maps of the Provinces of Ireland Viz.t Ulster, Leinster, Connaught & Munster, Divided into its Counties & Baronies wherein are Distinguish'd, the Bishopricks, Barracks, Bogs, Passes, Bridges, &c. with the principal Roads, & common reputed Miles.
There will be also Inserted.
An Account of the time & place, when & where Coaches & Waggons Sett out, with the Price for Passengers; The Fares for Hackney Coach Men, & Water-Men, in the Cities of London & Westminster. What Markets & Fairs are kept at every City & Town, & on what Days of the Week & Year.
Together with many other additional Improvements never yet Publish'd, or Propos'd in any Work of this Nature, which will be no less Usefull & Necessary, than Entertaining. The whole being Illustrated with such Marginal Notes, as are Peculier to every Place, in their proper Order, as they Occur thro' the whole of these Roads.
N.B. This Book will Contain 150 Leaves, Engraven by the best Hands, which being Printed (tho' from Copper Plates) on both Sides, will Contain twice as much Matter, & in a narrower Compass, than any Printed on Alternate Pages (as is commonly Used from Copper Plates) and as M.r Ogilby's Survey of the Roads is.

The Gentlemen that Subscribe to Pay ½ : 6. down & ½ more on Delivery of the Book which being now in hand, & very forward, will be delivered, Compleatly finish'd, about Midsummer 1719, & Publick Notice given Sometime before by an Advertisement. Subscriptions taken in by T. Bowles in S.t Pauls Ch. Yard & H. Overton without Newgate & the Print Sellers of London & Westm.

Advertisement.

Whereas, since the Publishing M.r Ogilby's Survey, the Names of several Gentlemen's Seats on the Roads are alter'd, & others since that time built: Such Gentlemen are desired to transmit an Account thereof (with their Arms which shall likewise be inserted near their Seats) to the Undertaker Tho: Bowles, Print & Map Seller, near the Chapter House, in S.t Pauls Church Yard; where a Book of M.r Ogilby's is kept, to the end the said Seats & Arms may be Sett down in their proper Places, on or near the several Roads.
At which Place is to be had 25 New Maps of the World by H. Moll Geographer.

Proposals for printing by subscription, Britannia Depicta, or Ogilby improv'd, and contracted into a neat pocket volume, London, [*c.* 1718] (Maps 187.l.1.(24)).

The Pleasures and Perils of Travel by Stagecoach

Stagecoaches were horse-drawn carriages that ran daily and moved goods or passengers around the country. They came into use in London in the early seventeenth century. They were often former private coaches that were probably obsolete in design and were no longer in use. When business picked up and more people used them to travel around the country, the stagecoaches were usually especially designed and had baskets attached to the back for lower-class passengers or luggage.

Travelling in stagecoaches could prove an endurance test. A journey from London to Edinburgh in 1780 took fourteen days. The coaches could be cramped and smelly, and passengers were very much exposed to the elements such as flooding or snow, as well as to highwaymen and robbers. Passengers who could afford the fee would travel inside the coaches, leaving those who were poorer to travel on the outside.

The single sheet opposite looks very much like a modern timetable, and it provided very similar information to eighteenth-century travellers as our timetables do today. The list is subtitled 'Very useful for shopkeepers, tradesmen, and others; adorn'd with the arms of all the counties of England' and has a legend explaining the abbreviations used: 'Note, m. signifies Monday; t. Tuesday; w. Wednesday; th. Thursday; f. Friday; s. Saturday; C. coach; Wa. waggon or Carrier.' Arranged alphabetically, the list supplies basic information on when a stagecoach or waggon departed, and from which place in London it travelled to a specific place in the country.

For example, travellers wishing to go to Barkhamstead (modern Berkhamsted) could travel by coach from the Bell in Holborn on Tuesdays, Thursdays or Fridays; or by waggon from the Bell in Warwick Lane on Tuesdays or Fridays. Those wishing to travel to York had the option of travelling by stagecoach from the Swan at Holborn Bridge on Mondays, Wednesdays or Fridays. Alternatively, they could take a waggon from the Red Lion in Aldersgate Street on Mondays, the Bear in Basinghall Street on Fridays, the White Horse in Cripplegate on Fridays or the Swan with two Necks in Lad Lane on Mondays.

Thomas Rowlandson, *A Stagecoach*, *c.* 1787 (British Museum Prints and Drawings, 1852,0214.164).

Woodstock Wa. bull, holborn, *f.*
Wooton Underhedge Wa. king's head, old cha. *f.*
Woolwich Caravan, ſtar, fiſh-ſtreet-hill, *m. t. w. th. f.*
Worceſter C. blue boar, holborn, *t. f.* ſum. *m. th.* win. Wa. bell, woodſtreet, *f.* bull and mouth, alderſgate-ſtreet, *f.*
Wrexham Wa. caſtle & falcon, alderſ.-ſtreet, *m. th.*
Wymondham Wa. 4 ſwans, biſhopſgate-ſtr. *t. th. f.*
YArmouth C. bull, biſhopſgate-ſtreet, *th.* Wa. ditto, *w. th.* green dragon, ditto, *th.*
Yeatly Wa. king's arms, holborn-bridge, *f.*
Yeldham Wa. pewter pot, leadenhall-ſtreet, *th.*
Yeovil Wa. gerard's-hall, baſing-lane, *m.*
York C. ſwan, holborn-bridge, *m. w. f.* Wa. red lion, alderſgate-ſtreet, *m.* bear, baſinghall-ſtreet, *f.* white horſe, cripplegate, *f.* ſwan with two necks, lad-lane, *m.*

KENT | LANCASTER

RIGHT AND OPPOSITE
A Correct List of all the Stage-Coaches and Carriers, [London, 1750?] (1881.c.6.(93)).

A Correct LIST of all the Stage-Coaches and Carriers;

With the Places where they Inn and the Days they set out from *LONDON*:

Very Useful for *Shopkeepers, Tradesmen,* and *Others*: Adorn'd with the ARMS of all the Counties in *ENGLAND*.

Note, *m.* signifies *Monday*; *t. Tuesday*; *w. Wednesday*; *th. Thursday*; *f. Friday*; *s. Saturday*; C. Coach; Wa. Waggon or Carrier.

Private Carriages for Sale

This publication is a catalogue designed to assist wealthier members of society to find any kind of carriage or coach they might wish to acquire for a variety of different uses. Similar to pattern books for furniture or other kinds of goods, this catalogue was probably used by people who could afford to have their own means of transport made to order. The volume consists of illustrations only. There are no explanations, so it is to be assumed that the people consulting it knew what they were looking at, and what they wanted to order.

When this book was published in the middle of the eighteenth century, less wealthy members of society still travelled in stagecoaches. Richer people were increasingly able to afford their own means of transport, however, and the roads, although usually still in a very poor state of repair, became much busier.

The nobleman and gentleman's director and assistant, in the true choice of their wheel-carriages, London, 1763 (62.a.33).

A Coach Ahead of its Time

The surgeon and engineer Sir Goldsworthy Gurney (1793–1875) had become interested in engineering while still at school. He moved from Cornwall to London with his family in the early nineteenth century, becoming a lecturer in chemistry and natural philosophy at the Surrey Institution in London, which was devoted to scientific, literary and musical education and research. While in London he also experimented with steam power, finally resulting in the production of the steam carriage described in *Fairburn's account of the new steam carriage, invented by Mr. Gurney*. Gurney began by building a small model of his carriage; once he had established that his invention was going to work, he obtained a pattern in 1825 and began to build his steam carriages. As they promised to move much faster than horse-drawn ones, other people became interested in the idea and a number of carriages were taken into use.

However, the general public was not keen on Gurney's new invention. They began to put obstacles in the carriages' way, or to throw stones at them. When taxes for motor-powered vehicles were raised considerably, the men who had taken to running his carriages could not afford the taxes. Gurney was forced to repay the men and fell into debt himself. This did not deter him from inventing other things, however. When the new Parliament was built between 1840 and 1870, Gurney's advice was sought on the ventilation of the building. He was subsequently employed and given the title 'inspector of ventilation'.

Fairburn's account of the new steam carriage, invented by Mr. Gurney, London, [1827?] (C.194.b.312).

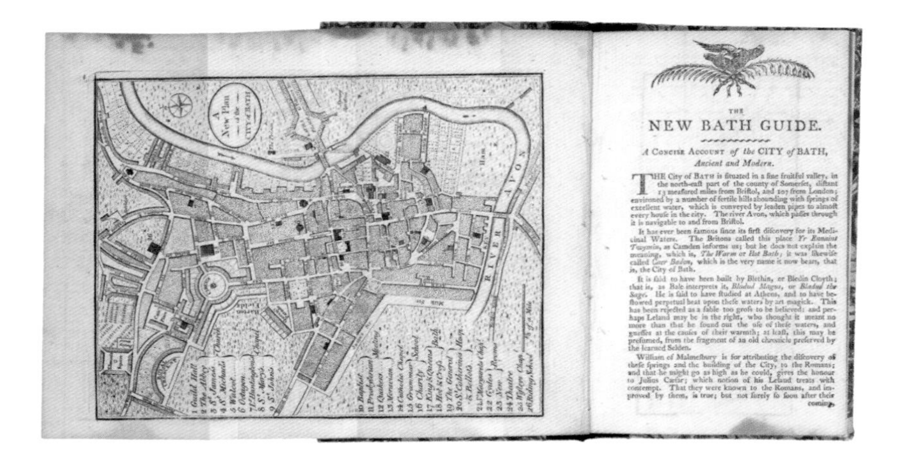
THE
NEW BATH GUIDE.

A CONCISE ACCOUNT *of the* CITY *of* BATH,
Ancient and Modern.

THE City of BATH is situated in a fine fruitful valley, in the north-east part of the county of Somerset, distant 13 measured miles from Bristol, and 107 from London; environed by a number of fertile hills abounding with springs of excellent water, which is conveyed by leaden pipes to almost every house in the city. The river Avon, which passes through it is navigable to and from Bristol.

It has ever been famous since its first discovery for its Medicinal Waters. The Britons called this place *Yr Ennaint Twymin*, as Camden informs us; but he does not explain the meaning, which is, *The Warm or Hot Bath*; it was likewise called *Caer Badon*, which is the very name it now bears, that is, the City of Bath.

It is said to have been built by Blethin, or Bledin Cloyth; that is, as Bale interprets it, *Bladud Magus*, or *Bladud the Sage*. He is said to have studied at Athens, and to have bestowed perpetual heat upon these waters by art magick. This has been rejected as a fable too gross to be believed: and perhaps Leland may be in the right, who thought it meant no more than that he found out the use of these waters, and guesses at the causes of their warmth; at least, this may be presumed, from the fragment of an old chronicle preserved by the learned Selden.

William of Malmesbury is for attributing the discovery of these springs and the building of the City, to the Romans; and that he might go as high as he could, gives the honour to Julius Cæsar; which notion of his Leland treats with contempt. That they were known to the Romans, and improved by them, is true; but not surely so soon after their

coming,

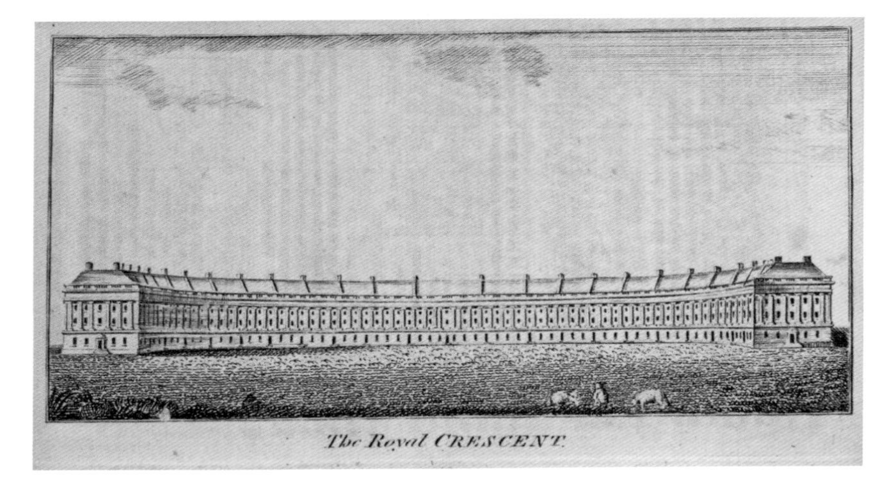

Spa Towns and Seaside Resorts

Travel to towns outside London became increasingly popular and affordable in the eighteenth century, with Bath and Margate probably the most popular destinations. Bath had begun to develop into a fashionable spa resort after Queen Anne had taken the waters there in the late seventeenth and early eighteenth centuries. The city's architecture continued to develop throughout the eighteenth century, and several key buildings – now the town's landmarks and a draw for tourists – were constructed at this time. The famous Circus was begun by John Wood the Elder (bap. 1704, d. 1754) in 1754, the year of his death. It was completed by his son, John Wood the Younger (bap. 1728, d. 1781), who also designed the Royal Crescent, built between 1767 and 1775. Another fine structure, Pulteney Bridge, was designed by Robert Adam (1728–1792) and built between 1770 and 1774.

The famous seaside resort of Margate owes part of its fame to the invention of the bathing machine by Benjamin Beale in 1753. This resembled a wooden hut on wheels, normally drawn by horses but occasionally also by humans. People entered the bathing machine in their street clothes on the beach, and it was then pulled into the sea, allowing bathers to change in privacy while inside the machine. Once it was in position in the water, the driver pulled down a canvas screen at the rear of the machine. This formed a little tent, under cover of which bathers could discreetly slip into

ABOVE
The New Bath Guide, Bath, 1797 (1607/4532).

RIGHT
The Margate Guide, [London], 1770 (11643.e.48.(2)).

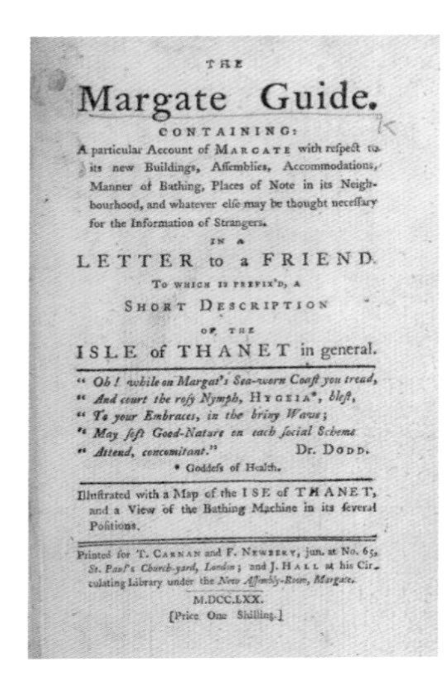
THE
Margate Guide.

CONTAINING:
A particular Account of MARGATE with respect to its new Buildings, Assemblies, Accommodations, Manner of Bathing, Places of Note in its Neighbourhood, and whatever else may be thought necessary for the Information of Strangers.

IN A
LETTER to a FRIEND.
TO WHICH IS PREFIX'D, A
SHORT DESCRIPTION
OF THE
ISLE of THANET in general.

" *Oh! while on Margat's Sea-worn Coast you tread,*
" *And court the rosy Nymph,* HYGEIA*, *blest,*
" *To your Embraces, in the briny Wave;*
" *May soft Good-Nature on each social Scheme*
" *Attend, concomitant.*" Dr. DODD.

* Goddess of Health.

Illustrated with a Map of the ISLE of THANET, and a View of the Bathing Machine in its several Positions.

Printed for T. CARNAN and F. NEWBERY, jun. at No. 65, *St. Paul's Church-yard, London*; and J. HALL at his Circulating Library under the *New Assembly-Room, Margate.*

M.DCC.LXX.
[Price One Shilling.]

the sea. The machines quickly found favour among the social elite. Another famous seaside town was Weymouth, which was first visited by George III in 1789 when he was recovering from porphyria; he had his own bathing machine there.

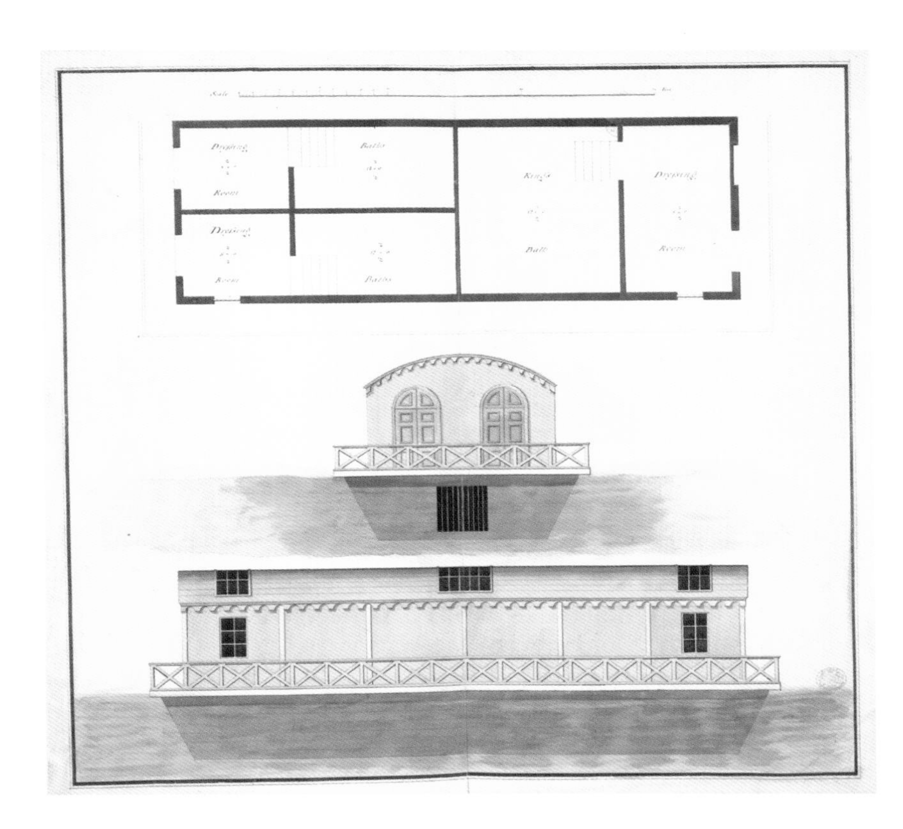

RIGHT
John William Hiort, plan and side elevations of the King's Floating Baths at Weymouth, 1782 (K Top XII 12h).

BELOW
Detail from J. Wells, *View of Margate with bathing machines*, 1786 (K Top XVII 4a).

Celebrating the Sights of Wales

Thomas Pennant (1726–1798), a naturalist, traveller and writer, made tours of several parts of the British Isles in the 1770s and 1780s. His travels through Wales took place in the early 1770s (the one described in this volume actually occurred in 1773, and the date has been corrected by hand in a number of copies), and they were published in three volumes between 1778 and 1783. Pennant was a fellow of the Society of Antiquaries, and his first major publication was *The British Zoology*, the first volume of which was published in London in 1766. It was followed by five editions between 1766 and 1812.

Pennant's first book on travel in the British Isles described the tours of Scotland that he undertook in 1769 and 1772. Both the 1769 and 1772 editions of his book *A tour in Scotland* influenced the great Samuel Johnson, himself working on the publication of his own journal featuring his tours to the Hebrides with James Boswell. Pennant's travel writing is very observant and was presumed, when his descriptions were published, to be close to the facts. In the volume shown here he describes the different parts of Wales that he visited, including a number of ruined castles, such as Hawarden Castle, pictured below.

The Satirist's View of Travel

James Gillray's satirical engraving shows a man and his wife seated in their carriage, driving along a country road. The carriage is drawn by a rather ill-looking horse, and is accompanied by a dog carrying a large bone and by birds flying above. Both passengers are smartly dressed, and the wife grasps her husband's arm as their carriage swings along the road. She wears long gloves and holds a closed parasol. A milestone they have just passed shows the vehicle's distance from London, but the figures have broken off so we cannot tell how far the couple are from home, or how close to their destination.

In journeying to Wycombe, the pair probably want to see as much as be seen. Such visits had become popular entertainments, and the fact that the couple could make the trip in their own carriage shows that travelling for pleasure had come within the reach of more and more people by the early nineteenth century.

The text underneath the image reads: 'Vednesday was a week, my Vife & I vent to Vest-Vycombe, vhether it was the Vind, or vhether it was the \ "Veather, – or Vat it vas! – ve vhip'd & vhip'd – & vhip'd! – & could not get off a Valk!.'

100 HAWARDEN.

any proceeding that might tend to affect the fortunes of themſelves or friends. Numbers of ſales were made by the loyaliſts themſelves, under the influence of fear. They were content to receive a trifle for the purchaſe, rather than loſe the whole by violence; for there were very few who had not incurred a premunire under the ruling powers: which they were glad to get clear of by a ſeemingly voluntary ſale. When they were thus diſappointed in the hope of re-enjoyment of their fortunes, they laid the blame on the king, and invented the calumny of his rejecting this bill, after it had been paſſed unanimouſly by both houſes.

Besieged in 1643.

During the civil wars, this caſtle ſuffered the uſual viciſſitudes of fortune. It was early poſſeſſed by the parlement, being betrayed by the governor, a neighboring gentleman of the name of *Ravenſcroft* *; and kept for its uſe till the year 1643, at which time a ceſſation of arms being agreed to, on the part of the king, with the *Iriſh* rebels, a number of the forces were drawn from *Ireland*, and landed at *Moſtyn* in this county, in the month of *November*. Theſe were immediately employed to reduce the caſtle of *Hawarden*, garriſoned by a hundred and twenty men of Sir *Thomas Middleton's* regiment. The garriſon received, by a trumpet, a verbal ſummons; which gave occaſion to the following letters between lieutenant-colonel *Marrow*, and *John Warren* and *Alexander Elliot*, the commanders on the part of the parlement. I omit the immediate anſwer to the ſummons, written in the religious ſtrain affected by the party; which *Marrow* replies to like a true *Cavalier*.

* *Life of the Duke of Ormond*, ii. 471; iii. 204.

'GENTLEMEN,

Thomas Pennant, *A tour in Wales. MDCCLXX*, London, 1778–81 (187.a.18–19).

James Gillray, *A Cockney & his Wife going to Wycombe*, 1805 (British Museum, Prints and Drawings, 1868,0808.7371).

Famille Anglaise en Voyage, 1815 (British Museum, Prints and Drawings, 1991,0720.131).

By the early nineteenth century, travel in the British Isles and to destinations abroad had come within the reach of the middle classes. This satirical print shows an English family, in descending order of height, somewhere on their journey. The father at the front carries one child, while behind him the mother holds a younger one. Their older daughter follows her mother, bearing the family's provisions. Even the dog carries a wrapped bundle, but its contents remain hidden from the viewer.

'Professor of Earthquakes'

For male offspring of the upper classes in the eighteenth century the Grand Tour was a must. While it usually lasted for a year or two, the diplomatist and art collector Sir William Hamilton (1731–1803) is said to have been on the Grand Tour for about thirty-five years. His decision to accept the post of envoy to Naples in 1764 was influenced by a desire to move to a climate that would benefit the fragile health of his wife, Catherine Barlow, but it was also an area that would allow him to study antiquities. He had always been interested in this field, and moving to Naples gave him the ideal opportunity to combine his work with his favourite leisure activities. His diplomatic duties were not very time-consuming and gave him plenty of space to pursue his studying and collecting of art and antiquities. With his proximity to Pompeii and Herculaneum, where excavations were going on at the time, he was in an ideal place to live the life of an antiquary. Unfortunately, he never really had the resources to be able to afford all the objects he collected; throughout his life he was often in debt and was forced to sell items from his collection. His financial troubles, however, did not prevent Hamilton from amassing not one but two large collections of vases, paintings and other assorted objects during his lifetime.

Hamilton was a very good self-publicist who made it his business to make his collection accessible. The Hamiltons' house in Naples became a very popular destination, and seeing the collection was almost compulsory for any visitor considering himself important and of refined taste. Hamilton also pursued the publication of a catalogue of his vases to promote his collection in Naples as well as abroad. His first important publication was his *Antiquités étrusques, grecques et romaines*, which was published in four volumes dated 1766, but in fact published between 1767 and 1776. This publication, featuring high-quality colour plates of his vases, was influential not only among fellow collectors and antiquaries, but also among members of the trade and industries, above all Josiah Wedgwood. The work was published just as Wedgwood had opened his pottery works in Staffordshire, and he used the plates of Hamilton's vases to throw six black basal 'first day vases' based on the patterns. Wedgwood continued to be inspired by the plates in future pieces of pottery.

In 1766 Hamilton was elected to the Royal Society, and in 1772 he was made a knight of the Bath and elected a Fellow of the Society of Antiquaries. In the same year he negotiated for his first collection to be sold to the British Museum, and in 1777 he was elected to the Society of Dilettanti. He did not resume collecting until 1789, when he began to amass his second collection of vases. This was described in *Engravings from Ancient Vases*, published in four volumes between 1791 and 1795. Hamilton tried to sell his second collection to ensure his pension, but much of it was lost in a shipwreck off the Scilly Isles in August 1798.

Today, Hamilton's fame is based not only on his collections of vases and other antiquities, but also on his strong interest in volcanoes. This he developed during his time in Naples where he witnessed the eruptions of Vesuvius in 1767, 1779 and 1794; it earned him the nickname of 'Professor of Earthquakes'. On each occasion Hamilton made careful observations and drawings, which he transmitted in letters to the Royal Society and in particular to Sir Joseph Banks, its president from 1778 to 1820. They were published in the Society's journal, the *Philosophical Transactions*, between 1767 and 1795. Hamilton became obsessed with ascending Vesuvius, and during his time in Naples he is said to have climbed the mountain more than sixty-five times. He used his ascents to make observations and drawings, and to collect samples of rock and ash which he sent to London. He often ascended the mountain in the company of friends or men who visited him on the Grand Tour.

Hamilton's most famous work, the *Campi Phlegraei: Observations on the volcanos of the two Sicilies*, was published in 1776. The text is in English and French and features over fifty hand-coloured illustrations of Vesuvius by Pietro Fabris, portraying its eruptions, rocks and scenes around the area of the volcanoes. Hamilton used the publication to promote his research, and he missed no opportunity to have himself depicted in the drawings. He usually appeared in the foreground, either on his own or in the company of one of the many people he guided to the volcano.

The volumes reprint some of the letters which Hamilton had sent to the Royal Society, and throughout the text he repeatedly stresses the accuracy of his descriptions, based on first-hand observations of nature. In this he agreed with Sir Joseph Banks, who also believed that reliable scientific evidence could only be taken from accurate observations of nature itself.

Hamilton's publication contains a map of the area around the volcanoes, marking the Campi

William Hamilton, *Campi Phlegraei. Observations on the volcanos of the two Sicilies*, Naples, 1776 (Tab.435.a.15).

III

Phlegraei and Mount Vesuvius in particular. Most of the spectacular and vividly coloured plates are in the second volume: for example, the 'State of the Top and Crater of Vesuvius Octr. the 29th. when the great eruption of 1767. Ceased'; a 'View of an eruption of lava from the Crater of Mount Vesuvius taken from an original painting of Mr. Fabris's done from nature about 22. years ago; a 'View of the great eruption of Vesuvius from the mole of Naples in the night of the 20th. of Oct.r 1767'; the 'Interiour of the Crater of Mount Vesuvius, as it was before the great eruption of 1767'; a 'View of the first discovery of the Temple of Isis at Pompeii, which City was buried by showers of pumice stones and other volcanick matter, during the great eruption of mount Vesuvius in the year 79 of the christian Æra'; a 'Piece of lava cover'd with sulphur taken from the inside of the crater of Vesuvius'; 'Specimens of curious stones found by the Author on Mount Vesuvius'; and the most famous plate, 'A Night view of a current of lava, that ran from Mount Vesuvius towards Resina, the 11th of May 1771. When the Author had the honor of conducting Their Sicilian Majesties to see that curious phenomenon' (opposite top).

The *Campi Phlegraei* is probably the most spectacular publication produced in the eighteenth century to illustrate people's growing fascination with natural phenomena and classical antiquity. It uses the medium of the printed book as a means of spreading this information and influencing taste.

William Hamilton, *Campi Phlegraei. Observations on the volcanos of the two Sicilies, Naples,* 1776 (Tab.435.a.15).

Further Reading

Black, Jeremy, *George III: America's Last King* (New Haven and London, 2006)

Brewer, John, *The Pleasures of the Imagination: English Culture in the Eighteenth Century* (London, 1997)

Burrows, Donald, *Handel* (New York, 2012)

Colley, Linda, *Britons: Forging the Nation, 1707–1837* (London, 1994)

Curl, James Stevens, *Georgian Architecture in the British Isles, 1714–1830* (Swindon, 2011)

Curl, James Stevens, *Spas, Wells and Pleasure-Gardens of London* (London, 2010)

Farrington, Anthony, *Trading Places: The East India Company and Asia 1600–1834* (London, 2002)

Greig, Hannah, *The Beau Monde: Fashionable Society in Georgian London* (Oxford, 2013)

Harman, Claire, *Fanny Burney: A Biography* (London, 2000)

Hatton, Ragnhild, *George I* (New Haven and London, 2001)

Hilton, Boyd, *A Mad, Bad, and Dangerous People? England, 1783–1846* (Oxford, 2006)

Hoppit, Julian, *A Land of Liberty? England 1689–1727* (Oxford, 2000)

Inglis, Lucy, *Georgian London: Into the Streets* (London, 2013)

Kelly, Ian, *Beau Brummell: The Ultimate Dandy* (London, 2006)

Langford, Paul, *A Polite and Commercial People: England, 1727–1783* (Oxford, 1989)

McIntyre, Ian, *Garrick* (London, 1999)

McIntyre, Ian, *Joshua Reynolds: The Life and Times of the First President of the Royal Academy* (London, 2003)

Morgan, Kenneth O. (ed.), *The Oxford Illustrated History of Britain* (Oxford, 2009)

O' Brien, John, *Harlequin Britain: Pantomime and Entertainment, 1690–1760* (Baltimore and London, 2004)

Porter, Roy, *English Society in the Eighteenth Century* (Harmondsworth, 1990)

Porter, Roy, *Enlightenment: Britain and the Creation of the Modern World* (London, 2000)

Pugh, Gillian, *London's Forgotten Children: Thomas Coram and the Foundling Hospital* (Stroud, 2007)

Richardson, Tim, *The Arcadian Friends: Inventing the English Landscape Garden* (London, 2008)

Rubenhold, Hallie, *The Covent Garden Ladies: Pimp General Jack & the Extraordinary Story of Harris's List* (Stroud, 2006)

Smith, E. A., *George IV* (New Haven and London, 1999)

Stott, Andrew McConnell, *The Pantomime Life of Joseph Grimaldi* (Edinburgh, 2009)

Styles, John, *The Dress of the People: Everyday Fashion in Eighteenth-Century England* (New Haven and London, 2007)

Summers, Judith, *The Empress of Pleasure: The Life and Adventures of Teresa Cornelys – Queen of Masquerades and Casanova's Lover* (London, 2003)

Summerson, John, *Georgian London* (New Haven and London, 2003)

Thompson, Andrew C., *George II: King and Elector* (New Haven and London, 2011)

Tomalin, Claire, *Mrs Jordan's Profession: The Story of a Great Actress and a Future King* (London, 1995)

Uglow, Jenny, *Hogarth: A Life and a World* (London, 1997)

Uglow, Jenny, *The Lunar Men: The Friends Who Made the Future, 1730–1810* (London, 2003)

Vickery, Amanda, *Behind Closed Doors: At Home in Georgian England* (New Haven and London, 2009)

White, Jerry, *London in the Eighteenth Century: A Great and Monstrous Thing* (London, 2012)

Index

Page numbers in *italics* refer to illustrations